Land and Territoriality

BERG

Ethnicity and Identity

SERIES

ISSN: 1354–3628

General Editors:
Shirley Ardener, *Founding Director, Centre for Cross-Cultural Research on Women, University of Oxford*

Tamara Dragadze, *School of Slavonic and East European Studies, University of London*

Jonathan Webber, *Institute of Social and Cultural Anthropology, University of Oxford*

Books previously published in the Series

Sharon Macdonald (ed.), *Inside European Identities: Ethnography in Western Europe*

Joanne Eicher (ed.), *Dress and Ethnicity*

Martin Stokes (ed.), *Ethnicity, Identity and Music: The Musical Constructions of Place*

Jeremy MacClancy (ed.), *Sport, Identity and Ethnicity*

Simone Abram, Jackie Waldren and Donald Macleod (eds), *Tourists and Tourism: Identifying with People and Places*

Jeremy MacClancy (ed.), *Contesting Art: Art, Politics and Identity in the Modern World*

Sharon Macdonald, *Reimaging Culture: Histories, Identities and the Gaelic Renaissance*

Nigel Rapport and Andrew Dawson (eds), *Migrants of Identity: Perceptions of Home in a World of Movement*

Land and Territoriality

EDITED BY
Michael Saltman

BERG

Oxford • New York

First published in 2002 by
Berg
Editorial offices:
150 Cowley Road, Oxford, OX4 1JJ, UK
838 Broadway, Third Floor, New York, NY 10003-4812, USA

Berg is the imprint of Oxford International Publishers Ltd.

Library of Congress Cataloging-in-Publication Data

A catalogue record for this book is available from the Library of Congress.

British Library Cataloguing-in-Publication Data

Land and territoriality / edited by Michael Saltman.
p. cm. -- (Ethnicity and identity, ISSN 1354-3628)
Includes bibliographical references and index.
ISBN 1-85973-564-9 (cloth) -- ISBN 1-85973-569-X (paper)
1. Ethnicity. 2. Ethnic conflict. 3. Human territoriality. 4. Territorial
expansion. 5. Genocide. I. Saltman, Michael. II. Berg ethnic identities
series.
GN495.6 .L35 2002
305.8--dc21

2001007466

ISBN 1 85973 564 9 (Cloth)
1 85973 569 X (Paper)

Typeset by JS Typesetting, Wellingborough, Northants
Printed in Great Britain by Antony Rowe Ltd, Chippenham, Wiltshire

Contents

Acknowledgements

Most of the papers in this book derive from presentations at the ongoing seminar series on Ethnicity and Identity at the Institute of Social and Cultural Anthropology at Oxford University. The two exceptions are the papers by Jean Besson and Shulamit Carmi and Henry Rosenfeld, who submitted their papers to this volume at my request.

My own presence in Oxford during the academic year 1997/8, when the seminar on Land and Territoriality took place, was facilitated by a Visiting Fellowship at St. Antony's College. Most of the editing work was done a year later at the Institute of Commonwealth Studies of the University of London, where I also had a Visiting Fellowship during the summer months. For this my thanks are due to Professor Pat Caplan.

The conveners of the seminar at Oxford – Shirley Ardener, Tamara Dragadze, Jonathan Webber and Ian Fowler – have been supportive and have given much helpful advice. Finally, thanks are due to the Research Authority at the University of Haifa, which funded the solution to some of the problems encountered in the word processing, as well as the compilation of the index for this volume.

1

Introduction

Michael Saltman

One advantage of a long-term, ongoing seminar such as the Ethnicity and Identity Seminar, held under the auspices of Oxford University's Institute of Social and Cultural Anthropology, is the accumulation, over time, of extensive ethnographic data within the scope of the seminar's fixed parameters. Each seminar establishes a link between the constant variables of ethnicity and identity and another specific variable. The chapters in this volume consider the concepts of land and territoriality in their relationship to ethnicity and identity.

One might expect that the accumulated data, since the inception of the seminar, would shed some light on the relationship between the two constant variables – ethnicity and identity. But what appears to emerge from the chapters in this volume is that the relationship between them is indeterminate. Insofar as land and territoriality are concerned, the ethnic characteristics within territorial boundaries are mostly definable. On the other hand, identity emerges as a factor in situations of conflicting claims between ethnic groups and the consequential mobilization of people for the political cause. This raises the obvious question as to whether the phenomena of ethnicity and identity are of the same ontological order? Ethnicity is a socio-cultural phenomenon, whereas identity, at a lower level of abstraction, has usually been associated with individual cognition and perception. Various attempts to bridge this gap have been employed. In its heyday, social psychology attempted this feat. Today it is popular to speak of 'collective identities' but the very idea of a collectivity seems to merge within the general idea of ethnicity. Furthermore, it is not clear what added value is achieved in the use of the term 'collective identity', above and beyond the concept of ethnicity.

A previous volume in this series, *Migrants of Identity: Perceptions of Home in a World of Movement* (Rapport and Dawson 1998), relates ethnicity and identity to the shifting locations of migrants. Their emphasis is clearly on identity as a major issue in the subject of migration. They stress that they 'discuss and analyse the search for identity in terms of the conceptualizatons of "home"' (1998: 4). If 'home' is the issue, then there is a genuine cognitive level where individuals perceive 'home' under the differing circumstances of migration, identifying to a greater or lesser degree with the differing realities of their past and present circumstances. But Rapport and Dawson also go beyond this by claiming that social reality is in a universally, constant state of movement both in time and space. This is the element of the 'World of Movement' stressed in the title of the volume. The editors admit to their polemical stand and speculate 'upon some of the possible relations between movement (physical and cognitive)and identity (individual and social), and how these relations may be seen to be changing in a contemporary cultural milieu of globalization' (1998: 9). This indeed may be true, but is not a necessary and sufficient justification for their critique, which states,

> A traditional concern of anthropological description and analysis has been the ident-
> ification of socio-cultural 'places': fixities of social relations and cultural routines
> localized in time and space. Societies were identified with cultures conceived as complete
> wholes; here were localized universes of meaning, with individuals and groups as their
> transparent components, their representative expressions. Of late, this localizing image
> of separate and self-sufficient worlds (of relations, culture, identity and history) has
> come in for much criticism (1998: 4)

There is inevitably a price to be paid for engaging in polemics, for it pits one argument against another to the complete exclusion of the opposing contentions. There is as much a legitimate place for perceiving cultures 'as complete wholes' and 'localized universes of meaning' as there is for individual and group cognition of cultural reality. It is not cultures, societies, groups and individuals that require and produce theories, but rather the questions we ask about these phenomena. Thus, I take no issue with Rapport and Dawson when they espouse a theoretical stand *vis-à-vis* questions of migration, but reserve the right to adopt a different theoretical perspective when dealing with questions of land and territoriality, the subject of the present volume.

Likewise, a second volume in this series, *Tourists and Tourism: Identifying with People and Places* (Abram *et al.* 1997), by the very nature of its subject matter, stresses the relationship between tourism, tourists and motion through time and space as advocated by Rapport and Dawson. The editors of this volume cite a perceptive insight of Zygmunt Bauman's which 'asserts that identity has the ontological status of a project and a postulate and, hence, "identity", though ostensibly a noun behaves like a verb'. This may provide a hint as to the relative statuses of ethnicity and identity, whereby the former is a static phenomenon as opposed to the dynamism of the latter. No verb, however, derives from the word 'ethnicity'. An understanding of the concepts of land and territoriality is perhaps more closely linked to the idea of ethnicity, while the topics of migration and tourism may be better perceived under the rubric of identity. There are distinct ontological levels involved here and polemical arguments have the tendency to rule out the value of other levels, especially in terms of their theoretical implications.

A piece of land, a stretch of territory, are neutral items fixed in time and space. It is true that an individual can 'identify' with a plot of land that is his or with the nation-state boundaries of the territory within which he lives. However, his 'identification' or 'non-identification' with land and territory is of a different order from the social realities of the circumstances that face a migrant or a tourist.

In the steady state of normal everyday life, people are not actively engaged in identifying with their immediate physical surroundings, nor with nationalistic sentiments towards the territory within which they reside. The ethnicity associated with a piece of land, a territory, refers to the characteristics of the people who live there. The naming of a territory is inextricably linked with the ethnic group occupying that territory: England – Englishmen; Scotland – Scots; Serbia – Serbians and so on. There are symbols and rituals that reinforce this connection but it is primarily when this so-called 'ethnic correlation' is called into question that identity with the land is mobilized into a nationalistic cause. The periodic 'ethnic cleansing' of the Balkans is an example of when the validity of the 'ethnic correlation' is challenged and the people living there mobilize into conflicting social groupings that are ethnically constituted. The issue of conflict is that of rights over land and territory. This is clearly an issue of nationalism, in which ethnicity is called upon as a contention to substantiate the right and as a basis of identification for rallying politically in order to establish a right.

Part of the problem seems to stem from the fact that the term 'ethnicity' no longer enjoys the exclusive status of an anthropological analytical concept, but has rather become a word of common parlance used in non-anthropological discourse. 'Ethnic-cleansing' is only one such example. An 'ethnic' Albanian is one who lives in Kosovo or Macedonia, but an Albanian who lives in Albania is just a straightforward, ordinary, presumably non-ethnic Albanian. Nonetheless, the latter can be described by all the criteria which Rapport and Dawson designate as 'cultures conceived as complete wholes'.

The point of departure, from hereon, is that identity achieves its strongest expression within the political context of conflicting rights over land and territory. The chapters in this volume cover a variety of situations that emphasize or de-emphasize the relative importance of ethnicity and identity. There are chapters that demonstrate the connection between land and territory and the social system, or a specific part of the social system. This relatively static relationship between behaviour and land, albeit progressing through time, are still constant variables. Other chapters relate ethnicity to nationalism, in which identity is expressed in terms of mobilization to a political cause. In Chapter 3, Carmi and Rosenfeld show how decisions were taken in a political system over the issue of land conquered in a war. Two national groups, Arabs and Jews, who coexisted in an uneasy and occasionally broken truce under the *Pax Britannica* of colonialist rule, claimed political sovereignty over the disputed territory of Palestine. The competing claims of the protagonists, Arabs and Jews, that gave rise to the war, are not issues of identity; rather, they are clear expressions of nationalism that coincide with ethnicity. The winners were divided among themselves. There were those who wished to abide by coexistence by allowing the refugees to return to their lands. But military power, and the capacity to maintain it, in the hands of those who denied the return of the Arab refugees and demanded exclusive control over all territories captured, won the day. The potential for ethnic coexistence was lost. Specifically, Carmi and Rosenfeld discuss non-return of the refugees and land take-over in terms of the nation-state undercutting the historic democratic and socialist movements that were politically hegemonic in the Jewish community.

But it is not only war that brings ethnicity to the forefront. Other contentious situations over land highlight the factor of ethnicity. Kennedy, in her chapter, describes how North American Indians, both in Canada and the United States, assert their rights in court in order to regain possession of land taken from them by the colonial authorities. The courts have become an arena, in which the submission of expert ethnographic evidence is allowed. The definition of 'traditional use sites' and 'traditional cultural properties' in Canada and the United States, respectively, has become a legal issue in which ethnicity plays a dominant role. It is insufficient for a group to lay claim to a place solely on the fact that they mystically identify with it. They must bring more solid evidence before the courts, based on their history, or purported history, in order to establish their claims.

Even though the two chapters cited above deal specifically with conflicts between two clearly defined ethnic groups, other chapters in the volume concern themselves with conflicts, wherein the ethnic boundaries are less clearly defined. These are conflicts between culturally defined groups over very specific issues that relate to land and territoriality. The common denominator underlying both ethnicity and culture is that they are of the same ontological order, for they are of sociological rather than cognitive importance.

Cooper's chapter is an example of a situation wherein the ethnic boundaries are less clearly defined in territorial terms. The territory in question is a borough in London, in which ultra-orthodox Jews and non-orthodox Jews live in a steady state of everyday normal existence with the non-Jewish majority. The equilibrium within the borough, in which ethnicity (although identifiable) played a minimal role, was shaken when a group of ultra-orthodox Jews symbolically bounded the area by placing poles connected by wire around the borough. This was done as a ritual measure to enable the religious Jews to carry objects or push perambulators on the sabbath in the public domain, both of which would normally be perceived as working on the Sabbath day, which is, of course, forbidden. Carrying objects within the private domain is not a transgression. A physical boundary, such as a wall, or in lieu of a wall, connected poles, ritually transforms all space within it to the private domain.

In the steady state of everyday equilibrium within the borough, each ethnic group of residents could be described in classical ethnographic terms. But the 'incident' became a political issue and groups, organized politically on defined ethnic lines, mobilized in order to identify with their respective causes. The action of the ultra-orthodox Jews brought them into conflict with some of the non-Jewish residents of the Borough who, although possibly tolerant of what Jews might do in their private domain, were unwilling to accept a visible Jewish ritual presence in the public domain. A second group of opponents to the ultra-orthodox was made up of non-orthodox Jews, or Jews with a strong secular orientation. Clearly, these latter not only wanted to disassociate themselves from their more orthodox co-religionists, but it might be fairly assumed that they also preferred to be identified with the gentile majority. This is the point at which identity becomes an issue, but even if it is an issue, the root cause of the problem is one of conflict between ethnic or cultural groups.

Abram's chapter joins Cooper's on the basis of a number of common features. In the first place, we are not talking of Ethnicity in its narrowest anthropological sense of groups set apart by different origins. It also encompasses groups set apart by different cultural characteristics. In Abram's case study we are talking of two culturally distinct groups that are in potential conflict with each other. One of the groups is a well-defined group, the inhabitants of an English village, who perceive themselves threatened by an influx of outsiders into a planned housing estate within the village environs. While this is the basis of the conflict, the actual conflict is taking place between the villagers and the planning authorities. It is a classic case of the virtual 'high culture' of the old-established village gentry attempting to resist what is seen as the intrusion of the 'low culture' of the interlopers. Abram correctly presents the issue as a moral problem, concerned with the 'rights' and 'wrongs' of the situation. A moral issue, however abstract, is still not a question of identity on a cognitive psychological plane. It is grounded in values, which, in turn, are grounded in social and cultural reality. The moral positions are invariably presented in terms of rational argumentation that draw on empirical social and cultural facts. Thus, the dominant framework of reference still remains ethnicity, in the sense of its broad meaning.

Two more chapters focus on ritualized relationships that obtain between people and land. Pfaff-Czarnecka looks at a complex ritual in Nepal that demonstrates the linkage between claims over land and power struggles within the caste system. Again, we are talking of social relationships, and only incidentally of individual perceptions. As long as the issue is one of power politics and inequitable forms of land distribution, one has to fall back on conventional anthropological analysis that seeks explanatory variables at the level of ethnicity, culture and society. But when this same issue is placed into a ritual context, then, clearly, the actors in the ritual are acting out their identification or non-identification with what is taking place in reality. The situation, described by Pfaff-Czarnecka, is thus reflected at both levels of analysis, for even if the conflict situation is played out symbolically, in ritual, the political identification with a cause is patently clear.

Armitage has also focused on a situation that requires analysis both in terms of ethnicity and identity. She looks at the connection between the Zionist Christian Church in Swaziland and land, the latter both as a practical asset and as a perceived landscape. Similar to what is presented in Pfaff-Czarnecka's chapter on Nepal, Armitage notes the situation of the 'haves' and the 'have nots' *vis-à-vis* land and political status in Swaziland. She states that until quite recently the members of the Swazi Zionist churches have not had control over land, and that women church members had no rights whatsoever either over land or cattle. Even though the church membership is not ethnically homogeneous, she argues that it effectively 'imitates' ethnicity. The Church's own internal system of power relationships and concepts of territoriality compensate for past exclusion from traditional and state political systems of power. Unlike the Nepalese situation, in which a ritual inspired a revolt of the excluded, the Swazi Zionists have developed a perception of their own landscape based on their reading of biblical texts that describe scenes and places in the Holy Land. This reflection of biblical landscapes reinforces the identity of the church membership, not only within their own ranks but also the members' perceptions of land and territoriality. Again, we have here political mobilization for a given end, but in a much weaker form than in some of the other cases in this volume.

Saltman's chapter on the Kipsigis of Kenya describes a situation in which a group of cattle herders were transformed over a relatively short time into cultivators. One of the consequences of this transformation is a conceptual shift as to the meaning of land under the two different sets of economic circumstances. Under conditions of pastoralism, land is territory over which the whole group roams and herds its cattle. Under conditions of cultivation and land enclosure, however, land becomes property, and rights of ownership, previously alien to Kipsigis thinking, now emerge with all the consequential problems. As land is enclosed and grows scarce, disputes over land increase in frequency and intensity. Traditional customary law had no solutions for these problems, but the traditional remedy agents sought a means to resolve these disputes. Adopting a principle of tort from their indigenous legal thinking, they adapted it and applied it to the resolution of disputes over rights of land ownership. The chapter argues a contention in the philosophy of law that the law and its remedies are reflected in the spirit of the people, in something that is inherent within their culture. Land, territoriality and people's attitudes towards them are firmly grounded in their culture. The solutions adopted by the Kipsigis to meet changing socio-economic conditions were characteristically Kipsigis in their conception. They were grounded in Kipsigis shared understandings as to how problems are to be solved. The whole issue of this case study is bounded solely by the ethnicity of the single group associated with the territory. There is no contingent nor associated problem of identity involved here.

This last point emphasizes the contrast with Besson's chapter, which depicts an interesting situation from the Caribbean. She employs concepts that characterize the area as one of 'deterritorialization, flight, exile, invention and creolization' and that ancestral lands, inherited cognatically, supply the linkage between people dispersed throughout time and space. Of all the chapters in this volume, hers is the hardest to accommodate to the framework of reference suggested in this Introduction, a framework that pits the analytical concepts of ethnicity and identity against each other. It is the present writer's contention that land and territoriality are concepts more closely linked to the idea of ethnicity rather than to identity. But the Caribbean presents a situation of great historical specificity, in which identity may indeed be playing a larger role than elsewhere. The syncretism of creolization, the history of what Besson calls 'circulatory migration', is symptomatic of a situation for which classical theories of society and culture may not be able to provide a complete understanding. That element of migration, so characteristic of Caribbean society, places Besson's chapter not only within the context of this volume but could also easily ascribe it a place in Rapport and Dawson's volume. Family land in the eyes of a West Indian 'transnational' is not necessarily seen as an economic resource that would allow for one type of analysis. It is just as much an emotional resource, a symbol with which to identify, and, as such, a cognitive phenomenon.

If, in the context of land and territoriality, identity can be construed as shared understandings between persons of the same culture, enabling them to rally together for a political cause, it remains a straightforward, non-polemical issue, not to be pitted against ethnicity. The latter is, rather, an expression of a similar cultural response that members of a society employ to cope with situations of everyday living. Shared understandings have little to do with the exotic jargon that has emerged in recent years in the pursuit of the concept of identity – deconstructionism, anti-essentialism, structuration and a plethora of other bewildering terms. People are socialized within their cultures. The cultures enable them, as individuals and groups, to both define and face problems of everyday life and to deal with them in culturally normative ways.

This volume tries to make a contribution by drawing the lines between ethnicity and identity in such a way that neither one excludes the legitimacy of the other. Rather than positing generalizations about the conceptual inadequacy of 'socio-cultural places' that imply fixed social relations and cultural routines, it might prove more useful to commence with a question and, only then, to apply the most appropriate theoretical framework to achieve an answer. Theories, however exalted they may be, are no more than an assemblage of tools brought together in order to solve a problem. The chapters in this volume all relate to people's attitudes towards either land or territoriality, or both. By virtue of the situations posed in these chapters, most appear to gravitate towards conventional, or, *mirabile dictu,* traditional anthropological theory in order to explicate their data. Ethnicity, culture and society as discrete sets of variables appear to take precedence over identity as appropriate frameworks of reference for dealing with land and territoriality.

References

Abram, S., Waldren, W. and Macleod, D. (eds) (1997), *Tourists and Tourism: Identifying with People and Places*, Oxford: Berg.

Rapport, N. and Dawson, A. (1998) *Migrants of Identity: Perceptions of Home in a World of Movement*, Oxford: Berg.

2

Culture and Politics in the Aboriginal Landscape: Reflections on the Identification of Culturally Significant Places in Western North America

Dorothy Kennedy

Introduction

Anthropologists have recently emphasized 'landscape' as a means by which indigenous people encapsulate and transmit historical and personal knowledge. Studies highlighting toponymic systems (Basso 1984, 1988, 1996; Hunn 1990, 1991, 1994, 1996; Thornton 1995), space and place (Tuan 1977; Tilley 1994; Eves 1997), boundary markers (Berndt 1976; Rappaport 1989), myth and ritual (Santos-Granero 1998), and other associations of past and current social action, reveal how aboriginal people imbue the land with cultural significance.

Places of cultural importance to indigenous peoples have, for the past decade, received acknowledgement and protection through policies and regulations formulated by various government agencies in Canada and the United States. Such places are called 'traditional use sites' in western Canada, and 'traditional cultural properties' in the United States. Assuredly, the voiced concerns of Native people, together with heritage impact statements and cultural resource assessments, have influenced the formulation of land-use policy in both countries; regulations are conceived in response to decisions in land-claims litigation based substantially on anthropological data. Yet despite good-faith efforts, conflicts between governments, developers and indigenous people continue over access and use of the land. Cultural resource specialists implementing policies and regulations find themselves targets of criticism from disgruntled parties on all sides of the debate.

On the resource-rich north-west coast of North America, where the stakes of land use are unquestionably high, the land-use rhetoric is malleable and changeable, resulting often in discursive polarization open to debate and interpretation. The discourse of land use is not by any means one-sided. Governments speak of 'multiuse', emphasizing the professed inclusiveness of their policies by calling competing interests 'stakeholders', as they try to reconcile the needs and concerns of indigenous communities – possessing special legal rights – with those of other citizens. Increasingly present in these deliberations is the aboriginal people's reliance upon equivocal metaphors to assert, within a localized political arena, positions accenting 'tradition'. Reference to the past, is, of course, mandatory, although the symbols invoked have varying relationships to past cultural practices and beliefs. For example, in a recent article on the use of tree symbolism in north-west coast political discourse, anthropologist Marie Mauzé writes:

> forests symbolise cultural renewal, as well as the strength of Indian identity. Trees and forests, as synecdoche or metonymy for the whole Northwest Coast Indian culture, are today endowed with a mystical aura. Doubtless these representations are influenced by ideas borrowed from the North American pan-Indian movement and from the many environmentalist groups now existing throughout North America (Mauzé 1998: 234).

We can extend Mauzé's comments on the use of tree symbolism in contemporary Native political life more generally to the association of Native people with the landscape. Just as the traditional and contemporary differ in the way of concept-ualizing the mode of relation between trees and human beings (Mauzé 1998: 235) so, too, do traditional and contemporary discourses differ in the way they speak of the 'landscape', and, in particular, places of cultural significance. Native people and governments alike employ the concept of 'tradition' to identify which places and resources within a colonized landscape warrant recognition. However, as incidents in other parts of the world have recently demonstrated (e.g., Hanson 1989; Linnekin 1992; Thomas 1992; Gable et al. 1992), the pragmatic and political aspects of defining 'traditional' raise issues of cultural construction that often become focal points of discussion.

Though these general remarks could apply to any area of the north-west coast, I focus here on the territory of the Coast Salish, a region some 300 miles long, transected by the Canada–US border and hemmed by the Pacific Ocean and the Coastal Mountains. This is an area where I have extensive experience conducting land-use research for First Nations,[1] governments and corporations.

The topic of the present chapter brings to the fore some of the thornier issues inherent in land-use disputes that have occurred in the north-west. My intent is to look at why, from an anthropological perspective, some of these problems occur.

In this chapter I outline the situation of the Coast Salish of British Columbia and Washington State, and in this context identify some issues that have followed from the ambiguously defined guidelines and regulations conceived to direct research and, ultimately, to acknowledge indigenous, land-based cultural resources within these people's territories. I begin by summarizing the American and western Canadian approaches to the identification of culturally significant sites and examine some of the legal underpinnings for this recognition. Then I present a few of the more pertinent aspects of the aboriginal Coast Salish that provide an understanding of their traditional land use, and follow with a discussion of some historical variables that have shaped the contemporary indigenous communities. A discussion follows of the ways various parties conceptualize 'tradition' and employ it strategically for diverse aims – a situation with parallels in other parts of the Western world where the emergence of highly contentious issues has divided both aboriginal and academic communities. Reference to a few significant cases illustrates salient points where land-use disputes have resulted in litigation and judicial review. Though I have no panacea to offer, solutions for resolving these disputes in ways that evidently meet the expectations of all citizens on the north-west coast remain far on the horizon.

Recognition of Culturally Significant Places

The experience of colonialism in both Canada and the US incorporated formerly autonomous groups of indigenous people within the nation-states. Colonialism imposed upon aboriginal groups socio-cultural systems under which they have striven to maintain distinct aboriginal identities, and to carry on transformed cultural practises—now regarded as 'traditional' – in areas they consider to be their own. Both Canada's and the US's acknowledgement of culturally significant places grew from a recognition that aboriginal peoples have unique legally protected rights not enjoyed by other citizens, and that some of these rights are land and resource based. They expressly derive such rights from treaties, constitutional provisions, statutes, common law, or express undertakings applicable to particular aboriginal groups. While the US treaties of the mid-1850s conceded the land and resource rights of the American Coast Salish, the precise interpretation of the treaty language was to be determined later by the Courts. Some Washington State tribes have, with the Court's liberal interpretation of treaty language, found themselves wielding a sizeable legal hammer to protect places of cultural significance.

The American Way

American Indian people were incorporated into the environmental impact assess-ment process through a 1978 update of the 1969 National Environmental Policy

Act (NEPA). At that time, Native Americans were invited to participate in the review of draft Environmental Impact Statements prior to their public release. The passage that same year of the American Indian Religious Freedom Act (AIRFA) provided further recognition of aboriginal concerns.

A considerable step towards defining sites of cultural importance and providing guidelines for their documentation came in 1990 with the publication of the National Parks Service's *National Register of Historic Places, Bulletin 38*, a document, entitled *Guidelines for Evaluating and Documenting Traditional Cultural Properties*, written by anthropologists Patricia Parker and Thomas King (Parker and King 1990). 'Traditional Cultural Properties,' or 'TCPs' as they are popularly known in the US, were thus given definition. In *Bulletin 38*, 'traditional' is said to refer to 'beliefs, customs and practices of a living community of people that they have passed down through the generations, usually orally or through practice'. Therefore, a 'traditional cultural property' is a place with significance to a community derived from 'the role the property plays in a community's historically rooted beliefs, customs and practices' (Parker and King 1990: 1). Properties or places deemed to qualify as TCPs (based on *Bulletin 38* guidelines) can be registered and accorded protection by legislation. Properties thought or alleged to have traditional cultural significance that might be impacted by federally funded, licensed or regulated activities, are subject to a review process prescribed by the Advisory Council on Historic Preservation (ACHP) under the authority of Section 106 of the National Historic Preservation Act (NHPA).

Section 106 of the NHPA stipulates that American federal agencies must take into account the effects of their undertakings on historic properties. As well, Section 106 affords the Advisory Council a reasonable opportunity to comment on such undertakings.

This 'Section 106 process', as it is commonly known, seeks to accommodate historic preservation concerns with the needs of federal undertakings through consultation. The goal of this consultation is to identify historic properties potentially affected by the undertaking, to assess effects of the undertaking, and to seek ways to avoid, minimize or mitigate any adverse effects on historic properties. Agencies are required to complete the Section 106 process prior to approval of the expenditure of federal funds on the undertaking or prior to the issuance of any licence.

Amendments to the National Historic Preservation Act in October 1992 strengthened the role of Native Americans in the national preservation programme. Advisory Council revisions to Section 106 regulations in February 1999 significantly increased the role of Native Americans throughout the consultation process, especially concerning TCPs.

As *Bulletin 38* notes, Traditional Cultural Properties are often difficult to recognize. Identification may not necessarily emerge from archaeological, historical or architectural studies, but generally requires the application of ethnographic methodology including consultation with members of the relevant indigenous community. *Bulletin 38* presents guidelines for documenting and evaluating TCPs, though this booklet is meant to be used with other National Register Bulletins. According to its authors, *Bulletin 38* is also responsive to the American Indian Religious Freedom Act (1978) which requires Federal agencies to reconcile their procedures in accordance with this legislation (Parker and King 1990: 2).

Qualities that give significance to places are often intangible, and thus evaluation must reflect the community's opinion of these sites within their own cultural framework. An evaluation procedure considers foremost the assertions of the community – an ambiguously defined group – and is complemented with critical analysis of supporting documentation. Places then considered eligible for listing in the US National Register of Historic Places are those that have 'integrity of location, design, setting, materials, workmanship, feelings, and association' and meet one or more specified criteria set out by the National Register regulations. Not all properties having cultural value are eligible for federal registration. Those properties considered ineligible for inclusion in the National Register include seven classes of sites, among them 'relocated properties' and 'birthplaces and graves' (Parker and King 1990: 11–12).

When sites in the United States are eligible for inclusion in the National Register of Historic Places it does not mean the government automatically protects them from disturbance. However, registration or a 'determination of eligibility' does mean these places must be considered in all planning programmes involving federally sponsored projects. Advisory Council regulations establish a process of consultation to resolve conflicts between project goals and the traditional community's desire to preserve and protect Traditional Cultural Properties. If, after consultation with the community according to federal guidelines, the involved federal agency determines that they should sacrifice a property to the needs of a project, then the National Historic Preservation Act cannot prohibit the federal agency's decision to proceed. The effects to the property, however, are still subject to mitigation. This principle is especially important with respect to TCPs, as 'such properties may be valued by a relatively small segment of a community that, on the whole, favours a project that will damage or destroy it' (Parker and King 1990: 4). The community's willingness to dispense with a property does not mean that it is not significant, but significance alone does not obstruct disturbance.

Recognition of Traditional Use Sites in British Columbia

Governmental acknowledgement of places possessing cultural significance to aboriginal people has been less forthcoming in British Columbia (BC) than in the

United States. Complicating matters is the fact that while the Canadian federal Crown has the primary, fiduciary relationship with Native people, as set out in Article 13 of the Confederation Act of 1871, Canada does not have jurisdiction over provincial Crown lands, which remain in the hands of BC. They therefore require the province's participation in a land allotment process. Historically, however, the BC government has been reluctant to acknowledge that aboriginal title to land and special rights ever existed. Despite BC's attitude, for the past two decades the BC Archaeology Branch has actively promoted ethnographic documentation to complement archaeological studies. By policy, the Archaeology Branch has advocated piggybacking ethnographic investigations onto archaeological studies, although the statutory definitions of the BC Heritage Act did not extend recognition of heritage value to sites lacking archaeological evidence. Canada's 1982 Constitution Act, to which BC was a signatory, nevertheless entrenched the affirmation of existing aboriginal and treaty rights, thereby providing the legal footings to subsequent claims of unresolved aboriginal interest. The Constitution Act also awakened in government the realization that aboriginal land claims would not just fade away.

Several landmark court cases in British Columbia crystallized what aboriginal rights might encompass and, importantly, if infringement of those rights could be justified. Especially pivotal was the case of *Regina* v. *Sparrow* where in 1990 the Supreme Court of Canada upheld the aboriginal right to fish for subsistence and ceremonial use. The Court also acknowledged that the constitutional protection of this right had to be reconciled with the federal government's legislative power – in this instance, the Crown's overriding, justifiable infringement where they may endanger conservation of the resource if the aboriginal right takes precedence. The *Sparrow* decision specified the Crown's fiduciary duty to consult with legally recognized aboriginal groups prior to that infringement.

The 1996 *Van der Peet* decision in the Supreme Court of Canada determined that to constitute an aboriginal right, a practice, tradition or custom must be 'integral' to the distinctive culture of an aboriginal society. Furthermore, the activity in question must have been integral prior to that society's contact with Europeans. Excluded from such rights are aspects of indigenous life that are true of every society, such as eating, or drinking fresh water to survive.

It was the Supreme Court of Canada's December 1997 *Delgamuukw* decision, however, that forever changed the relationship between governments and aboriginal people concerning lands of cultural significance, from one based on policy to one based on law. The 1993 Appeal Court of BC made a finding in this same case that existing legislation had not extinguished aboriginal rights. This decision meant that the province itself was required to take a greater role in considering sites of cultural importance not included within the statutory definitions of the Heritage Act. Now, if the province wished to engage in activities on Crown land, the ruling required that it consult with First Nations to ascertain whether aboriginal rights existed in that area and to determine if the proposed activity could coexist with those rights. The 1997 Supreme Court of Canada decision upheld the 1993 Appeal Court ruling.

Delgamuukw established several principles and placed an obligation on the provincial Crown to consult with First Nations concerning land activities on BC Crown lands (which comprise most of the lands of the province). As aboriginal and commercial law specialist John Hunter, QC, recently pointed out, the Supreme Court of Canada found that aboriginal title far exceeded the right to pick berries – it was a right to the land itself:

> The decision of the Supreme Court of Canada in Delgamuukw which was released last December [1997] required a reconsideration of the consultation policies, as it became clear that aboriginal title was not simply a bundle of aboriginal rights to engage in specific activities, as the Province had understood, but a distinct right to an interest in land, independent of the activities carried out on the land (Hunter 1998).

Notwithstanding, the Supreme Court of Canada has not made a determination that any aboriginal group in BC has aboriginal title. Proof of aboriginal title in Canadian law requires fulfilment of a number of criteria set out in the 1979 *Baker Lake* case.[2] Among these 'tests' are that the plaintiffs are: (1) members of an organized society; (2) that the society occupied the specific territory over which they assert title; (3) that the occupation was to the exclusion of other organized societies; and (4) that the occupation was an established fact at the time sovereignty was asserted by England. In effect, the Supreme Court of Canada's *Delgamuukw* decision upheld these *Baker Lake* tests.

A 1995 paper by aboriginal rights lawyer Robert Freedman discusses the four principles that make up the *Baker Lake* test. He notes that flexibility is needed in the way in which the Court applies *Baker Lake* in British Columbia, where patterns of aboriginal land use and occupancy differ significantly from those of the Inuit (Eskimo), in relation to whom the *Baker Lake* test was developed. Freedman (1995: 31) suggests that the 'test' be viewed as a broad outline and that the particular circumstances or complexity of a case might call for a modification of this test, appropriate to the area in which they are asserting a right.

The onus for proving title remains with the First Nations; still, the Court requires the province of BC to consult with aboriginal peoples, as government activities cannot infringe upon an aboriginal right without justification. Consequently, the province released consultation guidelines for BC government staff in September 1998 setting out a mandatory protocol (BC, Ministry of Aboriginal Affairs 1998).

'Consultation' for the purposes of fulfilling the distinct fiduciary obligations identified by *Delgamuukw* requires that the affected and interested aboriginal group have an informed opportunity to present their position and perspective on the range of options under consideration. BC government guidelines specify that where lands and resources are concerned, this must include informed consent, with appropriate legal and professional advice, on the part of the aboriginal groups concerned. What constitutes 'meaningful consultation' continues to be fiercely debated, although the Court has imparted some direction in that area.[3]

Coincident with land claims litigation and an evolving policy recognizing culturally significant sites in BC are attempts to define aboriginal rights more clearly by means of tripartite treaty negotiations. The process is slow. In February 1999, 111 years after the Nisga'a Nation of north-western BC first pleaded for recognition of the 'Indian Land Question', the provincial and federal governments stand prepared to ratify BC's first modern treaty. While opinion polls indicate BC citizens' overwhelming support for the settlement of land claims and the treaty process, the public are less easy with the costly terms of the agreement and how much autonomy it provides to the Nisga'a. These views undoubtedly contributed to the opposition party's Supreme Court of BC challenge to the treaty's legitimacy.[4] What is salient to this present discussion of culturally significant places is the Nisga'a treaty's inclusion of clauses providing for the future identification of, and formal exchange of, information relating to Nisga'a heritage sites. The treaty additionally recognizes a couple of sites presently identified as places significant in Nisga'a cultural history.[5]

A process designed for more effective consultation with First Nations prior to land alteration was initiated by the province of BC beginning in the mid-1990s. Modelled partly on the American recognition of 'Traditional Cultural Properties' (see Parker and King 1990), the province's process aims to document locations of indigenous cultural significance for inclusion in a provincial inter-agency database of heritage resources. The province hoped that funding First Nations directly to compile ethnographic site inventories through a 'Traditional Use Study' (TUS)[6] programme (as it is now called) would assist regional land- use planning by early consideration of aboriginal cultural values, and alleviate conflicts over specific places. The five-year programme, costing approximately 30 million dollars, provides funding for First Nations to inventory 'Traditional Use Sites' and participate in the compilation of databases managed both locally and provincially. Locations of all places identified as possessing cultural significance are categorized as to the site's use. Such site-type categories include ceremonial use, subsistence, domestic use, mythological and legendary associations, landmarks, cross-cultural interaction, and resource and materials harvesting, among others.

A central objective of BC's TUS programme is to address the need for more effective consultation with First Nations. The need for this consultation had arisen since the mid-1980s when civil disobedience targeting logging companies had been threatening the province's economic and social stability. There had been a marked increase in First Nations' own objections to provincial land-use planning and new alliances formed between aboriginal people and environmentalists. The rhetoric of the largely urban-based, non-Native environmental protesters increasingly invoked the image of the environmentally attuned aboriginal in opposition to Western development and what they perceived to be its march towards global degradation. The environmental protesters attempted to unite with indigenous leaders, who themselves recognized the public platform such demonstrations provided for aboriginal rights, even if the goals of their pursuits differed. The media linked First Nations with environmental sustainability, for, as the argument goes, aboriginal people are closer to nature than other Canadians, and imbue the land and its resources with a spirituality lost to Western society. Subsequent years have shown that aboriginal outlooks on logging, shopping centres and other land-altering activities are not homogeneous, while attitudes towards consultation remain firm.

Aboriginal Coast Salish

Aboriginally, the area of the Pacific north-west encompassing the Gulf of Georgia and Puget Sound was a biological and social continuum where at least sixteen mutually incomprehensible languages were spoken and cultural diversity was evident.[7] Multilingualism was common, however, as a high rate of village-exogamous marriages united villages into a network of kin. Thus, every village was related to neighbouring villages, some of which participated jointly in a rich ceremonial life.

Coast Salish villages consisted of one or more cedar plank structures, situated on seashores of sheltered bays and inlets and along riverbanks. Behind the coastal villages stood dense cedar and Douglas-fir forests, transected by trails and used by hunters and by those seeking plant resources and spiritual power. As the vegetation was lush, travel in the Coast Salish area was mostly by canoe and by trails situated along riverbanks.

Indigenous Coast Salish speak of villages, resource sites and prominent landscape features, distinguished by the application of Native place-names, while the naming systems de-emphasize undifferentiated landforms and remote forest land. Studies of toponymic systems increasingly indicate that as names set apart meaning-laden spaces from the landscape overall, cultural principles embedded in names illustrate a people's cognitive relationship with their surroundings. Place-names, therefore, are a good indicator of locations possessing cultural significance. Tilley (1994: 18) clearly notes this when he writes, 'without a name culturally significant sites would not exist, but only as a raw void, a natural environment'.

Named sites in the Coast Salish area include those used and those avoided, for Native people identify certain places that are the haunts of nebulous beings that may be threatening to humans. Place-names on this part of the coast often have very focused referents, nevertheless, though this characteristic varies from place to place. Some names contain specific descriptions regarding the physical properties of the referent site, providing information on an attribute of the site or topographical peculiarity, while they name others for the presence of plants or animals. These latter names frequently have metonymic associations, singling out places where resources are particularly abundant, or distinctive because of their uncommon occurrence.

Coast Salish traditional discourse also speaks of a time when the world was different from what it is today. It is said that a Transformer came through and set things right, changing animals and plants into their present form and leaving a landscape marked with rocks and cliffs where transformations occurred. These locations, far from being seemingly innocuous places, are hubs of cultural significance within a vast aboriginal landscape, possessing meaning for those who know the associated traditional stories.

Knowledge of places named and the associated cultural meanings are generally restricted to those specific groups of Coast Salish people who live or regularly visit a particular area. The extent to which notions of land and resource ownership prevailed varies throughout Coast Salish society, but do have implications for determining who can speak with authority about a specific area. Ownership of land and resources was conceptually different from the ownership of other types of property, with considerable diversity evident in what resource, site or type of technology was owned, and who did the owning.

To understand the application and efficacy of laws and regulations designed to facilitate protection of the Coast Salish landscape, and the problems that have emerged, it is necessary to consider two aspects of Coast Salish society: social organization and religion.

Social Organization

The Coast Salish, like many hunting, fishing and gathering societies, had no clans or confederations such as are found among their indisputably structured northern neighbours. Only residential groups provided for social, spiritual and economic needs, but membership in these groups was fluid and certainly they were not self-sufficient units. The term 'tribe', applied to individual Coast Salish societies, refers to a cluster of villages having enough social unity, and sometimes a common distinct dialect or language, to be recognized as a named group. Yet the tribe was not a political or an economic unit until the nineteenth century, and thus it had less consequence aboriginally in the daily lives of individuals than the independent family, or even the village. Nor was the village a self-sufficient unit, but only a link in an extensive regional network.

The prevailing anthropological theory set out by anthropologists Wayne Suttles (1960, 1963) and William Elmendorf (1960, 1971) characterizes Coast Salish social and economic relations as adaptations to an environment where resources were spatially and temporally concentrated and variable. Hence, recognition of the productivity cycles of salmon, along with the relative availability of other foodstuffs affected sporadically by environmental factors, led to Coast Salish families seeking ties with more distant villages. A series of obligatory affinal exchanges promoted the distribution of food and wealth. When things were tough, people changed their village membership. This was facilitated by a bilateral reckoning of kinship that permitted individuals to be socially related to one's father's and mother's relatives in the same way. Coast Salish kin terms are widely extended and may be said to provide the fundamental referents for most social interaction. Hence, kinship lays before each individual an array of possible ties to others. Once a choice has been made among several potential groups of kin, the acquisition of an ancestral name and the public validation of rights through potlatching activate it.

In theory, not all members of the Coast Salish kin group were localized in one dwelling, or even one village, as all who regarded themselves as descendants of the acclaimed progenitor were recognized as 'family'. Yet in practice, control of the family prerogatives became concentrated in the hands of a resident elite (Suttles 1990: 464).

Coast Salish people did not regard themselves as social equals and each tried to better his or her own status by establishing ties with other good families in other villages. Social control was maintained through the exercise of power by leading men (and to some extent, women) who controlled access to productive resources and proclaimed changes in status through potlatching. These elite individuals and their resource property were highly localized, but not associated with bounded groups of kin. Through a shared value system that emphasized the correct mode of behaviour, people of high class conformed to a particular conduct, for to do otherwise would result in gossiping neighbours commenting on an individual's low class. Low-class people had lost their history and had no advice to offer (Suttles 1958: 501).

Aboriginal theory thus highlights the potential for actuating membership in distant villages in order to gain access to dispersed resources; it also emphasizes control over access to specific resources in known locations. With many homes from which to choose, an individual's loyalties were constantly divided, and unlike the more structured groups to the north, the Coast Salish individual stood alone (Suttles 1981).

Coast Salish Religion

The blessings bestowed upon persons of high status included both tangible and intangible rewards. Ancestral names, songs, private family knowledge, and the use of ceremonial rights were manifestations of prestige, as was the preferred access to a few uncommonly productive resource sites. All of these were inherited possessions. Birth order was significant in the acquisition and recognition of status, but the possession of an appropriately powerful guardian spirit was critical in a man's proficiency to accumulate wealth, at least according to Coast Salish theory (Suttles 1951: 55, and 1958: 502; Barnett 1955: 250–1). Coast Salish people, not maintaining the discrete social groups that could give an individual perpetual support, sought help from outside of human society, in what Suttles (1981) has called the unnatural part of the world.

In earlier times, all boys and many girls were sent alone into the wilderness where they fasted, bathed themselves in cold water, and scrubbed their bodies with conifer boughs. The activity had to be conducted away from humanity, in a pure place, as the objective was to find a non-human helper. The Coast Salish, until recently, had no belief in a single Creator, a Mother Earth or a Great Spirit. Each individual person trained and entered into a partnership with a new helper that appeared in a vision. This guardian spirit power, once obtained, was a private possession that was never discussed but sometimes hinted at by the manner in which a person danced or painted his or her face at a winter spirit dance. At such dances, an individual was overcome by his or her power and danced alone around the longhouse. While the manner of acquisition of spirit power has transformed over the years, Coast Salish people continue to exhibit their helper's presence during winter spiritual dances. Religion for the Coast Salish is thus an individual affair that requires access to areas of wilderness – places away from humanity, but not necessarily the same place for all persons.[8]

Historical Variables

Historical evidence shows that maritime fur traders made calls at points along the north-west coast beginning in the 1770s, but none of these early expeditions remained long in the area. These early visitors engaged in trading with local Natives, but initiated no permanent establishments. The initial explorations would, however, establish independent European claims to the region. Under the theoretical premise that the north-west coast was *terra nullius*, European nations justified their property claims and title, eventually dividing the territory of the Coast Salish between the British and the Americans.

Over the next decades (1790s–1830s) considerable exploration by fur trade companies took place on the east side of the Cascade and Coastal Mountains, but little direct contact with Coast Salish people occurred to the west, other than the sporadic presence of trading vessels plying the coast. Of more consequence was the indirect effect of epidemics that decimated entire populations prior to and during this early historic period.[9] By the 1830s, a handful of fur trade posts had been established on the coast, but the few dozen men required to manage each of these depots did not dominate Native society. Diversification of the land-based fur trade on the coast in the 1840s changed this situation and resulted in a more direct impact on aboriginal lifeways. With the fur trade now in decline, the companies found new products of export – salmon, timber, agricultural products and coal – and introduced a new economy that competed with the aboriginal Coast Salish residents for both land and resources.

Competition between Natives and settlers took a different form in the British territory than in the American possessions, the latter being those lands delineated more precisely by the 1846 Treaty of Oregon which identified the area south of the 49th parallel as belonging to what subsequently became the United States. North of the border settlement was restricted largely to a few places around the trading forts. The presence of the forts affected Native settlement patterns as some Indian people shifted villages to locations more accessible to the trade, but for the most part Native people remained in their aboriginal villages. As what became British Columbia was a sparsely populated area situated a long way from London, the Imperial Colonial Office actively encouraged the development of locally specific policies, which would reflect the regional dynamics and character of aboriginal–white relations. Britain's concern was that aboriginal title be extinguished through measures of liberality and justice, and that 'the honour of the Crown' be preserved.

For several years, beginning in 1850, the British representative on the ground, Governor James Douglas, set about negotiating treaties, starting in areas where settlement was anticipated. These treaties reflected clearly their European authors' notion of land use, for while the purchase included all of what was deemed to be a particular group's territory, they reserved village sites and cultivated lands for Native use. They also made provision for 'liberty to hunt over the unoccupied lands, and to carry on our fisheries as formerly'. The colonial governor had little knowledge or appreciation of the complexity of Coast Salish social organization and typically had difficulty distinguishing which group of people belonged to a particular tract of land, and which headman should represent the group. This resulted in the treaties creating ethnographic absurdities (see Duff 1969).

Once London refused to advance the new colony the funds for distinguishing aboriginal title, the governor was left to his own devices to protect the interests of the indigenous people. His policy then was to balance the protection and development of Natives with the requirements of expected settlement by creating 'anticipatory reserves' ahead of white colonists. Native people would remain in their villages and be allocated agricultural land adequate to enable self-sufficiency.

The extent of colonial reserves set aside was generous, but the large landholdings in the hands of the aboriginal people were soon felt to be counter-productive to the development of a new colony, and their size was reduced.

In the colonial view, the land's productivity was dependent upon the intervention of humankind. There was no consideration that a landscape was being lost through colonization and development, only that it provided an environment upon which improvement could be made and civilization developed. Archibald Barclay (1849) of the Colonial Office illustrated this point with his command that uncultivated land was 'to be regarded as waste, and applicable to the purposes of colonization'. The aboriginal occupants – called by the colony's governor, the 'wandering denizens of the forest' – required protection from the 'aggressions of the immigrants' (Douglas 1859), and, consequently, traditional village sites became 'reserves'.

Most Indian reserves in British Columbia were not set aside until British Columbia's entry into the Confederation of Canada in 1871, and in 1876 the newly introduced Indian Act created the legal foundation by which Indians and Indian affairs were administered. The indigenous people remained displeased, having been dispossessed of most of their traditional territories without having either their aboriginal title extinguished or their aboriginal rights acknowledged. Moreover, an imposed administrative system that included an elected chief and council for each 'Band' – itself a foreign social unit – ignored, and often conflicted with, the aboriginal form of leadership.

The American approach to Natives and settlement in the north-west differed significantly from that of the British. A reconnaissance survey for a railway helped open up the area and soon the region was being settled by whites whose claims to land conflicted with Congress's recognition of aboriginal title. One historian observed that the early pattern of settlement of the American west resembled superficially that of the Indians[10] they were displacing. They spread over the prairie lands and grouped themselves on tracts adjoining rivers and bays where their domestic animals competed with the Indians for camas bulbs, a staple food of the aboriginal people (White 1972: 32). Still, legal assurance was given to the indigenous residents that their lands would not be taken without their consent. Once the new territory of Washington was defined in 1853, the government recognized the critical need to extinguish Indian title.

The newly appointed governor of Washington Territory, Isaac Stevens, was requested to treat with the resident Indians and set aside lands reserved for their use. It was soon recommended, however, that reservations be established away from white settlement, outside of the various tribes' aboriginal territories if necessary, and on as few tracts of land as possible. The task, of course, created an ethnographic and administrative nightmare, as groups with sometimes little former contact were brought together to share lands and resources, and to be represented by one head chief. Where 'chiefs' did not exist aboriginally, the governor appointed individuals with whom he could negotiate treaties (White 1991: 93). Some groups refused to participate, and others fled into the hills, but within a few months time the governor had met with thousands of Indians and had negotiated treaties encompassing most of Washington State (Cohen 1986: 37).

Allegations of fraud and forgery are common concerning the representation of the aboriginal groups said to be party to the treaties however (Trafzer 1986: 4), resulting in so much unrest being created by this work that war broke out in Puget Sound. Those Natives not already on reservations were soon removed from their lands and settled on temporary reserves. One writer on this period of Washington State history remarked that: 'By 1859, those who survived war, removal, and poverty had lost both their cultural distinctiveness and their tribal cohesion' (Seeman 1986: 19). While the level of cohesiveness that existed in aboriginal Puget Sound 'tribes' may be questioned, Seeman's comment does underscore the devastating results of the US Indian policy at this time. It also illustrates the place of aboriginal people within the American world-view – they were conquered and demoralized.

Each treaty stated that the affected Indians ceded, relinquished and conveyed forever to the United States all their right, title and interest in the lands defined. In addition to an anti-slavery clause, specific clauses set out protection of Indian fishing, hunting and gathering rights. The courts throughout the twentieth century would uphold these rights and a 1970 court decision established that ambiguous treaty language must be resolved in favour of the Indians. Hence, when the interpretation of treaty language was an issue debated in a recent hunting case (*State of Washington* v. *Buchanan 1997*) highlighting the right to hunt on 'open and unclaimed lands', the Appeals Court of the State of Washington found that a liberal interpretation of the clause was warranted. In this case, it was found that a tribe's hunting rights were not to be delineated by 'usual and accustomed' grounds, such as the manner in which the treaty defined reserved fishing rights. The treaty's specification of a 'privilege of hunting and gathering roots and berries on open and unclaimed lands' was, in the Court's view, not to be limited to traditional areas. This decision has considerable ramifications for cultural resource managers.

Issues Concerning Land and Heritage

Common to both Canadian and United States government policies concerning the identification of culturally significant locations is reliance upon the notion that an ethnographic site's importance is rooted in the place it occupies in a group's cultural 'traditions'. Determining what is 'traditional' is never without problems. While few anthropologists today would seek the purity of pre-contact cultures in contemporary aboriginal societies, and most accept the inherently dynamic nature of 'tradition', members of indigenous societies assert its constancy in legitimizing land claims, just as governments call for its presence before rights can be admitted.

Anthropologist James Waldram (1997: 132) recently wrote: 'Despite over 300 years of colonialism in Canada, there remain aboriginal people who can still be described as "traditional."' They retain their Native language, using it in the home and for ceremonial purposes, and engage in a hunting, fishing and gathering economy, supplemented by Western commodities. However, such communities as Waldram describes are few and generally isolated. In the Coast Salish area – in the midst of which are situated the immense cities of Vancouver and Seattle – three of the indigenous languages are extinct, most are moribund, and only one continues to be used in the longhouse, and when old people gather. There is, nevertheless, a widespread use of a distinctive dialect of Aboriginal English, a situation noted by Tonkinson (1997: 9) among certain Australian indigenous groups. Traditional subsistence activities remain prominent, at least for those Coast Salish members residing on Indian reserves (in Canada) and reservations (in the US). Former systems of ownership and access to resources are seldom acknowledged, having being replaced by regulatory mechanisms under band or tribal control, and, ultimately, under the control of the dominant society.

In the past several decades Coast Salish people have drawn upon their own oral traditions – or upon those of their neighbours whose cultural traditions persisted – in consolidating what they now regard as 'traditional' culture. This is largely focused on the winter spirit dances described above, and on an emphasis of family relations extending throughout the Coast Salish community. Of course, the cultural orientation of Canadian aboriginal people, as Waldram (1997: 133) points out, 'runs the broad range from the traditional in the Aboriginal context to more-or-less completely Euro-Canadian'. It is my observation that Canadian Coast Salish communities maintain a more conservative cultural orientation (to use Waldram's terminology) than those Coast Salish groups residing south of the international border. The early US policy of concentrating formerly distinct groups onto large, single reservations contributed greatly to language death and to these people's considerable integration into mainstream American society.[11] Washington State's Coast Salish people, in general, exhibit a greater acceptance of eclectic, pan-Indian beliefs than their northern neighbours. Both, nevertheless, employ 'tradition' as a metaphor for cultural identity and distinctiveness, just as non-Native governments on both sides of the border require adherence to tradition as the foundation for recognition of aboriginal attachment to specific lands.

While 'tradition' relies upon elements from the past, this 'past', as Linnekin (1993: 242) observes, 'is equivocal: it does not correspond to the experience of any particular generation'. Hobsbawm and Ranger also address its ephemeral nature (1983: 1) and remark that 'traditions which appear or claim to be old are often quite recent in origin and sometimes invented'. Citing this quotation, Marie Mauzé (1997: 5) then asks, how we can be sure that a 'tradition' is really old? Her question is truly challenging. Anthropologists' responses to this question – as discussed for the past two decades, particularly with reference to Oceania – depend largely upon their theoretical orientation. This is evident in the lively exchange resulting from Hanson's (1989) examination of the logic of 'cultural invention' or 'construction' with respect to the Maori of New Zealand, and, more recently, from the critical debate focusing on the highly contentious Hindmarsh Island Bridge Affair in Australia (see Tonkinson 1997).

In Canada and the US, 'tradition', as applied to recognition of 'traditional cultural properties' and 'traditional use sites', has been given a temporal benchmark. US guidelines for documenting the locations of culturally important places state that associated 'traditions' must be more than fifty years old, though there is a provision for traditions revived within the last fifty years to be associated with specific areas if the community used the land formerly for that activity. From the Canadian courts' perspective, 'tradition' dates to the time of British sovereignty, set by the court for BC as 1846. Yet our best descriptions of aboriginal society come from people interviewed after the turn of the twentieth century. These individuals did not themselves participate in aboriginal culture, and learned its content mostly through oral transmission.

Contemporary cultural revival movements model their notions of tradition on both extant oral tradition and on earlier accounts of Coast Salish society. The selective reappropriation of certain elements associated with the past favours grand emblematic displays of property distribution and Indian-naming over less congenial practices such as infanticide and slavery, although in Canada, at least, they have not challenged the aboriginal right to do so. Recent public outrage in British Columbia and Washington State concerning the neighbouring Makah and Nuu-chah-nulth tribes' proposed revitalization of whale hunting suggests that tolerance of aboriginal rights depends largely upon their affinity with the values accorded to them by mainstream society. These values highlight the spiritual. They also tend to ossify indigenous people as exotic specimens requiring preservation in their idealized state, along with trees and rivers.

The privileging of the 'sacred' was reflected in the guidelines established for the province of BC's Traditional Use Study programme and the initial explanation of its objectives. There was a presumption by the government ministry that the aboriginal communities would consider a large number of sites to be 'sacred', and thus kept confidential. So they arranged for the First Nations to send the government funders maps showing only the locations of these sacred sites (or any other site type considered secret), without a requirement for supporting documentation, whereas prior to the initiation of the TUS programme it was common for anthropologists and their First Nations' collaborators to compile studies providing detailed knowledge of place-names and resource use. One year after the inception of the programme, and the expenditure of millions of dollars, all parties involved in the TUS programme voiced mistrust of the process. The First Nations have subsequently disclosed little data.

First Nations' mistrust of the TUS programme focused on its potential use of the information that the Native people felt might compromise their land claims or treaty rights. As well, the aboriginal groups were concerned about the potential for site exploitation or desecration by the public, and they felt there had not been sufficient consultation in land-use planning and decision-making. The fears of industry concerning this programme centred upon the veracity of the data, especially since the government's TUS agreements with the First Nations permitted any information deemed to be 'sensitive' to be withheld, providing they plotted the extent of the sites. When industry was presented with maps containing large, amorphous, unexplained polygons said to represent areas of aboriginal use *so* sensitive that they could not reveal them, industry felt anxious about the implications for future development.

The use of tradition as a political instrument for regulating both internal and external relations has recently gained attention (see Mauzé 1997). In Tonkinson's (1997) review of the Hindmarsh Bridge Affair in Australia, for example, he suggests that we best conceptualize tradition as a resource to be used (or not used) strategically by certain (but not all) members of a society in defence or furtherance of aboriginal interests. Tonkinson (1997: 12) notes, with reference to the work of anthropologist Homer Barnett on the transition from innovation to tradition, that 're-readings of the past have long been recognized as a universal aspect of social life'. Importantly, Tonkinson explains, 're-readings of the past do not necessarily entail any conscious fabrication or manipulation of fact' (1997: 12). Nevertheless, First Nations' secrecy, and thus restrictions on the validation of data, does not instil confidence in either industry or the courts that they are achieving a full consideration of the evidence. Arguably, from the aboriginal perspective, the Canadian court's view regarding the non-evolutionary nature of tradition fosters justifiable fears that changing land-use patterns, an incomplete database, or, simply, a lack of tradition-bearers from whom an aboriginal group could elicit such inform-ation, will jeopardize asserted rights. The logical response is to reveal nothing.

Levels of disclosure and the veracity of information relied upon to assert claims have become central issues in land-use disputes throughout British Columbia and Washington State. Some problems raised can be illustrated by examining a situation focused on a hydroelectric licensing application set before the Washington State Pollution Control Hearings Board. The applicant initiated a study to ascertain the locations of traditional cultural properties in the project's area of potential effect (APE). Following accepted guidelines, cultural resource management consultants acting for the company attempted to fulfil the first consideration for the evaluation of properties; that is, determining the identity of a specific area (a 'property') regarded by the local tribe as culturally significant. The anthropological consultants working on the project for several years attempted, without success, to engage the relevant tribe in preparing an inventory of traditional sites. When the licence was issued, the tribe filed a complaint, stating that the whole middle fork of the pertinent river valley was important for 'cultural and religious' reasons, particularly for the practice of ritual bathing. They provided no details of use or site locations. The Board subsequently determined that the tribe may indeed have cultural resources in the project area, but the fact that the tribe would not inventory such resources meant that the panel could not conclude that development would adversely affect the sites. Nor did the potential for ritual bathing rise to the level of a beneficial use, intended to be protected by the State's Department of Ecology in its anti-degradation regulations.

While they could not validate the tribe's claim that the area was important for 'religious use', a look at what we know about Coast Salish religious concepts suggests that a different level of discourse was operating in framing the tribe's response. This is an area of Coast Salish where recently introduced Plains-style religious activities are used in the treatment of drug and alcohol abuse. This took place at the same time that a group of individuals was promoting adherence to the longhouse religion, a practice that requires access to wilderness, although not necessarily a specific wilderness. In an interview I had with an official of this same tribe (concerning a different project) subsequent to the Pollution Control Board review, he emphasized his dislike of the concept of 'property'. In addition, he advised me that, in his words, 'Native Americans do not have specific properties that have religious significance, as we get the feeling wherever there is water and cedar trees.'

The tribal official's comment brings to mind Mauzé's (1998) discussion concerning the use of trees — particularly cedar trees — on the north-west coast 'as a political statement in defence of ancestral lands on the ground that they are sacred and essential for religious practices', a discourse inspired by an aboriginal world-view, but one that takes liberties in its interpretation. Contemporary discourse, in Mauzé's (1998: 243) analysis, ontologizes natural beings in a slightly different way from that in which traditional discourse does, for now cedar trees are seen as moral beings with an agency of their own. The argument is strengthened by using Christian analogies that serve to bolster trees to the exalted position of being the most prominent, contemporary symbol of Indian identity and survival, a metaphor employed more often for matters of cultural and political survival than for ecological survival (Mauzé 1998: 246). Thus, while the official position taken by the tribe finds support in the ethnographic literature, as far as the nonspecific nature of sites for the practice of Coast Salish religion is concerned, the US National Register of Historic Places requires a nominated site to be a specific property with a documented history of associated use. Here, assertions of religious association failed, as no evidence was forthcoming that these aboriginal people had used or continue to use the project area. As federal regulations acknowledge the traditional use of specific properties, where culturally appropriate boundaries can be defined, the land's position within the parameters of an area generally considered having been associated with this tribe's ancestors did not meet the test for recognition of a 'traditional cultural property'.

Recognition of properties can sometimes pit indigenous people against one another when the identity of the rightful group to be officially consulted in the TCP process becomes an issue. Recently, in another area of Washington State, a group of people of Coast Salish descent, then not recognized by the US government as a legally constituted 'tribe', used the public forum provided by the TCP process to assert the group's association with a particular waterfall and thereby express their feelings of religious and political cohesion. The tribe's anthropologist entered a report in the proceedings arguing that the waterfalls have played a central position in the culture of these people 'since time immemorial'. The site was eventually determined eligible for listing in the US National Register of Historic Places. Research indicated that not just Native Americans visit the site, but that an estimated 1.5 million tourists view the waterfalls each year.

Moreover, fans of a popular television show, which was filmed at the site, supported the nomination, saying that they, too, had a spiritual attachment to the falls. Thus, the site's National Register eligibility could be determined quite readily, and the issue of 'integrity of association' did not become an external issue. What did emerge, however, was a charge of 'self-invention' levelled against the unrecognized group by a neighbouring officially recognized tribe. The latter tribe mounted an equally vocal attack against the anthropologist for his role in what they viewed as the creation of a new political entity and of the bogus authenticity ascribed to that group's past ties. It was their position that at the time of the treaty the ancestors of these people had chosen not to move onto their reservation. Thus, they alleged that these contemporary individuals were 'imposters' usurping an identity, which legally belonged to the descendants of Indian people enrolled as members of the federally recognized tribe.

As this situation illustrates, the politics of authenticity determining who is considered more *real* than the other can selectively divide communities by calling upon differing membership criteria: in this case, a recognized tribe whose political and social cohesiveness was formed by an imposed treaty, versus a group seeking recognition of Indian tribal status – and all the federal funding that flows with it – based partly on religious cohesion.[12]

The anthropologist attributed the non-recognized group an association with the falls that extended to 'time immemorial'. By doing so, he noted the US Department of the Interior's fifty-year age requirement for 'tradition'. But, importantly for their defence against the protestations of their recognized kin, the assertion fixed their specific tribal identity beyond the backward reach of the treaty – which consolidated a new social organization – to a time when their 'tribal' name had a more discrete, if not political, meaning. The political manoeuvring of the opposing groups, therefore, relied strategically upon 'tradition' fixed at distinct times to further their own interests.

Discussion

The model of 'tradition' recognized in Canadian and American policies and regulations concerning the recognition of culturally significant places is not necessarily the view exemplified in Kroeber's classic definition of tradition being 'internal handing on through time'. The Supreme Court of Canada does not say that a tradition must have remained static, only that it was an integral aspect of the antecedent culture and that it bears a direct relationship to its contemporary form. This is reflected in the guidelines for the BC government's Traditional Use Study programme. US regulations call for tradition to be older than fifty years. There is no explicit expectation that timeless values and beliefs are out there to be discovered by dedicated anthropologists; there is, nonetheless, an expectation that processes of social reproduction operate to transmit knowledge of the past to the present. Yet as the Coast Salish cases summarized above illustrate, 'tradition' is reached through inductive reasoning that takes place in the present, and is used to justify the present through remembering the past (Mauzé 1997: 6–7).

The present historic preservation policies and regulations in Canada and the US differ little from the Australian situation described by Tonkinson (1997). There, too, definitions of heritage and tradition may be broad, yet the parameters of the regulations shape the discourse through which aboriginal groups must frame their claims. In western North America, these call for identification of bounded properties or sites associated with the legally recognized entities of First Nations or tribes, and privileging specific places deemed to be sacred and expressed in terms of tradition. Importantly, the regulations also privilege groups possessing a more conservative cultural orientation, for programmes designed to promote cultural retention emphasize the past and call for proof of the aboriginal relationship and an assessment of its integrity. Public sentiment thus encourages the recognition of cultural diversity and religious expression, enabling governments to identify specific places of cultural importance and to confer upon them special safeguards. It is evident, however, that tolerance of aboriginal customs extends to land and resource uses that are in accord with the dominant society's values, and which emphasize a view of aboriginal people as morally superior beings intent upon maintaining a 'traditional' landscape.

As examined here, the specific cultural practice of the aboriginal groups may not fit well with the regulatory requirements. Sometimes this leads to a reliance upon metaphors for the development of a politically charged discourse, potentially perceived by discordant parties as constructed or invented tradition, lacking veracity. In one Coast Salish dispute examined here, the use of an asserted discourse failed when they could not meet demands for certain types of evidence. Though the indigenous litigants drew upon potent symbols of identity to assert general rights of association to a distinct area, the nation-state's requirement for 'proof' rested in disclosure of facts that the aboriginal group could not, or would not, provide. Indigenous people sometimes view identification of specific places within the indigenous landscape as an abrogation of one's heritage and one's ancestral rights.

A great debate in anthropology focuses on the nature of tradition. Its potency as a contestable resource (to use Tonkinson's terminology) in land-use planning is readily apparent. There are anthropologists who would have us not test the veracity of indigenous claims, instead only deciding whether he or she believed one's informant (Fergie, cited in Tonkinson 1997: 11). However, the acceptance of everything contemporary, especially in the politically charged atmosphere of the north-west coast, would be an absurd form of positivism that we must avoid if special legal rights are to be maintained. Rereading of the past may be universal, but 'one story is not as good as another', as noted by Haraway (1989: 33; quoted in Linnekin 1992), who advises that 'attention to narrative, is not instead of attention to science'.

The Supreme Court of Canada in December 1997 brought down a decision that authorized for *Delgamuukw* a new trial that would take into account the aboriginal oral traditions that the lower court trial judge had quickly rebuffed. It was the Supreme Court of Canada's ruling that courts are to adapt the laws of evidence so that they give due weight to the aboriginal views on their practices, customs, and traditions, and on their relationship with the land. It means that this evidence, as hearsay evidence, is not automatically inferior to documentary evidence. It does *not* mean that the courts must automatically accept oral history, or consider it superior to other types of evidence – only that they give it due weight. Already, aboriginal groups are marshalling evidence; some are mounting challenges to one another's claims to territory, based on oral records of land use. So now the question becomes, 'which story to believe?'

The 'battle for the control over the definition and content of tradition', as Tonkinson (1997: 603) so aptly states, will continue. There is not necessarily any mutually agreeable resolution to land-use disputes. It is here, nevertheless, where anthropological methodology will be necessary to interpret the concepts and traditions of all interested parties, and to assist both the courts and petitioners in assessing and analysing the data presented. Choosing not to participate in the process abandons the anthropologists' role to lawyers, who without our methodology are blinded by their role of advocacy in the unfriendly adversarial arena. Legal requirements look upon facts in more precise terms than our anthropological accounts of social practices that are open to various interpretations, but still anthropologists have the tools for evaluating the empirical from the empirically false. One fact we can all agree upon, however, is that the stakes in the cultural landscape are high, and there are many stakeholders competing for identification and association with the same land.

Notes

The Social Sciences and Humanities Research Council of Canada facilitated my research between 1997 and 2000 at the Institute of Social and Cultural Anthropology and Exeter College, Oxford, during which time I presented this paper. I am grateful to all who provided information and to those who offered comment on the original paper, particularly Randy Bouchard, Bob Freedman and Gail Thompson.

1. 'First Nation(s)' is currently the preferred term used in western Canada to refer to indigenous groups, although the terms 'Indian' and 'Native' continue to be used by aboriginal people themselves in daily communication.
2. *Hamlet of Baker Lake* v. *Minister of Indian Affairs and Northern Development* (1979), 107 D.L.R. (3d) 513.
3. The courts have found consultation to be a two-way street. In one instance, the Gitksan people (litigants in the *Delgamuukw* case) in north-western BC asked that a logging permit be quashed on the basis that it unlawfully interfered with an aboriginal right and that the Ministry of Forests had failed to properly consult with the tribe. The court found that the consultation process had been adequate and that the failure was entirely due to the refusal of the tribe to take part in the consultation process unless preconditions relating to a transfer of jurisdiction were met. The court found that there was little cooperation by the tribe and great persistence by the Ministry, therefore satisfying the demand for consultation.
4. The Supreme Court of BC ruled on 5 February 1999 that the Court challenge could not proceed until the Nisga'a Treaty had been ratified by both the federal and provincial governments. The Treaty received Royal Assent in May 2000. In August 2001 the Liberal Party of BC, who as of June 2001 formed the provincial government, dropped their legal challenge to the Treaty, although they announced their intention to proceed with a referendum focused on treaty issues.
5. A neighbouring group asserting an overlapping claim alleges that one of these sites is associated only with their own history, and not that of the Nisga'a.
6. The acronym 'TUS', as used by the province, refers both to 'Traditional Use Study' and also to 'Traditional Use Site'.

7. This summary of Coast Salish society is based on Kennedy and Bouchard (1990), Suttles (1990), Suttles and Lane (1990) and Hajda (1990).
8. This point was argued by Wayne Suttles in a statement on the contemporary land needs of Coast Salish people for religious purposes that he prepared in conjunction with a cultural resource inventory focusing on one of Washington State's National Forests (Suttles 1981).
9. The consequences of the initial epidemics have been examined by Boyd (1985, 1990, 1994), Acheson (1995) and Harris (1994).
10. The term 'Indian' continues to be preferred by Americans of aboriginal ancestry.
11. A 1941–2 study by Elizabeth Colson (1967) among an American Coast Salish group – identified by the author as the 'Fishers' – described their 'assimilation' by means of American government policies designed to promote incorporation into mainstream US society. The Fishers 'borrowed, adapted and rejected, in line with their own interests' (Colson 1967: 212). Yet though they partly evaded the authoritarian control of the Indian agent by practising ceremonial rituals in modified form, the cessation of prohibited rituals eventually resulted in associated changes in the Native social organization. The most important changes, according to the author, resulted from the establishment of a boarding school which removed the children from the community, providing only restricted visits with the home community.
12. Though it was not important for the federally recognized tribe to assert their own 'traditionalism' in the debate, inasmuch as they are a 'political entity', they, too, are undergoing cultural rejuvenation with the help of anthropologists and linguists. More recently, another neighbouring tribal group who have also opposed the granting of status recognition to the the non-treaty group, became litigants when their plans for a new amphitheatre to be built on their reservation were challenged by environmentally minded citizens, including a senior representative of the US government.

References

Acheson, S. (1995), 'Culture Contact, Demography and Health Among the Aboriginal Peoples of British Columbia', *Canadian Western Geographical Series*, 31: 1–42. (Victoria: University of Victoria, Department of Geography.)

Barclay, A. (1849), 'Memorandum to James Douglas, December 17th, 1849', Hudson's Bay Company Archives, Provincial Archives of Manitoba, Winnipeg, Manitoba, A.5/28, folios 90d–92.

Barnett, H. (1955), *The Coast Salish of British Columbia*, University of Oregon Monographs, Studies in Anthropology 4, Eugene. (Reprinted: Greenwood Press, Westport, Conn., 1975.)

Basso, K. (1984), 'Western Apache Place-Name Hierarchies', *Naming Systems: The 1980 Proceedings of the American Ethnological Society* (eds Elizabeth Tooker and Harold C. Conklin), Washington, DC: The American Ethnological Society.

—— (1988), '"Speaking With Names"': Language and Landscape Among the Western Apache', *Cultural Anthropology*, 3(2): 99–130.

—— (1996), *Wisdom Sits in Places: Landscape and Language Among the Western Apache*, Albuquerque, N.Mex.: University of New Mexico Press.

Berndt, R. (1976), 'Territoriality and the Problem of Demarcating Socio-cultural Space', in N. Peterson (ed.), *Tribes and Boundaries in Australia*, London: Angus and Robertson.

Boyd, R. (1985), 'The Introduction of Infectious Diseases Among the Indians of the Pacific Northwest, 1774–1874', Unpublished Ph.D. dissertation in Anthropology, University of Washington, Seattle.

—— (1990), 'Demographic History, 1774–1874', in W. Suttles (ed.), *Handbook of North American Indians*, Vol. 7: *Northwest Coast*, pp. 135–48, Washington, DC: Smithsonian Institution.

—— (1994), 'The Pacific Northwest Measles Epidemic of 1847–1848', *Oregon Historical Quarterly*, 95(1): 6–47.

British Columbia, Ministry of Aboriginal Affairs (1998), 'Consultation Guidelines', September.

Cohen, F. (1986), *Treaties on Trial: The Continuing Controversy over Northwest Indian Fishing Rights*, Seattle and London: University of Washington Press.

Colson, E. (1967), 'Assimilation of an American Indian Group', *Beyond the Frontier: Social Progress and Cultural Change*, New York: The Natural History Press.

Douglas, J. (1859), Letter to the Hon. Sir E.B. Lytton, March 14th, 1859, British Columbia Papers, 16–17.

Duff, W. (1969), 'The Fort Victoria Treaties', *British Columbia Studies*, 3 (Fall): 3–57.

Elmendorf, W. W. (1960), 'The Structure of Twana Culture', *Washington State University Research Studies*, 23(3), Monographic Supplement 2, Pullman.

—— (1971), 'Coast Salish Status Ranking and Intergroup Ties', *Southwestern Journal of Anthropology*, 27(4): 353–80.

Eves, R. (1997), 'Seating the Place: Tropes of Body, Movement and Space for the People of Lelet Plateau, New Ireland (Papua New Guinea)', in J. Fox (ed.), *The Poetic Power of Place: Comparative Perspectives on Austronesian Ideas of Locality*, pp. 174–96, Canberra: Department of Anthropology in Association with the Comparative Austronesian Project, Research School of Pacific and Asian Studies, the Australian National University.

Fox, J. (1997), 'Place and Landscape in Comparative Austronesian Perspective', in J. Fox (ed.), *The Poetic Power of Place: Comparative Perspectives on Austronesian Ideas of Locality*, pp. 1–21, Canberra: Department of Anthropology in Association with the Comparative Austronesian Project, Research School of Pacific and Asian Studies, the Australian National University.

Freedman, R. (1995), 'Reconsidering the *Baker Lake* Test', Paper presented at the Sovereignty Symposium, Tulsa, Oklahoma, 8 June. (Original in possession of author, Vancouver, British Columbia.)

Gable, E., Handler, R. and Lawson, A. (1992), 'On the Uses of Relativism: Fact, Conjecture, and Black and White Histories at Colonial Williamsburg', *American Ethnologist*, 19(4): 791–805.

Hajda, Y. (1990), 'Southwestern Coast Salish', in W. Suttles (ed.), *Handbook of North American Indians*, Vol. 7: *Northwest Coast*, pp. 503–17, Washington, DC: Smithsonian Institution.

Hanson, A. (1989), 'The Making of the Maori: Culture Invention and its Logic', *American Anthropologist*, 91(4): 890–902.

—— (1991), 'Reply to Langdon, Levine and Linnekin', *American Anthropologist*, 93(1): 449–50.

Harris, C. (1994), 'Voices of Disaster: Smallpox Around the Strait of Georgia in 1782', *Ethnohistory*, 41(4): 591–626.

Hobsbawm, E. and Ranger, T. (1983), *The Invention of Tradition*, Cambridge: Cambridge University Press.

Hunn, E. (1990), *Nch'i-Wana: The Big River: Mid-Columbia Indians and their Land*, Seattle: University of Washington Press.

—— (1991), 'Native Place Names on the Columbia Plateau', in *A Time of Gathering: Native Heritage in Washington State*, pp. 170–7, Seattle: Burke Museum.

—— (1994), 'Place-Names, Population Density, and the Magic Number 500', *Current Anthropology*, 35(1): 81–5, 232.

—— (1996), 'Columbia Plateau Indian Placenames: What Can They Teach Us?' *Journal of Linguistic Anthropology*, 6(1): 3–26.

Hunter, J. (1998), 'Doing Business on Crown Land: An Overview', Paper presented by John Hunter, QC, at a Conference entitled 'Doing Business on Crown Land' hosted by the Pacific Business & Law Institute, 15 October, Vancouver, British Columbia.

Kennedy, D. I. D. and Bouchard, R. (1990), 'Northern Coast Salish', in W. Suttles (ed.), *Handbook of North American Indians*, Vol. 7: *Northwest Coast*, pp. 441–52, Washington, DC: Smithsonian Institution.

Linnekin, J. (1991), 'Cultural Invention and the Dilemma of Authenticity', *American Anthropologist*, 93(1): 446–9.

—— (1992), 'On the Theory and Politics of Cultural Construction', *Oceania*, 62(4): 249–63.

—— (1993), 'Defining Tradition: Variations on Hawaiian Identity', *American Ethnologist*, 10(2): 241–52.

Mauzé, M. (1997), 'On Concepts of Tradition: An Introduction', in M. Mauzé (ed.), *Present is Past: Some Uses of Tradition in Native Societies*, New York: University Press of America.

—— (1998), 'Northwest Coast Trees: From Metaphors in Culture to Symbols for Culture', *The Social Life of Trees*, pp. 233–51, Oxford: Berg.

Parker, P. and King, T. (1990), *Guidelines for Evaluating and Documenting Traditional Cultural Properties*, National Register Bulletin No. 38, United States Department of the Interior, National Park Service (Interagency Resources Division), Washington, DC.

Rappaport, J. (1989), 'Geography and Historical Understanding in Indigenous Columbia', in R. Layton (ed.), *Who Needs the Past? Indigenous Values and Archaeology*, pp. 84–94, London and New York: Routledge.

Santos-Granero, F. (1998), 'Writing History into the Landscape: Space, Myth and Ritual in Contemporary Amazonia', *American Ethnologist*, 25(2): 128–48.

Schama, S. (1995), *Landscape and Memory*, London: HarperCollins.

Seeman, C. (1986), 'The Treaties of Puget Sound', in C. Trafzer (ed.), *Indians, Superintendents, and Councils: Northwest Indian Policy, 1850–1855*, Lanham, Md.: The University Press of America.

Suttles, W. (1951), 'Economic Life of the Coast Salish of Haro and Rosario Straits', Ph.D. Dissertation in Anthropology, University of Washington, Seattle.

—— (1954), 'Post-contact Culture Change Among the Lummi Indians', *British Columbia Historical Quarterly*, 18(1–2): 29–102.

—— (1955), *Katzie Ethnographic Notes*, Victoria: British Columbia Provincial Museum.

—— (1958), 'Private Knowledge, Morality, and Social Classes among the Coast Salish', *American Anthropologist*, 60: 497–507.

—— (1960), 'Affinal Ties, Subsistence, and Prestige Among the Coast Salish', *American Anthropologist*, 62(2): 296–305.

—— (1963), 'The Persistence of Intervillage Ties Among the Coast Salish', *Ethnology*, 2: 512–25.

—— (1981), 'The Coast Salish Need For Wilderness', Appendix in *Inventory of Native American Religious Use, Practices, Localities and Resources*, Report prepared by Astrida Blukis Onat and Jan Hollenbeck for the Mt. Baker–Snoqualmie National Forest, Washington State.

—— (1990), 'Central Coast Salish', in W. Suttles (ed.), *Handbook of North American Indians*: Vol. 7: *Northwest Coast*, pp. 453–75, Washington, DC: Smithsonian Institution.

Suttles, W. and Lane, B. (1990), 'Southern Coast Salish', in W. Suttles (ed.), *Handbook of North American Indians*, Vol. 7: *Northwest Coast*, pp. 485–502, Washington DC: Smithsonian Institution.

Thomas, N. (1992), 'The Inversion of Tradition', *American Ethnologist*, 19(2): 213–22.

Thornton, T. F. (1995), 'Place and Being Among the Tlingit', Ph.D. Dissertation in Anthropology, University of Washington.

Tilley, C. (1994), *Places, Paths and Monuments: A Phenomenology of Landscape*, Oxford: Berg.

Tonkinson, R. (1997), 'Anthropology and Aboriginal Tradition: the Hindmarsh Island Bridge Affair and the Politics of Interpretation', *Oceania*, 68(1): 1–25.

Trafzer, C. (ed.) (1986), *Indians, Superintendents, and Councils: Northwest Indian Policy, 1850–1855*, Lanham, Md.: The University Press of America.

Tuan, Y. F. (1977), *Space and Place: the Perspective of Experience*, London: Arnold.

Waldram, J. (1997), 'The Reification of Aboriginal Culture in Canadian Prison Spirituality Programs', in M. Mauzé (ed.), *Present is Past: Some Uses of Tradition in Native Societies*, New York: The University Press of America.

White, R. (1972), 'The Treaty at Medicine Creek: Indian–White Relations on Upper Puget Sound, 1830–1880', Unpublished Masters Thesis, University of Washington.

—— (1991), '"It's Your Misfortune and None of My Own," A History of the American West', Norman: University of Oklahoma Press.

3

The Time When the Majority in the Israeli 'Cabinet' Decided 'Not to Block the Possibility of the Return of the Arab Refugees' and How and Why This Policy was Defeated

Shulamit Carmi and Henry Rosenfeld

This is a study on a defeated social and political alternative. The alternative was return of the Arab refugees of the 1948 war. As is well known, 650,000 to 750,000 Palestinian Arab war refugees were denied return by the Israeli leadership that, at one and the same time (1948–49), adopted a political agenda embracing non-return of the refugees, take-over of their land and the imposition of a military government upon the remnant Palestinian population. We believe that this new orientation stood in contradiction to a historically wrought Jewish minority's 'wisdom' of what we call 'coexistence within conflict' with the Arabs in Palestine. Thinking it over, 'coexistence within conflict' could well be the human situation within which alternatives are considered. If so, and since culture is a historical production, we believe we have a case to present.[1]

In the first section of this paper we discuss and criticize briefly two approaches to Jewish–Arab relations in Palestine and to Jewish development leading to Israeli statehood. One approach, more or less in the mainstream, has it that the process of 'from Jewish community to Jewish state' was separate from parallel Arab developments, while the other approach, joined over the last decade to post-modernism and post-Zionism, claims a privileged European status for the Jews, their development causing Arab underdevelopment. We find that the maxim 'coexistence within conflict' comes closer to explaining the interrelationship between pre-state British rule, Arab majority rights and Jewish minority demands. Coexistence did not develop into outright cooperation because of the nature of the, essentially national, conflict. Conditions became extremely difficult for European Jews, while the currents of Arab nationalism in the Middle East became stronger and more militant at the same time. On top of this, the British were better at exploiting national divisions than in investing in mending them. But neither did social and economic existence between Jews and Arabs develop into stratified power relations. Among the main reasons for this were the political terms and ongoing restrictions imposed on the Jews by the ruling power and, no less important, the predominance of socialist movements and groups, and of pioneering voluntarism and democratic practices in the Zionist 'constructivist' project. In distinction from the portrayal of Jewish settlement in mandate Palestine as an instance of 'one . . . at the expense of the other' (Zureik 1979: 66; Asad 1975: 262), and of 'exclusion' (Asad 1975: 262), we say that, in many realms Jewish–Arab relations were 'one alongside the other', while politically usually 'one against the other'; 'one at the expense of the other' was a rare event.

How then did this Jewish orientation of 'coexistence within conflict' become, after the war, the Israeli almost, but-not-quite, pure nation-state? The two other approaches do not have to contend with the problem of extreme change, since the first arrives at statehood through gradual, constructive nation building, and the second by the progressive displacement of the other, Arab, nation. We say that if we put together the circumstances of the transition – the UN partition, war, Arab flight, Arab expulsion, 'British-made chaos', the mass Jewish immigration, security – we would arrive at important factors for explaining the pre-state to state change, but not at causes sufficient to account for the radical non-return policy; the more so, since this policy was not arrived at by right-wing parties or nationalistic military groups. Indeed, right-wing groups had no say in the government. We believe that we have 'evidence' that the decision not to return the Arabs and to upgrade the state to an almost, but-not-quite, pure nation-state was contrary to past ruling ideas, programmes, political practice or perspective. Nevertheless, the decision of non-return won out and became policy, while the historical principles became defeated social alternatives. That will form the second section of the paper.

Conceptualizing Transition from a National Community to a Nation-State: Nation-Building; Colonialism; Coexistence Within Conflict

In the discussion which follows, we give additional, although abbreviated, attention to the nation-building approach, since it has groups of people in action within complexes of events to commend it; we give less to the colonialist-capitalist projection, since, leaving nothing to chance, it sticks to its over-calibrated sights without respite. The 'from *Yishuv* to statehood' paradigm is guided by the idea of an evolutionary continuity, not necessarily simplistic, although romantic and positivist. From a small Jewish community living under conditions of privation it developed, by means of intensive group effort and high national investment, struggle and War of Liberation, into an independent nation-state enjoying territorial sovereignty accompanied by a distinct and unified national-religious identity (90 per cent Jewish), and allotted membership within the family of nations. True, it was surrounded by enemies, but was victorious and strong enough (Eisenstadt 1967; Horowitz and Lissak 1978, 1989; Safran 1978; Gorni 1987; Shapira 1992). The key to development in this inward-looking approach was to be found in the properties (self-sacrifice, discipline, innovation) of the Jewish Zionist pioneering movements; in planning, organization, financial aid, institution building, the labour movement, political parties. The totality constituted the embryo of a proto-state, 'the state in the making' ('the parliament in the making', 'the army in the making', etc.). 'It was the social and political character of the *Yishuv*, a "state in the making" under the Mandate, that enabled it to succeed in the armed struggle between Jews and Arabs and that made possible a gradual transition to statehood' (Horowitz and Lissak 1989: 3). 'The other [Arab] nation', brought the catastrophe on itself, mainly because their rejectionist politics prevented them from negotiating – be it over partition plans, or the entrance into the country of immigrant Jewish refugees from Nazism – with the position of Palestinian leadership, and that of the Arab League, being either the White Paper or war. When the partition into two states was adopted (Resolution 181) by the United Nations General Assembly (29 November 1947), they went to war (Louis 1986: 13–26).

The other group of studies views the Jews as a European colonial client becoming a dominant caste that weakened, impoverished, and dislocated the native population. Through economic and military power the Arabs were either pushed out or, as in the case of the remnant population, Jewish colonialist-capitalist settlers turned them into marginal labourers. Jewish expansion erased Arab identity and enforced its own identity over the whole territory (Rodinson 1973; Asad 1975; Zureik 1979; Said 1979; Migdal 1980; Schölch 1982; Shafir 1989; Ram 1993).

In spite of their different starting points and their relation to different parameters – 'historical particularity' for the first, the ' world-system' for the second, and that the 'virtues' of the Zionist national movement were the motor force of the one, its 'vices' of the other – both approaches drew a cumulative line from the beginning of the new Jewish settlement in the 1880s to the Israeli nation-state.

Although in both approaches factual observations and explanations are to be found, central issues regarding historical change go unaccounted for. Looking at examples from the region, especially that of Syria, we can say that conflicts and state militarization were endemic to the colonial partitions and divisions, and to the post-colonial states (Hurewitz 1950; Monroe 1963; Tibawi 1969; Louis and Stookey 1986). Clearly, such fragmented and imposed structures were a provocative invitation to war, much in the way that foreign conquest rouses resistance and liberation movements. The boundaries decided upon for the nations of the region were contended for in battle. This determining of new facts on the ground, most often in cities and villages with their civilian inhabitants, often resulted in mass flight (especially when the population was not organized for war, an easy prey to disinformation, as was the case of the Palestinians), uprooting and massacre.

To a great extent, the 1917 Balfour Declaration was the cause of both the ongoing coexistence and the conflict. Power and control remained exclusively British. Recognition of a Jewish National Home did not carry with it colonial concessions, especially in land or immigration; neither did it carry autonomy in taxation, military forces or administration. Land was a matter of purchase in the Arab land market and was linked to mandatory land laws. Immigration was dependent on British interpretation of the security situation, their categories of economic selection, and conditions in the local labour market. Without colonial concessions, development was only possible in terms of coexistence, such as mixed cities and regions, anomalous land–population ratios, joint government workplaces, (including police, common transport and electricity systems), and so on. That is, coexistence took on a bi-national pattern.

'Constructivism' stemmed from the same non-colonialist terms under which the Jewish community could grow, meaning it was pressed to rely on its own means, national and private, for investment, infrastructure, land purchase, settlement, and labour regulations (growth geared to economic development so as to conform to, while augmenting, British regulated 'absorptive capacity', in an attempt to reach demographic parity). Extraordinary conditions between two world wars, and social adaptation to British rule and Arab resistance, took on the form of a separate national project which also generated contradictions and conflict for both Jews and Arabs. Yet in coping with local and international conditions, the Zionist and socialist movements also restrained and controlled the Revisionist brand of militaristic Zionism.

We can go no further than to say that conflict remained a permanent feature of Arab–Jewish relations. There were ups and downs, certainly Arab strikes and the 1936 Arab Revolt were among its extreme expressions (and yet, very closely related in time, popular activism, and results, to the Syrian General Strike). In a way, the conflict goes back to square one: the Balfour Declaration and the division of the area between the British and French. (We could, but need not, push history back still further.) Jewish socialist and liberal, non-colonialist constructivism did not find a strong counterpart in the Arab national movement or in the Arab public, even though there were always groups, organizations, and individuals that were actively committed in that direction (Asaf 1967; Lockman 1996). The Palestinian Arabs were not party to the Balfour Declaration; their right to national self-determination was not respected. Moreover, their clear identification with Palestine as their homeland and their political rights as the majority population were put in jeopardy by the British and by the Jews, especially when Jewish immigration was pushing to parity (Kolinsky 1993: 220–3). These were among the causes for the ongoing political conflict between the three parties–partners. With this 'problematica' in mind, we say 'coexistence within conflict' was not simply a Jewish interim programme, a preliminary stage or stepping-stone, leading to a nation-state or to two nation-states. It was a way of active adaptation in a conflict situation and, taking into account national, religious and cultural complexities, certainly no less 'natural' than the nation-state.

Most obvious in the Palestine partition decision of 1947 was the physical, geographical severance into two or three separate political, territorial units detached from one another in communications and transport facilities, without consideration for economic viability and with little regard for ethnic, religious and national affiliations. The almost landlocked, tiny, mountainous state allotted to the Arabs, and the coastal-strip state allotted to the Jews with 40 per cent of its inhabitants Arabs, was a recipe for bloodshed, avoidable only if the United Nations, or Bernadotte, had had greater means of power, or if the British had remained, or had not given up their mandate (especially under such conditions), or if they had retreated in a manner safeguarding the UN partition and not in a fashion described as leading to 'Chaos, British-Made' (Cohen 1970: 404).[2]

The colonialist-capitalist version has it that the Arabs were already uprooted and impoverished prior to the 1948 war. However, it is enough to look at the estimated Arab land losses in order to see that the Arab nation was solidly rooted on its land: in 1947, the Jews, who were mostly urban, were one-third of the population in Palestine and owned 10–11 per cent of the land. And, for example, the relatively large plantation area, under intensive agriculture, and the main pre-1948 export branch, was owned, approximately, half by Arabs and half by Jews. The extent of other Arab immovable property in houses, urban land plots, stores, workshops, businesses in the mixed cities, etc., registered by the Israeli Custodian as Abandoned and Absentee Property (Shafrir 1975: 222–44), underlines rapid economic growth by the Arabs during the British mandate period.[3]

These are some of the details, but they should be considered as aspects of more complex phenomena, such as the bi-national character of growth and development, where the most populated Jewish area was equally the most populated Arab area (the coastal plain), and where, for the same and for different reasons, the most prosperous towns, cities, and regions were those that were mixed. Nor was this an instance of one displacing the other, a stratified picture of the exploiter on top and the exploited below. At the top of Arab urban society (and of Arab society in general, although additional factors are involved here) there were high-ranking civil servants in all government and municipal departments (above them, only the British), contractors, landowners, merchants, professionals (Shimoni 1947: 206–39).

In spite of the fact that the 'from community to state' studies were written from the vantage point of hindsight, their authors remained steadfast to their interpretation of a gradual, stage-like transition. This is a strange construction of social history, taking into consideration those most eventful, radical and swift population and territorial changes (Kimmerling 1989: 265–82) from a (Jewish) 'formative state' which, according to the partition division was to include a large Arab minority population (40 per cent, at the time), to what became an (Israeli) nation-state with a residual Arab population (10 per cent) in a territory that was two-fifths larger than that allotted Israel by the UN. To harness war gains, government-style, as do the authors, to the gradual approach of nation building, is a gross oversimplification. The area taken over, Arab land and property, was 'nationalized' as Israeli state land and property,[4] and the Arab population was turned into a refugee population outside the country's borders.

We can put aside the problem of territorial expansion, not an unusual occurrence for new states, especially when, as here, the map was drawn with the help of an ex-colonial superpower. According to the step-by-step ('another goat, another dunam') approach to state formation, the national home was built through labour, pioneering effort, leaching saline soil, draining swamps and input of national capital. The take-over of four to five million dunams of cultivated land (or as the Israeli Minister of Foreign Affairs put it 'land with . . . wells and water') hardly fits the 'virtuous' approach. And we can add 'nationalizing' on a national basis (the transfer of Arab private property into Jewish national property), and not on a class basis, adopted by a government headed by the veteran leaders of the socialist workers' party, Mapai, and of the workers' federation, the Histadruth, within which membership was closed to anyone who profited from any form of ownership or from the employment of hired labour. And how come a democratic state erased ownership and citizen rights of Arabs, both of the refugees and of those who remained within Israeli borders, many of the latter as 'present absentees'? Of course we know the answer: *Laws of the State of Israel*, among which was, LSI 4 (1949/50): 68, The Absentee's Property Law (Jiryis 1976: 83–8).

The claim of 'from community to state' continuity does not hold water. What should be obvious are the sharp contradictions between the two phases. When we say that the refugee phenomenon became the most important of factors, the factor of factors, we mean it in the same spirit (although, as we shall see, we draw opposite conclusions) that Moshe Sharett meant it when he said, 'This [the flight of the refugees] is a more extraordinary episode . . . than the establishment of a Jewish state'. We may add that the 'extraordinary episode' became a 'non-return'[5] policy, and the policy became a regime.

Why were the refugees not dealt with in the two approaches we have discussed? In the colonialist-capitalist one, as was said, the end result is catastrophic: though not physically annihilated, they are 'kick[ed] . . . out' (Frank 1975: 8). The refugees are not seen as such in their writings – one demise is like another, the actual is incidental. For those who saw state development as an inherent attribute, the refugees were regarded as a war phenomenon, an incident (neat, how the two approaches intersect!) of war, *force majeure*, that then dictated the (end result) relations between the two nations, the victors and the losers; equally, or alternatively, they started the war, or they were the enemy or part of the enemy, complicit in the heavy Jewish war casualties. Meanwhile, the war has not yet been terminated and so the refugee problem was a security problem and a matter of state.[6]

Unlike more realistic work on Israeli state policy towards Palestinian Arabs written in the 1950s (e.g., Gabbay 1959; Peretz 1958; Schwarz 1959), local studies were written from inside a country that had gone through a swift process of repopulation and resettlement by Jewish refugees and immigrants in which the human and social void left by the Arabs was obliterated, contributing to an atmosphere of irreversibility. Exclusivity and defence of the state's borders reigned. Harkabi, for example, provided elaborate reasoning, philosophical-psychological, political-military, that the Arabs would tolerate nothing less than the total annihilation of the Jewish state, and was of the opinion that Jewish 'moderates' who fail to recognize this suffer from 'autism' (1974: 239). Harkabi then presented a theory of the necessity for 'counter-enmity-that-should-not-be-quenched', as a must for Israeli national survival. Furthermore, 'Despite its negative aspects the conflict can become a great motivational force for greater national effort, internally and externally, and a powerful stimulus' (1977: 163). Critical, alternative writing was not absent during the same decades (e.g. the journal *New Outlook*), but political and judicial boundaries of compliance were very stringently applied, especially towards Arabs (e.g. Sabri Jiryis), but also towards Jews (e.g. Aharon Cohen, Israel Baer), and the academy tended to conform. True, something has changed since, the reverence for matters of security and State being relaxed somewhat after Sadat's visit to Jerusalem in 1977. Harkabi repented, supporting recognition of the PLO, a two-state solution, and deplored Israel for refusing to negotiate for peace (1988).

The transition from coexistence to a nation-state is still in process. Because of the many wars that followed the 1948 war, in every decade there have been re-evaluations of the starting points. 'New' studies, Flapan's *Birth of Israel*, Morris's *Birth of the Plaestinian Refugee Problem*, Pappé's *The Making of the Arab–Israeli Conflict*, which highlight Plan 'D' conspiracy ('a master plan for expulsion'), committees on transfer ('the old Zionist idea of population transfer'), acts of atrocity, the flight, the expulsions, whether 'flight or expulsion'(e.g. Finkelstein *et al.* 1991), the uprooting, 'blocking the return', and so on, miss the relevant issue (Flapan 1987: 93, 102–3; Morris 1990: 30–4, 35–66, 155; Pappé 1992: 54–5, 87–99). On their part, expulsion, no return, transfer, etc. were implicit in the Zionist logic, waiting the opportunity for realization, or to be explained as self-fulfilling necessities, 'the kibbutzim's need for more land', 'the *Yishuv*'s need', 'the new immigrant's need' (Morris 1987: 155). We say that refugees (those who fled and those who were expelled), this Plan, and those acts of brutality were war phenomena and have taken place in many countries that have gone through war. But there is also 'after the war', and not to return the refugees 'after the war' was a new political position, one not previously entertained. As we shall see, the decision of the government majority took into account that the refugees would return. It could have been otherwise. Non-return, then, was a most extreme and contradictory policy, a decision incongruent with the social history of those who made it and congruent only with the concept of the nation-state itself – one well-honed in the world by the 1940s.

We can tick-off a number of internal state factors (some of which we elaborate on) that were effected so as to turn the 'facts' of war into policy: monopolization and centralization of power and matters of security in the hands of the prime minister and his faction in the majority (Mapai) party; the dismantling of broad national alliances with the socialist left (their main partners), liberals, and other opposition groups (the dismantling of the Palmach, Mapam outside the government coalition); use of judicial and legislative power for state ends (establishment of a military government, a custodian for Arab property, the revival of the British Emergency Regulations, 1945, etc.). As well, political events of the time (which we cannot elaborate on here) helped promote the adoption of the policy of non-return: the assassination of Count Bernadotte (August 1948); the sanctionless UN General Assembly Resolution 194 (III) of 11 December 1948 recognizing the right of the Palestinian refugees to return; the removal of pressure by the United States in mid-1949 on Israel to return 100,000 refugees. Other factors were highly significant for the rapidity by which the 'non-return' and 'take-over' policy became a regime: Jewish mass immigration (1948–51); the reparations from Germany (beginning 1953–4); US support, French and English cooperation (Carmi and Rosenfeld 1989). The many factors which combined within a short time period, and which contributed to the swiftness and intensity of change and transformation, were conducive in the undermining of the principal social and political procedures within which decision-making and responsibility had been traditionally channelled and shared during the Yishuv period, and during most of the 1948 war, including the first months of statehood (Carmi and Rosenfeld 1991).

At a Mapai conference in February 1948 (less than three months after the UN partition decision, some three months before state declaration), where relations with the Arab population within the future state were discussed, central party leaders, among whom were members of the Provisional Government, proposed to terminate the closed-shop policy of Jewish labour (*avodah evrit*), to set up a number of

committees, the purpose of which was to encourage Arab workers to join the
Workers' Federation (the Histadruth), and to ease the representation of Arabs in
all municipal and central governmental institutions at all levels, including as
ministers and deputy ministers (Davar, 9 February 1948; see also Cohen 1970:
452; Segev 1986: 44–5). Ben-Gurion avowed that, 'still, even at this moment of
emergency, there are three things worth living, and dying, for – a Jewish State,
Jewish–Arab solidarity [or alliance], a socialist regime' (1957 [7 February 1948]:
62). Since Mapai was the majority party, we can also regard their decisions and
his remarks as political statements considered acceptable to the rank and file within
the wider public; the politically left parties, Mapam, Maki (with approximately 40
per cent of the votes in the Histadruth), with their territorialist (joint Jewish–Arab)
position, held even more progressive agendas.

We know that only four months later the policy of the same leading party (Mapai)
was to prevent the return of the refugees, and, soon after, the Arabs who remained
within the borders of the state were differentiated from the Jewish population and
placed under a military government which subsequently ordered their lives for
some twenty years. Segev relates to what transpired in the following fashion: 'The
war raged in the months that followed' and 'In view of all this the desire for the
integration of the remaining Arabs as equal citizens of the state had diminished'
(Segev 1986: 46).

Missing in Segev's work is the comprehension that the policy of integration of,
and equality for, the Arab national minority was not a 'desire', or a conference
slogan, but rather the outlook and stated position of the ruling workers' party, and
even of those to the right of it. For the same reason, he did not grasp that within the
briefest time-span, between February and June (the months of the war victories
and the mass flight), the policy of integration had not 'diminished'; rather, it was
turned on its head. Many of those who had backed integration in the winter (1948)
speedily quenched their 'desire' in the beginning of the summer of the same year;
nor did the 'desire' 'diminish' because of the war, since there were parties and
individuals that continued to support traditional policy during and after the war.[7]

'Our Joint City [Haifa] . . . Do Not Betray Her': Jewish Appeal for Coexistence in the Midst of Armed Conflict, April 1948

The mass flight of a population is always a civilian phenomenon. What is being
spoken of is hundreds of thousands of persons, not of an Arab army, or of 'terrorist
gangs', but of a people. The invading contingents from Arab states were estimated
at some 30,000 men in their entirety (Pappé 1992: 108–13), and the refugees as
between 650,000-750,000. The extreme change did not take place after years of
trench warfare or as a result of a scorched earth policy, but was enacted in a matter

of weeks and months. In March 1948 the condition of the Jews improved somewhat, but that of the Arabs, especially in the towns and cities, deteriorated and became critical.

A young researcher named Klein – and we discuss him not necessarily as an authority, but simply as a young researcher treating the issues in the 1980s – who was killed in the war in Lebanon before he could complete his study, wrote a brief historical, political overview in 1982 on the Arabs in his city, Haifa, up to the establishment of the state. He wished to provide a learned analysis, perhaps also a personal one, of the history of Arab Haifa which, from the end of April 1948, similar to Jaffa, essentially had been reduced to one of the worst and most crowded slum neighbourhoods in the country. It can be said that up to 1948 Haifa had been an exemplary mixed city: groups from different nationalities, denominations, sects, including its British administrators, lived around and above its port area, with 70,000 Arabs and an equal number of Jews being its main population groups; also, the periphery of the city was composed of several fairly large Arab villages.

There were still tens of thousands of Arab citizens in Haifa in early April. The Haganah held talks with the representatives of the Arabs on conditions for the latter's surrender. In the next couple of days the Haganah completed its take-over of different parts of the city (22 April), the contacts with the Haifa Arabs' representatives fell through and, three weeks later, at the time of the establishment of the state on 15 May, some 3,500 Arabs remained in the city (Al-Khatib 1954; Haifa 1968; Slutzky 1973: 3(B); Almogi 1980: 71–8; Asaf 1967: 182; Carmel 1949: 110–15; Kanafani [1970]1972; Habibi 1984; Morris 1987: 73–95; Goren 1998: 183–215).

According to Klein, the Arabs fled because they belonged to terrorist groups and they feared revenge; they believed Jewish defeat was near and hoped to return with the victorious invading Arab armies, and they rejected living in a Jewish state on principle, and so on. The researcher (in 1982) differed from his forerunners on one matter especially: he did not agree with the credit given by the *History of the Haganah* ('*Sepher Toldot Hahaganah*') to the Arab community of Haifa: 'The book [*History*] makes a total separation between the Arab inhabitants of Haifa and between the terrorists who are described as elements from the surrounding villages'; as far as he was concerned the distinction was unwarranted – that is, the Arabs of Haifa were also terrorists (Klein 1983: 44; cf. Slutzky 1973, 3: 1571–3).

Unlike the *History*, which regarded the dual community existence as a factual situation and a Jewish political achievement, the researcher writing in the first years of the 1980s focused strictly on conflict. He regarded Arab enmity as a natural condition and, as many others (like Harkabi, its leading proponent), thought in terms of contradictory essences, 'the Jews' and 'the Arabs', engaged in a struggle over absolute control, or until the extermination of one of the sides. This either-or viewpoint had, nevertheless, a certain advantage: one can find in it a reasonable balance between crime and punishment. Total enmity on the part of the Haifa Arab community seemingly justified the penalty of its almost total destruction.

However, those who inflicted the 'punishment', those who then administered control over the land area and property of Arab Haifa and who executed the actual policy with regard to the Arabs who remained and those who fled near and far – the town and district officers, the city authorities, the Custodian of Abandoned Property, and other leaders of the Haganah and the Yishuv – knew better. Their public experience and training, and even their military experience, had developed out of complex and not necessarily hostile, political-national and personal relations. The growth of Jewish Haifa had always involved mixed groupings: Jewish rent payers, Arab landlords, the British, the international petroleum complex, the joint municipality, as well as certain joint public services, large governmental workplaces, adjacent and some mixed neighbourhoods, an Arab section in the Histadruth, mixed membership in the Communist Party, and so on (Vashitz 1993).

Even during the winter of 1947–8, when the British failed in providing necessary measures of security in areas under their control – and they are to be blamed for one of its most serious consequences, the mass murder of Jewish workers in the Haifa refineries (Leibricht 1987: 170) – the two populations in Haifa were not completely separated. From the time of the departure of the British rearguard (14 May 1948), it was only a matter of a day or two before the Haganah gained full control over the city (Khalidi 1986: 127). The proclamation that appeared on the day of the British-to-Jewish changeover reflected the relative ease of the transfer. Its final paragraph pledged to the Arab citizens of Haifa that 'all property left behind . . . will be placed under control and will be returned in due time to its rightful owners' (Slutzky 1973, 3: 1571–3). There is not the slightest reference to the possibility that those who left will not return. On the contrary, the victors recognized the temporariness of the flight with regard to the entire population. (The evacuated villager of Ikrit and Biram received an explicit promise from the army that their return to their homes was a matter of days; this was not exceptional. They continue to be unexceptional, since despite the promise they have remained internal refugees within Israel and haven't been allowed to return to their villages to this day.[8])

However, the *History of the Haganah*, from which we quoted and which published the proclamation as an historical document, completely disregarded its meaning – to the degree that a reader reflecting on what was written there would consider the historian's intentions as little more than a moral alibi. In the *History* there is not even a hint as to what brought Jewish leadership to adopt a policy which, practically speaking, altered its position with regard to the Arabs and their rights overnight.

The assurance given by the Haganah to the Haifa Arabs was not an isolated event. During the very same days, at the end of April 1948, the Histadruth in Haifa turned to the Arab citizens with its own appeal: 'Workers, our joint city, Haifa, calls upon you to take part in its building, in its progress and development, do not betray her and do not betray yourselves' (Almogi 1980: 78). The flight of Haifa Arabs was regarded as failing a common enterprise. After 4–5 months of skirmishes, firing and general tension in the city, the language of non-denial remained – 'our joint city . . . we've lived together for years and years' – a testament on the part of the Jews who, while fully cognizant that their neighbours were weak, still believed national coexistence to be in the Jewish interest.

If up to the 22nd of April the Jews stuck to coexistence, how come the final wave of Arab flight, and their own military victory, could cancel Arab existence for them? And also, what replaced the Jewish policy and recognition of a historical interest in the perpetuation of (an avowedly complex) coexistence of populations, communities, cities, towns? Therefore, in our opinion, the central question is not what happened to the Arabs but what happened to the Jews?

First of all, we show that the change in policy was neither a casual unfolding of events nor a direct necessity of war. We remain with the example of Haifa because coexistence was most common there. Although Jerusalem, too, had a joint municipality, it was also the stronghold of the landed and religious Arab aristocracy, and of national leadership; and, in this centre of mandatory rule, British officialdom played a distinctive role in keeping the two communities apart. Jaffa and Tel Aviv had become separate cities and did not maintain joint municipal institutions. In Haifa, the populations of both nations grew simultaneously and at a rapid pace (Seikaly 1995). Between the two world wars Haifa became a centre for regional and countrywide communications, for the military and, to a lesser degree, for industry. The livelihood and jobs of the Haifa population were tightly enmeshed in the Mandatory government's war economy and the regional economy. The port, the refineries, the surrounding army camps and the railroad workshops were among the largest workplaces in the country; both population groups depended on them, though their direct importance was perhaps greater for Arab workers (Metzer and Kaplan 1985; Vashitz 1993; Bernstein 1996; Lockman 1996; Carmi and Rosenfeld 1974).

The Haifa municipality also operated a broad spectrum of services and was a place of employment for both Arabs and Jews; in addition, church-administered hospitals and schools served the Arab urban population. There is no doubt that successful urbanization was a most important feature in the relations between Jews and Arabs, with British investment and enterprises being a key factor. Haifa attracted not only merchants, contractors and *rentiers* but, as well, many Arab village workers found jobs alongside Jewish workers in government plants. Even during the 1948 war, each group feared losing its place to the other in government jobs (in the refineries and the port, etc.). However, during the war differences between the two communities in levels of political leadership and organization became far more important than similarities in the direction of their development (Morris 1987: 77; Pappe 1992: 56–69).

The pronouncements of the Haifa Arab National Committee during the war months (winter 1947–8) were quite similar to the public appeals of the Jewish Ad Hoc Committee. The Arab Committee also requested its public to maintain its daily routine, asking the workers to remain at their government and municipal jobs and not to abandon the city (Haifa 1968: 18-24). For the longest period, exit from the city became one of the main ways of releasing themselves and their families from fear, hardship, black market prices, etc. For a few piastres one could board a bus for Shafr Amr, Acre or Nazareth, or a taxi for Beirut, and escape the lines of fire and even the boundaries of the proposed Jewish state (Farah 1985: 194–8; Nakara 1985: 164–81). The final stage in the abandoning of the city indicated the extensive reliance of the Arab urban population on the Mandatory government. When the British evacuation became a certainty, the final mass flight of the Arab population, preceded by a brief battle, the rout of an Arab 'Rescue Army' and units of the Arab Legion, also took place. (Slutzky 1973, 3: 1569–73; Haifa 1968; Carmel 1949).

Only after a while were order and continuity restored. We know, after the fact, that the time of the British departure (the last ten days of April and the first days of May) had an earthshaking effect on the Arab population. The extent of the effect wasn't foreseen by the Arab leadership or, for that matter, by the main Jewish organizations, or even by the Jewish commanding general of the northern region. The city of Haifa was barely touched by fighting, but nevertheless people fled even from their hospital beds; they left their houses and belongings, and warehouses full of food (Carmel 1949: 110–15). Many Jews felt anguish 'unconsciously . . . from this flight and especially that the British were furthering it' (Weitz 1965, 3: 283); one way of 'furthering it' is documented by Cohen, who describes how the British government and British firms promised to re-employ evacuees in Beirut (1970: 463–4). Even though the weakness of Arab Haifa was evident, the flight astounded everyone.

The Prime Minister of the provisional government, Ben-Gurion, who visited Haifa shortly after its occupation, was amazed when he saw the vacant gun positions of the Rescue Army: 'Why didn't they fight?' (see Almogi 1980: 79). To both these unanticipated, unaccountable events: 'How come they fled?' and 'Why didn't they fight?' (and this doesn't mean that there were not good and sufficient answers such as 'fear and defeat', 'a search for refuge until the war's end', 'a failure of leadership', and that most of local Palestinian Arab fighting was done by villagers), a third unforeseen contingency is to be added: the actions of the British in Haifa which radically altered everything.

The British were the principal military power in the country and the region, and their armaments and the number of troops at their disposal guaranteed a convincing superiority over both the Jewish and Arab armies. British action could have altered the entire map, but their departure, and along with it the organized and methodical transfer of all Mandatory government property to the Jewish municipality (in the case of Haifa), was the third surprise (Cohen 1970: 463; Morris 1990: 18–21, 31–2). In recognition of and out of respect for the orderly transfer from regime to regime, the Jewish mayor (Shabtai Levi) wrote in *The Municipal Yearbook* that, 'In the coming days there will also be a city police force which will include Arabs and which will fulfill certain jobs now undertaken by the *Haganah*' (Haifa 1968: 38–40). Matters did not return to normal. Arabs were not permitted to come back to Haifa, and Shabtai Levi's term of office as mayor was shortly ended by the ruling party's candidate (Haifa 1968: 37).

Meanwhile, the statistics of the defeat and the flight began to accumulate. The commander of the northern front who described the Haifa flight also referred to the behaviour of the 'Rescue Army' with regard to Nazareth: 'Nobody knows why and how come the spirit of the Arab fighters broke after a few hours and the commanders secretly left the city' (Carmel 1949: 214). But it is interesting to note that the analogy ends here. Of all places, the population of Nazareth, swollen with refugees from Haifa, Tiberias, Beisan and surrounding villages, did not join the flight of the 'Rescue Army'. As the weeks passed, the fight of the population lessened greatly and expulsions became the order of the day. Where there were no expulsions the population remained, as in Nazareth.

Jaffa, like Haifa, was at the centre of the joint Jewish–Arab pattern of growth-in-tandem of the two national groups, a process which gave the 1948 war the aspect, in territorial terms, of a civil, as distinct from an anti-colonialist or nationalist, war. The population of Jaffa dwindled during the first months of the war (the end of 1947 until the end of April 1948). People left everything and fled to Lod and Ramle, or to Gaza or Egypt and, in the city, trucks were loaded with sugar and flour for the Jaffa refugees in Nablus (Abou Iyad 1979: 23–5). At the end of April and the beginning of May, there remained in Jaffa (out of some 90,000) just 5,000 persons 'who looked like ghosts' (Aricha 1959: 242, 250; see also Slutzky 1973, 3: 1551–3). The Tel Aviv poet, Alterman, in the eyes of many Jews certainly the outstanding poet of the War of Liberation, described Jaffa as 'crumbling without fight' (Aricha 1959: 243). Although written in biblical imagery, it fitted the tragedy of the city's inhabitants. Here he did not write that Jaffa was conquered or 'freed', or that there was a military victory, but that the city crumbled under the pressure of the difficulties of holding on, of mass flight or, as others have written, due to lack of food, water, electricity, of total civilian disintegration (Flapan 1987: 90–2; Morris 1989: 99–101). What should have been a temporary war calamity was turned into an ongoing tragedy. Close upon the date of the 15th of May (the declaration of the State's independence), the number of Arab refugees increased greatly, as did the number of captured towns: 'Jaffa has surrendered, Safed is ours, Beisan has surrendered, large and strong villages of our neighbours are increasingly disintegrating, the Arabs are fleeing in the tens and the hundreds of thousands' (Weitz 1965, 3: 283).

Jaffa and Haifa, and their environs, alone meant 200,000 refugees. But these were circumstances of war, and there were official Jewish pronouncements that pointed to the refugee situation as being temporary. The future president of Israel, Chaim Weitzman, stated in his visit to the White House on 15 May 1948 that, 'At the end of the war we'll return Jaffa and Acre' (see Ben-Gurion 1969: 108). (True enough, according to the UN partition, neither of these cities was to be within the borders of the Jewish state.) As for Haifa, approximately a month after the Arab flight the Jewish radio, 'The Voice of the Galilee', announced on 29 May that negotiations were being held with a delegation of Arab refugees in Beirut, and that procedures had been determined for the return of 20,000 (Weitz 1965, 3: 294). Clearly, then, the return of the war refugees was regarded as a concrete possibility by both Arabs and Jews.

'I Am Particularly Amazed by the Flight of the Arabs . . . This is One of Those Revolutionary Events that Alter the Course of History': Inspirational Reasoning Advancing the Nation-State Ideal

At a certain moment, perhaps as the number of empty villages and the area of vacated land increased, and the number of refugees grew, a new appreciation of the situation came into being. This comprehension went beyond the context of war operations and facts on the ground. There is no doubt that the most embracing political, and even historical, albeit pragmatic, expression of the conscious change in direction came at this time (16 June 1948, at a cabinet meeting) when the Minister of Foreign Affairs, Shertok-Sharett, said:

> there is also the problem of the Arab community that was inside Israeli territory before the fighting began. I am particularly amazed by the flight of the Arabs. This is a more extraordinary episode in the annals of this country than the establishment of a Jewish state. The latter while enormously important . . . is not really surprising after three generations of Jewish settlement, a Jewish National Home, and war (in Ben-Gurion 1971: 149).

But the Minister of Foreign Affairs, second in position of leadership of the leading workers' party (Mapai), explained to the members of the government that this occurrence was liable to alter with changing circumstances. Therefore, he said, 'There can be no return to the status quo ante', asking 'should we fight to maintain the present situation?' His answer was: '*they will not return. And that is our policy.*

They will not return' (in Ben-Gurion 1971: 149–50; 1969: 165; emphasis added). The Prime Minister continued the discussion: 'We cannot allow the Arabs to return to those places that they left' (Ben-Gurion 1971: 150); *'they will not return after the war either'* (Ben-Gurion 1969: 167; emphasis added).

When the question was asked, rhetorically, at the same cabinet meeting by the Minister of Foreign Affairs as to the number of Arabs remaining in the state, the Prime Minister (also Minister of Defence) interjected, 'I'd be surprised if there were even a hundred thousand.'[9] The Prime Minister's reasoning was blunt with regard to the military politics of 'I do not want those who fled to return' and 'We can stand up to the Arab world and the regular armies of the Arab states.' (More modestly, Ben-Gurion, 'doubted' Israel's ability 'to hold our own against the British Army', and thus emphasized that a conflict between the two was to be avoided (1971: 151).) In concert, the Minister of Foreign Affairs (although concerned over possible confrontations at the United Nations) heralded the facts of flight: 'and if we get the area abandoned by the Arabs . . . [we get] 'all land with villages with wells and water'[10] (in Ben-Gurion 1969: 165; 1971: 149).

On the scale of values of socialist Zionist vision, these were very early public, and even bombastic, statements announceing that some of the country's leaders had dispensed with 'constructivist' discipline, of respect for historic rights (not just of the Palestine Arab nation, but also of the Jewish) and with their own propensity for understanding history. Why? A strong element of national bribery was implicit within this new direction ('policy', in Sharett's words): 'with their abandoned land . . . wells and water'. In addition the 'policy' enjoyed the rationalizations given 'matters of security', and of creeping immunity from a public, open agenda. Foremost, and in formal terms, it was military power, and the state leadership's growing strength, that provided it with the capacity to transform the wishful 'policy' – refugees outside, abandoned property inside – into regulations and rules of the government bureaucracy and commands of the military. Israeli power politics was not the only factor; one must add the concurrent Jewish mass immigration, the weakness of the UN, the hesitancy, that turned into support, of the great powers – especially that of the US (Carmi and Rosenfeld 1989).

By the early summer it was already clear that the Arabs were weak, and that Israeli military strength had become definitive in determining political gains. The state's leaders showed a readiness to capitalize on these possibilities – treating the other nation as if it no longer existed, as if there had not been villages, towns, communities, peasants, workers, property owners: 'Truly astonishing is that the Arabs have ***disappeared*** from a whole section of the country' (Shertok-Sharett, in Ben-Gurion 1971: 149; emphasis added). Foreseeing the possible direction of the extreme shift, a prominent leader from the Mapam left, M. Ya'ari, warned in a 15 May 1948 speech at a mass meeting: 'Great fear has fallen on the Arab population . . . hundreds of thousands have fled . . . But do we want a refugee problem to be created with a belt of hatred surrounding us? We won't be able to maintain our independence if we are surrounded by eternal hatred' (Lahduth Haavodah 1948).

That history 'documents' a great switch in policy is not our main point. Indeed, it could well be that Ben-Gurion and Sharett were, more than anything else, pitching their statements in an effort to forestall and offset the recommendations demanding the return of the refugees they know would be forthcoming from the UN mediator Count Bernadotte. Our main point is that it had been otherwise – that a total political, economic, social, ideological framework of Zionist socialist and liberal, and non-Zionist, potential for coexistence had been present and had dominated the Yishuv up to the time of the 1948 war. It was these capabilities and forces that had to be overcome, defeated. We now explain the main ramifications of this process.

The Defeated Alternative

The new political direction, which many scholars apparently regard as proceeding either from old and preconceived tenets of Zionist nationalism, or out of the necessity of immigrant absorption and of an 'embattled state' – and therefore as either implicit or unavoidable – was considered differently at the time. A policy of permanent military supremacy, and of ongoing war or 'no peace', was unexpected, not fully comprehended and definitely not decided upon. There were those who were against the 'they will not return' and 'we will take the lands that we need' policy. Within the political alignment of the time, up until the first (not provisional) government of February 1949, committee members who did not comply came from all parties and were in the majority – although even earlier, in June–July 1948, it cannot be said that matters remained simply procedural. The Prime Minister's authority began to increase as he incorporated both the offices of the Military Government and that of the Custodian of Abandoned Property under his ministry. However, these measures still came under the rubric of *ad hoc* 'war management'.

The Majority Decision

How were matters concerning land and refugees dealt with after the pronouncements of Ben-Gurion and Sharett? Primarily, they were decided upon in pre-state fashion, democratically, in committees. These were *existing* and newly formed committees, the latter set up by the Provisional National Council on the basis of recognized constitutional procedures; that is, by proportional, party representation (Sharef 1962: 185–7). This meant that policy matters were not the prerogatives of the army, the bureaucracy, or of the Prime Minister. The multiplicity of committees, the manifold spheres they covered, and the 'committee way' of consent and appeal had a restraining effect on over-zealousness stemming from war victories.

For example, towards the end of July 1948 (during the second ceasefire) it was proposed that four settlements be established in the Jerusalem corridor. This was originally planned in the Committee for Settlement which then decided that a composite committee, consisting of members from committees from the Jewish Agency, the Jewish National Fund (JNF), the provisional government, and the Water Authority, would inspect the sites, authorize their settlement and provide a budget. Meanwhile, the chairman of the board of directors of the JNF, Granovsky-Granott 'doubted the legality of [the] settlement on Arab land . . . and it was decided to bring the matter before the [Central] Managing Committee for authorization'. At the Managing Committee's meeting (composed of cabinet ministers and the heads of settlement institutions such as the Jewish Agency), 'the Minister of Finance [Kaplan] announced the government's decision that all matters concerning the status of abandoned Arab property would be finalized by a ministerial committee [Sharett, Kaplan, Rosenblith, Shitreet, Zisling]'. Weitz, himself a member of one of the committees, and the director of the land department of the JNF, voiced the activist and minority grievance in his diary: 'It turns out that we are not authorized to establish the four settlements until the Ministerial Committee will permit it. I felt that we had been placed in chains' (Weitz 1965, 3: 318–22 [July 1948]).

The caution shown by the provision of cross-checking committees pointed to the broad understanding within the government that 'urgent needs of war should not be mixed with far-reaching policy' (Al Hamishmar, 18 June 1948). Even though there were numerous existing committees, committees that never ceased functioning during the height of the war, this additional newly formed Ministerial Committee, set up to formulate policy in regard to Arab property, decided (24 July 1948): 'to maintain a suitable reserve of land in each [abandoned] village, in accordance with a general (country-wide) plan of development, for the inhabitants of those villages when they will return, and if they will return'.

In each proposal for Jewish settlement on land, the guiding principle, according to the Minister of Finance, who was a member of the Managing Committee, was to be that 'the confiscation for this purpose [settlement] of the land from Arab villages should conform to the principles laid down by the Ministerial Committee'; meaning that land was to be kept in reserve for the Arab returnees, and that it would be included in a general development scheme (Weitz 1965, 3: 390–4). The three senior members of the Ministerial Committee – the (Mapai) Minister of Finance, the (Mapam) Minister of Agriculture and the (Liberal) Member of Knesset – were assured by a minority member of the Committee, who shared the views of Ben-Gurion and Eshkol on the matter (to take all the land), that 'the areas allotted for new Jewish settlement are very small and neither harms nor dispossesses the former [Arab] owners of their holdings' (Weitz 1965, 3: 318–19).

The chairman of the JNF, Granovsky-Granott, and Mapai member of the then Provisional Council of State, wrote in the JNF annual (1948–9): 'These days, many

Zionists in the world ask, "How will we get land in the Israeli state?" And they add, "Hasn't a tremendous and basic change taken place which fundamentally alters all the accepted ways of settlement . . . Thus, one who travels through the country and on his way sees abandoned and empty Arab villages, may well think in his heart . . . here we now have land, the land conquered by our soldiers." And he goes on to say: 'It is a mistake on the part of those who come to conclusions on such assumptions . . . Let us analyze the situation as it is. We'll look at our reality in regard to the land problem [Granott was a foremost specialist on questions of land].[11] In Israel, the Jews own 1,500,000 dunams of land which are 11% of its area. The majority of land does not belong to the Jewish National Fund or to private Jewish owners, or to the state [but] is abandoned Arab property. The vast majority of Arabs who ran away are not to be found in Arab states but rather in the Arab part of Palestine (in the original: *"b'aizorei Eratz-Israel sh'byadai ha'arvim"*) and they are concentrated a short distance from our borders.'

According to Granovsky-Granott, what was going to take place was that some of the refugees would not return, while those who did return would take part in an overall agrarian reform plan along with an accelerated pace of urbanization. The policy of the JNF would be to (a) buy land from the state; (b) buy land directly from Arab owners; (c) large-scale agrarian reform 'for Jews and Arabs alike'. He reached the conclusion that agrarian reform was the most important. State land had become practically non-existent, since the amount of land that was formerly British mandatory government property and which now belonged to the government of Israel was insignificant. The new state 'order' thereby cancelled the British land-laws, and enabled the Jews to treat the land anomaly through reform.

As to land purchase from Arabs: the idea was to contact Arab landowners who were possible candidates for selling their land. Since Granovsky-Granott was referring to refugees whose intentions were, at best, not known, he went on to state that the main source for getting land would be through agrarian reform, more or less as follows: Intensification, enforced on the returning villagers, would bring a reduction in the size of their farm units, and would thereby lead to a land surplus *'even if the entire population was to return'*. This surplus would then be sold to the government and bought by the Jewish National Fund. We add, almost as an aside, Granovsky-Granott's plea to world Jewry to make haste with their contributions, 'In order that we can reach a clear Jewish majority in the immediate coming years in the State of Israel (even if the Arab refugees will return in large numbers)' (Granovsky 1948/9: 199–201; emphasis added).

We may state that the most important feature implicit in this document were that 'return' and not 'non-return' was its starting point, that land and agricultural policy were not dependent on 'non-return', nor was there fear of coexistence in a state with its 'two nations'. In the Jewish state, Arab landownership would lose its political importance; that is, contrary to their position during the mandate, the Arabs would not be able to hinder Jewish immigration, land purchase, settlement and development, or agrarian reform. This understanding based itself on the preservation of Arab citizen and property rights. This, then was how it was visualized by the top people in the foremost institutions dealing with land.[12] They were knowledgeable in the intricacies of the land map, ownership with and without deeds, ownership in different categories, political limitations, and so on. The suggested agrarian reform took into consideration the detailed maps of the 5-6 million dunams or so of Arab village and bedouin land, held or cultivated by them under different conditions of fellah private ownership, tenancy, sharecropping, villages without land and villages with tens of thousands, and sometimes more, dunams of land, and major differences within and between different areas.

'They Will Not Return', 'Yes, to Take-over': The Minority Opinion that Became Policy

The majority recommendation was that even when planning new Jewish settlements enough land should be set aside for the Arab inhabitants of the villages when or if they returned. This was not an isolated opinion that we extracted after months of rummaging through files. Given the deep-seated ideological positions of *all* the members of the different committees, the majority opinion must be viewed as unexceptional and genuine, even when we take into consideration the complexities of war, refugees and land. This was the considered position that the minority had to overcome.

The minority opinion in the Managing Committee was voiced by the then head of the Settlement Department at the Jewish Agency, Levi Eshkol (Prime Minister 1963–9), 'In regard to entering [abandoned] Arab villages, I have a definite opinion. It is to enter those villages wherever possible.' Apparently Eshkol (18 December 1948) was at one with the Prime Minister/Minister of Defence: 'I asked [Ben-Gurion] if now we'll get only part of the village lands *in order to leave part for the returnees, as is the opinion of his colleagues in the government*, he replied: No, along the borders and in every village we'll take everything, according to our settlement needs, we won't return the Arabs' (emphasis added). Ben-Gurion also told Eshkol that a meeting had been arranged between him, Kaplan and Granovsky for next Tuesday, and then 'we'll write and sign our agreement' (in Weitz 1965, 3: 366, 372). The minority's plan of action thus ran contrary to the policy that had been endorsed.

And then, at the very same time that the government's position had been clarified in the Ministerial Committee and in the Managing Committee, the Prime Minister/ Defence Minister proposed to the Jewish National Fund that it purchase from the government one million dunams of land (Weitz 1965, 4: 90; Granovsky 1949/50: 162). In interpreting this development, it can be asked what was the importance of all that went before – the multiple committees, the people on them, their decisions, and so on – if we find that during the same month, at the end of December 1948, the chairman of the (Central) Managing Committee, a liberal and legalist, 'purchased' one million dunams of land? Ben-Gurion 'sold' and Granovsky-Granott 'bought'. And it was not only Ben-Gurion that 'sold'. So did Kaplan, Minister of Finance, who was part of the cautious majority on the aforementioned committee that advised that there should not be settlement that would be injurious to returnees, that land would be retained for them, and that there was to be an inclusive plan for both Jews and Arabs, and so on. Kaplan 'sold' to Granott, and Granott, who in July of the same year, as we have seen, doubted the possibility of establishing four sites in the Jerusalem corridor on 14,000 dunams, a few months later 'bought' one million dunams of village lands. (Yes, we are discussing the 'buying' and 'selling' of Arab land, now called Israeli state land, to be sold to the Jewish National Fund as Jewish national land, and/or the Prime Minister acting as custodian, taking steps to ensure that the owners do not return.)

The Jewish political establishment was very aware of the meaning of the sale of Arab lands with regard to peace, understanding between nations, and justice. The leaders of this establishment had publicly stated that the government did not own land, that military conquest did not carry with it rights of ownership, nor, specifically did it cancel prior rights. In the opinion of Grannott, if the state were to take the land of the Arabs, 'it would behave as the foulest of states'. And the director of the JNF Land Department, Weitz, continued, in July 1948, 'This land has owners, and they will not abandon it even if forced to live in exile for many years.' We add here that a new argument was raised at the time and later put to central use; namely, that there are those who promote the idea that we can exchange Arab property for that of Jews from Arab countries: 'There is no connection between the two. Robbery of the one can't be cancelled by the robbery of the other' (Weitz 1965, 3: 154–5).

If we began with the main report of the JNF for 1948, it is worth looking at the report for the year that followed. In the 1949 document we are told:

> The Jewish National Fund started immediately to redeem the owners [the government, not the Arabs!] of the land by payment and to bring it under national [Jewish National Fund] ownership. Following a special agreement with the state of Israel as the custodian of abandoned property in respect of one million dunams of abandoned land to the authority of the Jewish National Fund the JNF purchased 500,000 dunams (of this property) (Granovsky 1949/50: 162).

The first, 1948, document refers to real buying and selling – 'The [Arab] owners are not in Paris and not in the Arab states, they are on our borders' (Granovsky 1948/9: 199–201) – while in 1949 the government becomes the owner, and the Arabs are mentioned in ghost phrases – 'the abandoned land', 'the absentee property'. Now purchase became a *non sequitur* – Jews bought from Jews; in fact, by the close of 1949 'the land property of *the nation* rose to two million dunams' (Granovsky 1949/50: 162–3; emphasis added). (In a more inclusive agreement between the government and the JNF, signed in 1953, where the government was represented by the Development Authority, 'two million dunams of abandoned Arab land, mainly agricultural land' was purchased in the same way and thus land in JNF ownership reached more than three million dunams (JNF 1954: 259).)

The plans raised in 1948 for comprehensive agrarian reform for Jews and Arabs became obsolete or meaningless; barely two years passed and on 3 August 1950, the same Granott-Granovsky could say: 'The nation's land doesn't belong to the individual [owner] but to the nation as a whole.' We can understand why he failed to mention agrarian reform, since the land was already in the (Jewish) nation's hands. How did they get the land? He tells us: 'not by a social revolution, not through spilling of blood, but through building the country, educating the new generation', and so on (in Rotem 1951: 81). The establishment didn't cry, 'No!, Stop!, *Gevalt*!' to the act of dispossession. Nor did we hear that people resigned from the Jewish National Fund.

As a momentary aside (in a theme we continue to follow), it is fitting to notice that at exactly this time, January 1949, when the state 'sold' and the Jewish National Fund 'bought' one million dunams of Arab land, Levi Eshkol could intone another fiction: '40 years we laboured and stored particle [of earth] on particle until we arrived at this point' (in Erez 1969: 74).

Does the reversal indicate that the earlier decisions in the highest parliamentary offices were camouflage, window dressings, or what is termed today 'myths', and that those who sat on the committees had forked-tongues, as Flapan (1987: 113–18), Amitay (1988: 65–6), and Morris[13] intimate? Such reasoning is erroneous. The political direction first taken was real, in line with past commitments and conceptions, and had the power of the majority, including leading members of Mapai, to support it. However, the same committees did not stand fast against the 'sale', perhaps another instance of how democracy yields to state power, aided by chauvinism and the attraction of war spoils – the phenomenon of what can be called the caving-in of democracy. This is another way of saying that the practical crumbling of the majority was not, in our opinion, a Zionist dilemma; rather, it was a dilemma of democracy.

The chronological sequence of events brings us to the observation of the 'leaps' that occur in social existence. It was not imperceptible gradual development, but rather, as here, a brief political struggle, often little more than a political manoeuvre, that brought about an 'extreme change' (Carmi and Rosenfeld 1989, 1991). Change, in which the Arab non-return 'totality' (land take-over, closed borders, military government, etc.) was perhaps the most striking, but not the only, change. The committees had to confront a new force: the executive (military, administrative) and judicial power of their own state. Previously, committees, parties, movements, and their members and leaders, had confronted foreign rule. In the analyses of most of the researchers not enough attention was given to the means and possibilities introduced by the new state power and its specific methods in relation to other political forces including representative committees and legislative authority. This central point is discussed in the following section.

Whoever compares the first (1948) and the second (1949) reports/statements will find that the policy of the majority disappeared and what remained was that of the Prime Minister/Minister of Defence. That his purpose was to concentrate determination of policy and the means of effecting it in his own hands, and to make it the sole monopoly of his war office, was clear. What we wish to show is the combination of factors that eased Ben-Gurion's way in evading the majority's decisions, in dispensing with their interference by dividing them and when necessary removing the main 'obstacles' among them; how the majority was intimidated, brought to its knees, and how this permitted the monopolization of state power.

The question has arisen as to whether the Managing Committee was not something of a fiction, since it was formed more or less at the same time (summer 1948) that the British Emergency (Defence) Regulations (1945) were revived by Ben-Gurion. The simple answer is that with all their severity the Emergency Regulations did not then recognize the Prime Minister/Minister of Defence as sole authority in what concerns us here: matters of refugee return and/or expropriation of their land.

In May 1948 the provisional government had affirmed Ben-Gurion's proposal to declare a state of emergency. (As is known, emergencies are temporary, but the temporary proved to be a constant, and is still in force today.) The revival of the British Emergency (Defence) Regulations (1945) followed and served as the basis for the implementation of the Military government, as well as for the Abandoned Area Ordinance which was promulgated at the same time (less than two months, on 24 June 1948, after the establishment of the state). Soon after came the other ordinances imposed on the remnant Arab population and on the refugees – for example, Emergency Regulations, Cultivation of Waste Lands, 1948; The Absentee Property Regulations, 1949, etc. These were strengthened and expanded by new laws over the years that followed (see Saltman 1982; Kretzmer 1990; Hofnung 1991). Even though the Prime Minister, who spoke in the spirit (and perhaps with the cadences) of Joshua Ben-Nun and followed the practices of High Commissioners, activated 145 British Emergency Regulations which made possible the closure of certain areas, prohibition of entrance, temporary confiscation for purposes of security, and so on, these did not allow for transfer of ownership or entertain the possibility of land expropriation. That was the main reason why the British Mandatory government owned very little land; this was the state of affairs which the Managing Committee did not wish to transgress.

Ben-Gurion, on his part, was determined, by means of the Emergency Regulations and the Military government, to ensure that the Arabs would not return. The Managing Committee, as we have seen, represented the decision that 'there was enough room for all'. We relate, therefore, to a time period when these two contradictory positions and perspectives faced one another within the government, and within the ruling party (Mapai) itself. But the Prime Minister/Minister of Defence, and not the Managing Committee with its majority, had the political power and state means – military, judiciary, administrative, propaganda – to impose his policy. Ben-Gurion brought about the Committee's capitulation in December 1948, and thereby turned it from an independent political committee into an executive body. The ease with which Ben-Gurion turned his major decisions into policy was exemplified in the words of the state's first Attorney-General, his appointee, Ya'acov Shimshon Shapira, who, together with the then District Court judge, Moshe Landau, was assigned the task of 'putting law and order into the realm of abandoned property' (Ben-Porath 1981: 194). Together they redefined the British Emergency Regulations, the Abandoned Property Ordinance (12 December 1948), and reintroduced the Law of Military Courts.[14]

In the concluding section we return to the matter of rapid capitulation, presenting further, and synchronic, analogies to the same effect, with their synchronization serving, we believe, to write large the defeated alternative.

Synchronic Events Which Further Clarify Use of the Term 'Defeated Alternative'

What kind of force was applied to the Managing Committee? After all, the Committee was at a ministerial level, experts were among its members (on land, agriculture, economy, law), and each of them was either a representative or leader of a party. The Committee members had political experience, and the new state did not cease being a 'party-state'. In January, 1949 more than twenty parties, including those of Arabs, took part in the first general elections. Parties, then, were not dissolved, each maintained diversified establishments of political, administrative, cultural, settlement and security spheres. The members of the Managing Committee, therefore, could rely on 'backing' if forced to confront an attempt to undermine their authority. However, this framework proved weak and provided insufficient support to safeguard a 'constitutional' transition to statehood.[15]

The 'caving-in' of democracy has to be understood within the parameters of the struggle between movements and parties and their differential access to the new state apparatus. It was as if everything remained the same, including the recognized players (parties and their leaders). But the head of the state pyramid, the Prime Minister/Minister of Defence, and his party cohorts succeeded in using the state apparatus as an instrument to centralize administrative, military and judicial powers in their hands. The political struggle, especially between Mapai and the left, mainly Mapam, had a highly intensive pre-state history (Aderet and Becker n.d.). State means, meanwhile, were novel, and their implementation became definitive in achieving quick results – what we have called the capitulation of personages and the ignoring or disavowing of agreed-upon political principles (socialism, a political solution to the Arab–Jewish national problem), and the rights of recognized movements. Unlike the case of the Arabs, weak and helpless as they were, the internal Jewish political struggles involved strong formations and groups and holders of key positions (the Palmach and its headquarters, and the Head of the National Command).

At the same time that the Prime Minister/Minister of Defence began to concentrate Arab affairs in his offices, mainly by invoking the Emergency Regulations and instituting the Military government, and when 'They will not return' was still a declaration but not yet a policy decision, he was deeply immersed in the struggle over 'Either him or me'. The dismissal on 3 May 1948 of the Headquarters Commander, or Head of the National Command of the Haganah, Israel Galili, was a stage in the political struggle. Ben-Gurion's purpose was to strike at Mapam and its central position in military operations, units, and command, especially its command positions in the Palmach, probably the most significant army corps during the war. Galili's dismissal brought about the collective resignation of the Head-quarters Staff, the highest army command. The resignation was delivered in the middle of the war, on 5 May, ten days before the declaration of statehood. As a result of the resignation, Ben-Gurion cancelled the dismissal, and the first round ended with a Headquarters' victory. As in the case of Arab refugees and their land, a Ministerial Committee was appointed to clarify the functions of the Headquarters Commander and of the Minister of Defence, the forthcoming decision to be binding for both sides. But, in mid-June, Ben-Gurion reneged and dismissed Galili once again. The dismissal was again followed by the collective resignation of the Headquarters Staff (Ben-Porath 1981: 108–15). Thereupon, Ben-Gurion threatened to resign as Prime Minister/Minister of Defence (24 May). The head of the Ministerial Committee, who was Minister of Interior at the time, turned to Mapai to appoint a replacement for Ben-Gurion; the party refused, forcing an impasse. The Committee capitulated, Galili left, and the crisis was resolved (Ben-Porath 1981: 112; Shapira 1985: 239–43).

Mapai was the largest party (approximately 35 per cent of the electorate), but not a majority party. The use of its strength as a bloc vote – 'either you take Ben-Gurion, or there is no government' – enhanced control over state power by Ben-Gurion and his supporters, who applied it when necessary, even against Mapai leaders. Top Mapai leaders were members of the Managing Committee that reached a policy decision, during July and August, that 'there was enough land for all', 'not to enter the abandoned villages', and 'not to harm the possibility of refugee return' this, not only after the mass flight and expulsion of the Arabs, but also after the 'exhortations' of Ben-Gurion and Sharett ('They will not return'), and after the assassination of Bernadotte (among whose demands was the immediate return of Arab refugees). They arrived at their decision in spite of their earlier involvement as witnesses or participants in the caving-in of the Headquarters, the Ministerial Committee, the government, and Mapai itself over the removal/forced resignation of Galili (3 May to mid-July).

The decision of the Managing Committee was in line with the accepted historical understanding common to the main social movements and parties whose represent-atives sat in the government and on its committees. The new viewpoint was introduced and enforced by Ben-Gurion and his partisans; it was proclaimed less as policy than as the fortuitousness of military fortune: 'We come before the United Nations General Assembly . . . backed by an army . . . which is perhaps the most important military force in the Middle East' (Sharett, 27 September 1948, in Ben-Gurion 1971: 272). True enough, the strong nationalist-militarist and 'statist' line that gained the upper hand within Israeli politics (Rosenfeld and Carmi 1976; Carmi and Rosenfeld 1989) was definitive in deciding the resultant issues, as well as the (non-negotiable) 'non-issues' (refugees, borders, and Jerusalem) of the war.

Israeli polity is not to be treated as a closed system. The internal policy decision of non-return taken by Israel could have been cancelled quicker than it had been made. This would have been the case had the United Nations applied pressure, and had Great Britain or the United States issued an ultimatum (as did Britain towards the French presence in Syria in 1945, and the US with Israel in Sinai in 1956–7). Signs of such demands were not lacking. We have mentioned the December 1948 UN Resolution 194. In the winter of 1949, Sharett made a counter-offer of 100,000 returnees to the US suggestion of 250,000. *Mapam* proposed that the government make a positive numerical tender before the US apply pressure, when Truman showed signs that such were his intentions. In 1961, Kennedy proposed a referendum (to choose between return and reparations) among the Palestinian Arab refugees, and it appeared serious enough to give rise to a twelve-paragraph reply from Ben-Gurion (Medzini 1981: 207) – but nothing materialized. Without going deeply into the matter, it would seem that Israel's policy of non-return, which gave preference to ongoing war above concessions, was not out of keeping with the Cold War. The negotiated armistice agreements brought Israel decades of arms expenditures, wars, and ongoing, heavy military, economic and political dependence on the United States.

The Arab refugee problem gained international recognition. Bernadotte, a United Nations mediator, was sent immediately to deal with the situation, and Resolution 194, uncompromising about 'right of return', holds until today. But this is where it stands. Nevertheless, neither the weakness of the UN, nor the retreat of the US government, nor the caving-in of the democratic majority before state power were sufficient conditions in themselves to transform the policy of non-return into a major structural component of the Israeli regime. The mass arrival of Jewish refugees gave it the strongest push. Between the years 1948 and 1951, the number of Jewish refugees entering Israel equalled the number of Arab refugees outside its borders. The weight of their numbers, their social and ethnic makeup, the large percentage of Jews who survived Nazism and those who fought against it, provided the hasty repopulation with an air of irreversibility.

At the same time, the mass immigration created a highly problematic situation, since its economic absorption depended solely on state means. Ben-Gurion phrased (27 September 1948) the severity of the approaching situation with the words: 'Either militarization of our state, or immigrant absorption and settlement. There is no escape from this dilemma' (1957: 269). The state succeeded with partial solutions: outstanding were the yearly contributions of American Jewry, some help from the United States government, and in 1953–4, and most important, the signing of the Israel–Germany Reparations Agreement. The mobilization of economic aid, and the political backing accompanying it, provided the government with the breathing space needed to transform policy into a regime. In this, it succeeded in deferring the immediacy of Arab refugee return; what followed were the military expenditures and wars which have become an integral part of the regime until today. The Managing Committee's decision of 1948, that 'There is room for all', has never been reached again, but remains a Defeated Alternative to be renegotiated under new circumstances.

Notes

1. We present this paper to Lambros Comitas, in friendship. We gratefully acknowledge the RISM Landes Senior Fellowship awarded us for research on political economy and Arab–Jewish relations in Haifa. This work is an offshoot of that project.
2. Here are some of the possibilities considered by Isaac Deutscher: 'The outcome of the struggle might have been different if the Arabs had been less divided or better armed and better trained; if Britain had not been in retreat; and if either the Soviet Union or the United States had backed the Arab' (1968: 121).
3. For the 'condition of virtually full employment' in Palestine during the Second World War years, see *Survey of Palestine 1946*, III: 1308; for the real rise in income for both Jews and Arabs between 1939 and 1945, see Loftus (1948: 19).

4. For figures on 'abandoned' villages, land, and property, see Kamen (1987, 1988); Khalidi (1992); Peretz (1958: 165); Shafrir (1975); Carmi and Rosenfeld (1992: 19).

5. We use the term 'non-return' (for Arabs) as the negative for the 'Law of Return' coin (for Jews) (Carmi and Rosenfeld 1989).

6. See Buber's polemical use (March 1949) of '*raison d'état*' in an argument with Ben-Gurion at a symposium. Among much else: 'This morning . . . I read in the newspaper that the Palestine Conciliation Commission, which is presently in Beirut, intends to call an international meeting on the subject of the refugees. I hope that this information is false. They do not deserve that initiative. We deserve it. And if "raison d'etat" argues against such an initiative, then it suffers from myopia' (in Mendes-Flohr 1983: 243–4).

7. For example, the Socialist-Zionist Mapam newspaper, *Al Hamishmar*, published a proclamation, two-and-a-half months after the establishment of the state, turning to 'the intelligent and progressive [Arab] workers and peasant masses', and to 'the Arab Palestinian refugees wherever they may be' saying: 'The Jewish masses heard with satisfaction the voice of the democratic Arab groups calling for peace and cooperation between the two nations . . . on the basis of the decision of the United Nations Assembly from the 29th of November 1947 regarding the granting of independent states: a Jewish state and an Arab state linked in economic union' (in Amitay 1988: 48).

8. For a personal account seen first through the eyes of a child of eight in 1948, and then continued over the years, see Chacour (1985) and Shoufani (1972).

9. Two weeks previously (4 June 1948) the director of the JNF's colonization department had termed the 'situation' 'a de facto transfer' (in Ben-Gurion 1971: 122).

10. An English version (Ben-Gurion 1971: 149) shortens the last part of the sentence in Hebrew to 'well-watered lands'.

11. See, for example, Granott (1952).

12. For some of the proposals and plans envisaged see Hashomer Hatsair (1947); Jewish Plan (1947); Granovsky (1948).

13. 'Revisionist', 'new historian' studies regard such statements as expressions of political camouflage for an underlying policy of expulsion, confiscation, and take-over by force. Benny Morris's interpretation of double standards will serve: 'The "surplus lands" formula seemed to point the way to both having one's cake and eating it: strategic and agricultural–territorial interests could be safeguarded while at the same time lands could be set aside for a possible return of the refugees. In any case, the Arabs were to be compensated for the lands expropriated. Hence, it was to be "development for the benefit of both peoples", as Hazan described it; or "we must fight for development and against eviction", said party co-leader Ya'ari. Mapam had found a formula

that seemed to wed strategic and economic expediency with principle' (Morris 1989: 184).

14. Prior to Israeli statehood, Shapira, then a lawyer, had been an outspoken critic of the British Emergency Regulations; and Landau, a retired Supreme Court Justice, in 1990 wrote the judgement (the Landau Committee) for the use of 'moderate physical pressure' as being permissible in the interrogation of Palestinian detainees and prisoners.

15. Weitz complained that Zisling and Bentov, the two Mapam ministers, were concerned 'about our neighbours who fled'; and that Zisling told him that, as Minister of Agriculture, in his plan for settlement (for Jews and Arabs), he had made provision for 'constitutional law regarding land' (in Weitz 1965, 3: 319, 347); and at a meeting of the directorate of the JNF (7 December 1948) Hazan presented his position: 'Here Hazan found a place to present his views in regard to the Arabs, that in his opinion we should not do anything that will prevent their return. He agrees that there are security areas where Arabs cannot return, but then, we have immediately to prepare land and settlements for them to return to. He doesn't consider another possibility such as settling them outside the borders' (Weitz 1965, 3: 361).

References

Abou Iyad (Khalaf Salah) (1979), *Without A Homeland*, Jerusalem: Mifras Publishing House (Hebrew).

Al-Khatib, H. M. (1954), 'In the Wake of the Catastrophe', in *In the Eyes of Enemy*, pp. 7–68, Ma'arachot: Israel Defence Forces (Hebrew).

Almogi, Y. (1980), *Total Commitment*, Haifa: Adanim (Hebrew).

Amitay, Y. (1988), *The United Workers' Party (Mapam) 1948–1954: Attitudes on Palestinian–Arab Issues*, Tel Aviv: Tcherikover Publishers (Hebrew).

Aricha, Y. (ed.) (1959), *Tel Aviv-Jaffa (A Reader)*, Tel Aviv-Jaffa: Tel Aviv-Jaffa Municipality (Hebrew).

Asad, T. (1975), 'Anthropological Texts and Ideological Problems', *Economy and Society*, 4(3): 251–82.

Asaf, M. (1967), *History of the Arab Awakening in Palestine and Their Flight*, Tel Aviv: Tarbut Vehinuch (Hebrew).

Ben-Gurion, D. (1957), *Israel's Battles (Bhilachem Israel)*, Tel Aviv: Am Oved (Hebrew).

—— (1969), *The Restored State of Israel*, Tel Aviv: Am Oved (Hebrew).

—— (1971), *Israel: A Personal History*, New York: Funk & Wagnalls, Inc.

Ben-Porath, Y. (1981), *Dialogues*, Jerusalem: Edanim (Hebrew).

Bernadotte, F. (1951), *To Jerusalem*, London: Hodder and Stoughton.

Bernstein, D. S. (1996), 'Expanding the Split Labor Market Theory: Between and Within Sectors of the Split Labor Market of Mandatory Palestine', *Comparative Studies in Society and History*, 38(2): 243–66.

Carmel, M. (1949), *Northern Campaigns*, Tel Aviv: Hakibbutz Hameuchad (Hebrew).

Carmi, S. and Rosenfeld, H. (1974), 'The Origins of the Process of Proletarianization and Urbanization in Palestine', in A. L. Ruffa *et al* (eds), *City and Peasant: A Study in Socio-Cultural Dynamics*, pp. 470–85, New York: New York Academy of Sciences, Vol. 220.

—— (1989), 'The Emergence of Militaristic Nationalism in Israel', *International Journal of Politics, Culture and Society*, 3(1): 5–49.

—— (1991), 'The Radical Change: From a Socialist Perspective to Militarism', *International Journal of Politics, Culture and Society*, 4: 577–87.

—— (1992), 'Israel's Political Economy and the Widening Class Gap Between its Two National Groups', *Asian and African Studies*, 26: 15–61.

Chacour, E. (1985), *Blood Brothers*, Eastbourne, Sussex: Kingsway Publications Ltd.

Cohen, A. (1970), *Israel and the Arab World*, New York: Funk and Wagnalls.

Deutscher, I. (1968), *The Non-Jewish Jew and Other Essays*, London: Oxford University Press.

Eisenstadt, S. N. (1967), *Israeli Society*, London: Weidenfeld and Nicolson.

Erez, Y. (1969), *Land Covenant (Brit Adama)*, Tel Aviv: Tarbut Vehinuch (Hebrew).

Farah, B. (1985), *From Ottoman Times to the State of Israel*, Nazareth: As-salt (Arabic).

Finkelstein, N., Masalha, N. and Morris, B. (1991), 'Debate on the 1948 Exodus', *Journal of Palestine Studies*, 21(1): 66–114.

Flapan, S. (1987), *The Birth of Israel: Myths and Realities*, New York: Pantheon Books.

Frank, A. G. (1975), *On Capitalist Underdevelopment*, Bombay: Oxford University Press.

Gabbay, R. (1958), *A Political Study of the Arab–Jewish Conflict*, Geneve: E. Droz.

Goren, T. (1998), 'Arab Leaders Between the British Command and the Haganah and the History of the Negotiations Over the Surrender Document of Haifa's Arabs', in Y. Ben-Artzi (ed.), *Haifa, Local History*, pp. 183–215, Haifa: Haifa University/Zamora-Bitan (Hebrew).

Gorni, Y. (1987), *Zionism and the Arabs*, Oxford: Clarendon Press.

Granovsky (Granott), A. (1948), 'On the Threshold of the State', in N. Bistritski (ed.), *Kama*, pp. 11–34, Herzlia: Masada (Hebrew).

—— (1948/49), 'The Tasks of the Keren Kayemet on the Establishment of the State', in *The Journalists' Yearbook*, Tel Aviv: The Journalists' Association (Hebrew).

—— (1949/50), 'Hakeren Hakayemet Lyisrael', in *The Journalists' Yearbook*, Tel Aviv: The Journalists' Association (Hebrew).

Granott, A. (1952), *The Land System in Palestine*, London: Eyre and Spottiswoode.

Habibi, E. (1984), *Haopsimist*, Jerusalem: Miphras (Hebrew).

Haifa (1968), *Events of Twenty Years 1948–1968*, Haifa: Davar (Hebrew).

Harkabi, Y. (1974), *Palestinians and Israel*, New Brunswick, N.J.: Transaction Books.

—— (1977), *Arab Strategies and Israeli Responses*, New York: Free Press.

—— (1988), *Israel's Fateful Decisions*, London: I.B. Tauris.

Hashomer Hatzair (1947), *The Road to Bi-National Independence for Palestine*, Memorandum of the Hashomer Hatzair Workers' Party of Palestine, Tel Aviv: Hashomer Hatzair.

Hofnung, M. (1991), *Israel Security Needs vs. The Rule of Law*, Jerusalem: Nevo Publishing (Hebrew).

Horowitz, D. and Lissak, M. (1978), *Origins of the Israeli Polity: Palestine Under the Mandate*, Chicago: Chicago University Press.

—— (1989) 'The State of Israel at Forty', in Peter Y. Medding (ed.), *Israel State and Society, 1948–1988*, pp. 3–24, Institute of Contemporary Jewry, The Hebrew University of Jerusalem. New York/ Oxford: Oxford University Press.

Hurewitz, J. C. (1950), *The Struggle for Palestine*, New York: W.W. Norton.

Jewish Plan (1947), *The Jewish Plan for Palestine. Memorandum and Statements Presented by the Jewish Agency for Palestine to the United Nations Special Committee on Palestine*, Jerusalem: The Jewish Agency for Palestine.

Jiryis, S. (1976), *The Arabs in Israel*, New York and London: The Monthly Review Press.

JNF (1954), 'Hakeren Hakayemet Lyisrael', in *The Journalists' Yearbook,* Tel Aviv: The Journalists' Association (Hebrew).

Kamen, C. S. (1987), 'After The Catastrophe I: The Arabs in Israel, 1948–51', *Middle Eastern Studies*, 23(4): 453–95.

—— (1988), 'After the Catastrophe II: The Arabs in Israel, 1948–51', *Middle Eastern Studies*, 24(1): 68–109.

Kanafani, G. ([1970]1972), 'Returning to Haifa (Aid ila Haifa)', *Collected Works*, Vol. I, pp. 337–414. Beirut: Muasasat Al-Abhath Al-Arabiya (Arabic).

Khalidi, W. (1986), 'The Arab Perspective', in W. R. Louis and R. W. Stookey (eds), *The End of the Palestine Mandate*, pp. 104–36, London: I. B. Tauris.

—— (ed.) (1992), *All That Remained*, Washington, DC: Institute for Palestine Studies.

Kimmerling, B. (1989), *The Israeli State and Society*, Albany, N.Y.: State University of New York.

Klein, I. (1983), *The Arabs in Haifa Under the British Mandate: A Political Economic and Social Survey*, Occasional Papers on the Middle East (New Series) No. 5, Haifa: University of Haifa, The Jewish–Arab Center Institute of Middle Eastern Studies (Hebrew).

Kolinsky, M. (1993), *Law, Order, and Riots in Mandatory Palestine, 1928–35*, London: St. Martin's Press.

Kretzmer, D. (1990), *The Legal Status of the Arabs in Israel*, Boulder, Colo.: Westview.

Lahduth H. (1948), *United Workers' Party*, 1 (1) (Hebrew).

Leibricht, H. (1987), *The Palestinians Past and Present*, Tel Aviv: Miphalim Universataim (Hebrew).

Lockman, Z. (1996), *Comrades and Enemies*, Berkeley: University of California Press.

Loftus, P. J. (1948), *National Income of Palestine 1945*, Palestine: Government Printer.

Louis, W. R. (1986), 'British Imperialism and the End of the Palestine Mandate', in W. R. Louis and R. W. Stookey (eds), *The End of the Palestine Mandate*, pp. 1–31, London: I. B. Tauris.

—— and Stookey, R. W. (eds) (1986) *The End of the Palestine Mandate*, London: I. B. Tauris.

Mansur, G. (1937), *The Arab Worker Under the Palestine Mandate*, Jerusalem: The Arab Cultural Company Ltd.

Medzini, M. (ed.) (1981), *Documents in the History of the State*, Jerusalem: Ministry of Defence (Hebrew).

Mendes-Flohr, P. R. (ed.) (1983), *A Land of Two Peoples: Martin Buber on Jews and Arabs*, New York: Oxford University Press.

Metzer, J. and Kaplan, O. (1985), 'Jointly but Severally: Arab–Jewish Dualism and Economic Growth in Mandatory Palestine', *The Journal of Economic History*, 45(2): 327–45.

Migdal, J. S. (1980), *Palestinian Society and Politics*, Princeton, N.J.: Princeton University Press.

Monroe, E. (1963), *Britain's Moment in the Middle East, 1914–1956*, London: Methuen.

Morris, B. (1989), *The Birth of the Palestinian Refugee Problem, 1947–1949*, Cambridge: Cambridge University Press.

—— (1990), *1948 and After*. Oxford: Clarendon Press.

Nakara, H. (1985), *Advocate of the Land and the People*, Acre: Dar El Aswar (Arabic).

Pappé, I. (1992), *The Making of the Arab–Israeli Conflict, 1947–51*, London: I. B. Tauris

Peretz, D. (1958), *Israel and the Palestine Arabs*, Washington, DC: The Middle East Institute.

Ram, U. (1993), 'The Colonization Perspective in Israeli Sociology: Internal and External Comparisons', *Journal of Historical Sociology*, 6(3): 327–50.

Rodinson, M. (1973), *Israel : A Colonial Settler State?*, New York: Monad Press.

Rosenfeld, H. and Carmi, S. (1976), 'The Privatization of Public Means, The State-Made Middle Class, and the Realization of Family Value in Israel', in J. G. Peristiany (ed.), *Kinship and Modernization in Mediterranean Society*, pp. 131–59, Rome: The Center for Mediterranean Studies, American Universities Field Staff.

Rotem, Z. (1951) 'The Keren Kayemet Jubilee Year', in *The Journalists' Yearbook*, Tel Aviv: The Journalists' Association (Hebrew).

Safran, N. (1978), *Israel the Embattled Ally*, Cambridge, Mass.: The Belknap Press of Harvard University Press.

Said, E. W. (1979), *The Question of Palestine*, New York: Vintage Books.

Salomon, Y. (1982), *In My Own Way*, Haifa: The Gillie Salomon Foundation.

Saltman, M. (1982), 'The Use of Mandatory Emergency Laws by the Israeli Government', *International Journal of the Sociology of Law*, 10(3): 385–94.

Schölch, A. (1982), 'European Penetration and the Economic Development of Palestine, 1856–82', in R. Owen (ed.), *Studies in the Economic and Social History of Palestine in the Nineteenth and Twentieth Centuries*, pp. 10–87, Oxford: The Macmillan Press.

Schwarz, W. (1959) *The Arabs in Israel*, London: Faber and Faber.

Seikaly, M. (1995), *Haifa: Transformation of a Palestinian Arab Society 1918–1936*, London: I. B. Tauris.

Segev, T. (1986), *1949, The First Israelis*, New York: Free Press.

Shafir, G. (1989), *Land, Labor and the Origins of the Israeli–Palestinian Conflict*, Cambridge: Cambridge University Press.

Shafrir, D. (1975), *Life's Garden*, Tel Aviv: The Central Office of the Agricultural Histadruth (Hebrew).

Shapira, A. (1992), *Land and Power*. New York: Oxford University Press.

—— (1985), *From Dismissal of the Headquarters Command Up Until the Disbanding of the Palmach*, Tel Aviv: Hakibbutz Hameuchad (Hebrew).

Sharef, Z. (1962), *Three Days*, Garden City, N.Y.: Doubleday & Company.

Shimoni, Y. (1947), *The Arabs of Palestine*, Tel Aviv: Am Oved (Hebrew).

Shoufani, E. (1972), 'The Fall of a Village', *Journal of Palestine Studies*, 1(4): 108–21.

Slutzky, Y. (ed.) (1973), *The History of the Haganah (Sefer Toldot Hahaganah)*, Vol. III, Part B, Tel-Aviv: Am Oved (Hebrew).

Survey (1946), *A Survey of Palestine*, Vol. 3, Jerusalem: Government Printer.

Tibawi, Abd Al-Latif (1969), *A Modern History of Syria, Including Lebanon and Palestine*, London: Macmillan.

Vashitz, J. (1993), 'Social Changes in Haifa's Arab Society Under the British Mandate', Thesis submitted to the Senate of the Hebrew University towards a Ph.D. degree, Jerusalem (Hebrew).

Weitz, Y. (1965), *My Diary and Letter*, Vols 3 and 4, Tel Aviv: Masada (Hebrew).

Zureik, E. T. (1979), *The Palestinians in Israel: A Study in Internal Colonialism*, London: Routledge & Kegan Paul.

4

All that Fuss Over 100 Houses: Identities and Moralities of Building on Land

Simone Abram

Introduction

This chapter considers how apparently innocuous, narrowly defined planning proposals can provoke a plethora of moral conflicts over territorial ideals.

The scene is a well-appointed living room in a large, old house in a village in the Home Counties, some 40 miles north of London. Eight local residents (one a temporary resident: the ethnographer), each educated, articulate, professional, clink their wine glasses and get down to the business in hand: appointing a solicitor to represent them at a public enquiry.

The discussion covers the possibility of their local residents' group gaining charitable status. Will they be able to take funds from members as loans and later turn them into covenants? Should they take pledges rather than contributions? Where do they stand on tax liability? They accept the challenge to raise several thousands of pounds, possibly fifteen to twenty thousand, but they're confident they will raise it over the two years before the Public Enquiry, which will decide the plan for the village's future. They have already been given a total of £2,000 from sympathetic members, and they previous handled accounts for a campaign against the building of a motorway alongside the village which raised over £30,000. A fund-raising committee is already forming, with initiatives afoot, hosting garden openings, dinners, walking tours.

And what is the crisis that heralds this meeting? A threat to demolish an ancient monument? A new airport to be built alongside the village perhaps? Or a new road to blast through the middle of the village, dividing families and threatening the safety of children? No; the issue is whether the District Council will include a policy in its new forward plan to allow about 150 houses to be built in a field on the edge of the village over the next twenty years. For a village with a population of 4,000–5,000 inhabitants, where in the previous five years over a hundred houses were built while the population dropped, this should not, on the surface, seem to be so dreadful a fate. It is a small percentage growth, not even 5 per cent, in a village that has grown tenfold in forty years. So why are these people so incensed? Why are they prepared to put up thousands of pounds to pay a solicitor to represent them for the sake of a few more houses?

The answer, of course, depends on to whom you ask the question. The players to be asked here include the members of the group, other village groups, including the Parish Council, local politicians of the District Council, District Council planning officers and others. The aim of this chapter is to explore the variety of moral frames that are implicated in the negotiations over local policy, in this case planning for the housing of the future.

These moralities are taken here to be emblematic of the different assumed social identities of people involved in different ways with the preparation of policy. In this way, the chapter links the notions of identity and morality as interdependent concepts, with each defining the other. The chapter therefore assumes that the morality of public service is implicit in individuals' relationships with their roles as public servants or politicians as well as citizens. However, it seems that competing moral priorities and discursive frameworks act to divide participants to planning policy processes, leading arguments to become tangles of misunderstanding rather than constructive debates. For example, planners arguing for ways to distribute housing allocations are frustrated by residents' complaints over the loss of fields and meadows, and their discussions often do not move towards consensus, but rather towards dissent, since each is arguing a different case. What is at stake here is not simply control over territory, or ownership of property, or even competition over property values and exclusivity, but the very meaning of territory and its significance in certain organizational relationships and forms of society. The argument over the use of land is, I contend, a concretization of differences in moral priorities. We have here a struggle between different interpretations of nature, of public interest (which is intrinsically a dispute over who constitutes the public), of democracy (since we have competing versions of who the state represents and who represents the state) and of development (since notions of development as progress are increasingly threatened).

Planning

In order to explain how this situation has come about, it will help to know why the District Local Plan includes this allocation of housing, and why the plan is important. We will need to consider briefly what planning is in England, and how it operates, in order to understand how local demands come to be made, before we can understand the tight constraints within which local politicians make decisions. We must also consult the District Local Plan for the district of Aylesbury Vale, in Buckinghamshire, where this village is located (see Figure 4.1).

The District Local Plan for Aylesbury Vale (AVDLP) emerged from a changing statutory planning process. Until 1995, districts were obliged to produce separate

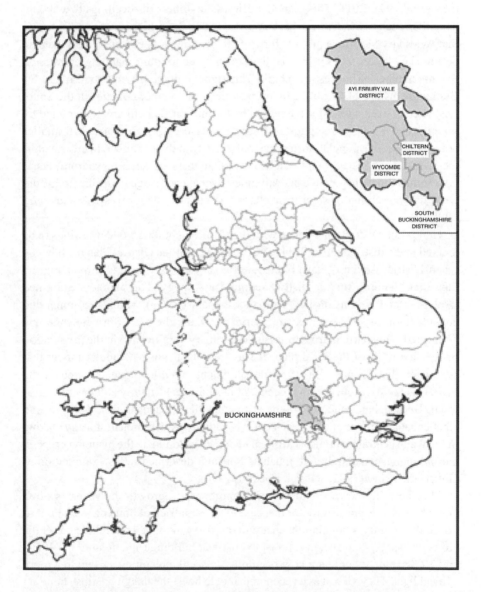

Figure 4.1 *Map of Buckinhamshire showing constituent districts.*

plans for urban areas and rural areas. When new requirements appeared for district-wide local plans, Aylesbury Vale District Council began to merge their existing documents with the requirements of the County Structure Plan for Buckinghamshire, the county of which Aylesbury Vale district is a part. The immediate process of developing the DLP was prompted within the hierarchical British planning system by the confirmation of a new strategic County Plan for Buckinghamshire, covering the period 1991–2011. This plan identifies the numbers of dwellings that should be built in each of the districts that belong to Buckinghamshire county, and specifies that Aylesbury Vale must provide for 15,600 'dwellings' to be built within the plan period (i.e., before 2011). That is, they must agree to grant planning permission for this number of houses to be built. This figure emerged from a total figure for Buckinghamshire of 64,000, a figure negotiated with other counties in the South East region, from a total for the region of 1.1 million. This figure, determined by government forecasts, suggests a large increase in the formation of smaller households from a population growing only very slightly in number. In other words, the planning of housing follows a hierarchy of numbers that spills down from central government, to be negotiated and struggled over at each stage in the hierarchy, but with little possibility of significant change within any one level (see Abram *et al.* 1998).

Hence, the District Plan began with the requirement for 15,600 dwellings to be located in the district before 2011. The preparation of the District Plan itself began when District Council planners prepared a set of issues papers introducing the idea that planning for the district required a strategy. The planners examined Government Planning Policy Guidance papers (PPGs) which recommended consideration of sites with existing services, where the use of private cars may be limited. This particular factor assumed primary significance in the preparation of the first draft of the local plan. It was 'tested', using a computer model that suggested that 75 per cent of all development should be concentrated in the main town of Aylesbury, with 25 per cent in rural areas, mainly at the next largest town, Buckingham, and with some at two smaller villages/towns, Winslow and Haddenham. This use of technical models is particularly common in strategy making in local and central planning. Statistical approaches dominate the planning process, and in doing so also define it, much as Foucault described in his examination of Governmentality (1991; see also Hacking 1990).

The moral framework underlying commitment to growth, however, is often described as a responsibility for the state to allow sufficient housing to be built to house the country's population, an argument that cannot be contradicted directly. However, as we shall see, in contrast to post-war building right up until the 1960s and 1970s, more people are now beginning to see the planning system in a more cynical light. They view it as an economic tool to boost the flagging British building industry, and this rather more Thatcherite 'rationality' is less persuasive, chiming significantly less with the dominant Christian morality in areas such as the one considered here.

Haddenham, the village we are concerned with, presented itself to planners as an 'obvious' choice for supplying land for housing in the Vale. It has two primary schools and a 'middle' school, a health centre, library, lively village hall, a number of shops, several pubs, a fairly large industrial site, a bus service and a station on the adjacent railway line that also serves the nearby town of Thame (which is just over the administrative border, in Oxfordshire). All these conditions drew planners to assume that Haddenham would be an appropriate place to site some of the District's rural housing requirement. Indeed, interviews conducted with county and district planners in the mid-1990s indicated that they had mentally allocated housing to Haddenham even before they had elaborated planning policies.

In the early 1990s, the District Council planners had worked with County Council planners to prepare the County Structure Plan mentioned above, a strategic plan that distributed development throughout the county and issued general policies for all the districts. Drafts of the Structure Plan had included policies identifying Haddenham as a 'Key Rural Settlement', since its qualities (such as services, location, size) coincided with the policies for housing and employment location under the County's interpretation of 'sustainable development'. However, after complaints from the Haddenham Village Society (whom we shall meet later in the paper) who objected to this label as a form of blight on the village's future, and with the support of the District Council who felt it was the District's role to identify sites rather than the County's, mention of Haddenham was removed from the Structure Plan.

However, the District Council planners, and politicians (see pp. 77–80) did not remove Haddenham from their mental scheme, and it reappeared in the draft versions of the District Plan as a key site for rural housing and employment. In short, the District set out criteria for rural development, based mainly on the County's policies, and these criteria were met by Haddenham. It became more apparent later that this supposedly straightforward technical process was in fact heavily influenced by political and business pressure. From the planners' perspective, however, their recommendation of Haddenham for development appeared to satisfy their requirement for development that they could call 'sustainable' and solved the 'problem' of where to locate the housing required of them by the County Structure Plan.

The specific policies also identified a site within the village for this allocation of housing. This site was also identified earlier, rather optimistically, as a site for a secondary school in a Village Plan drawn up in 1971 by the District Council. At present, Buckinghamshire still follows a segregated education system, with children tested at age 12 for entry to Grammar Schools or High Schools, so that children from Haddenham do not all go to the same secondary school. Furthermore, as

Haddenham is closer to Thame, in Oxfordshire county, which has Comprehensive schooling, many parents choose to send their children at age 11 to the highly regarded nearby Comprehensive school in Thame. Some other families send their children for private education. After leaving the village 'Middle School' (ages 10-12), pupils from the village disperse to a wide range of secondary schools. To date no secondary school has been built in the village, or ever thought feasible, given the conditions. Consequently, the site has never been built on, and, when read from a map, appears as a 'hole' in the developed boundary of the village.

To planners (and some politicians), the site appeared from the map to be the 'obvious' site for housing development, and hence it appears as such in the DLP. Therefore, planners appeared at exhibitions in the village, stating to villagers that the fields to be developed constituted the site that planners felt was 'most appropriate' within the village. This opinion seemed to be based on an understanding of territory having potential for building. The fields appear to planners not as economically productive land occupied by crops (or indeed by other flora and fauna), or as recreational land essential to village cohesion; rather, they are perceived as empty potential for building – a missing part of a jigsaw that will satisfy governmental demand for housing figures to be met. Before we dismiss planners as narrow or technocratic, however, we must remember that the planners at Aylesbury Vale considered their role as rather more heroic, since their overarching priority was to ensure that the country's housing needs were met. That is, in the current Labour government's terms, to ensure that a 'decent' home was within reach of every citizen.

Not surprisingly, the planners' authority to make judgements about the 'most appropriate' use of land in and around the village from their offices in Aylesbury town was frequently challenged by villagers, and their statements of these preferences were considered by many villagers, at the very least, to be presumptuous. The allocation of authority to make such judgements rests on a set of beliefs about who has the right to govern what. Here, perhaps, one could argue that there are not simply different conclusions about who can make better decisions being made here, but that broader beliefs about governance are coming into conflict. The residents believe that they hold some right to control their immediate surroundings through the planning system. But this is denied by the planners' conviction that they are in a better position to make strategies that will satisfy the 'needs' of a broader section of the population than merely the current residents of the village. The right to make decisions on others' behalf is a crucial component of governmental systems, and once the legitimacy of this right is in question, a whole range of competing governmental moralities come to the surface.

It is at times when policy is in question, such as during the preparation of new policies, that people make public their moral beliefs. The question of the future plan for the District therefore brought into the open the beliefs of these various people about the meaning of democracy and governance and about the importance, or otherwise, of local social organization. In the next sections, the actions and stances of the local politicians and village groups are contrasted with those of the planners outlined above, to illustrate how these different approaches developed throughout the preparation of the plan for Aylesbury Vale.

Politicians

The beginning of the preparation of the AVDLP coincided with a change in political control of the District Council, from Conservative to Liberal Democrat. Many of the Liberal Democrat councillors were therefore newly elected, and many had very little experience of planning. This change also affected planners, since they had to adapt to the different political approach of the new councillors, and to help them to understand the background to DLP policies and the workings of the planning system. The new Lib Dem politicians found themselves required to fulfil housing requirements formulated by their Conservative predecessors, when their own attitudes towards growth were quite different. With their style of grass-roots representation contrasting strongly with Conservative corporatism, the Lib Dems seemed to struggle more visibly with the need to reconcile the competing pressures from constituents in different wards with a more strategic, general approach from which local site-specific details followed. Some politicians in the same party took opposite stances, one suggesting that he was elected to represent his constituents and that was what he would do. Whereas others felt that upon joining the council, it was their duty to take a more strategic view of the whole district, rather than a more partizan, directly representative approach to District-wide issues such as the DLP.

Early on in the preparation of the DLP, planning was reviewed by a lowly sub-committee of the elected council, which discussed strategic approaches to the location of development in Aylesbury Vale. As mentioned above, planners presented the committee with a set of alternative strategies, based on the results of its transport model. The committee voted to follow a strategy of 'urban concentration' whereby development in the rural area of the Vale would still be concentrated in the larger settlements, agreeing that this constituted a 'sustainable' approach in accordance with government advice. The approach also seemed to suit the majority of councillors, since most wards would not be subject to any specific housing policies, thereby reducing local opposition.

After the election which saw the Liberal Democrats (Lib Dems) take control of the District Council, the new Lib Dem members of the forward planning committee began to recognize the importance of the forward plan. A general reorganization of District Council committees allowed them to increase the status of the plan by creating a new forward plans committee to report directly to the full District Council. Shortly after this, the first draft plan was published, identifying housing and other development sites in the District. At this point, various constituents began to respond to proposals in the plan, and politicians began to come under pressure from unhappy residents. Most of these unhappy residents came from Haddenham, objecting to the construction of new housing estates on so-called greenfield land. Indeed, out of less than 3,000 letters of objection received by the Council, over 1,800 came from Haddenham.

The consultation period over the draft plan fell into the period leading up to the General Election of 1997, and one of the village's councillors was standing for parliament. All the local parties began to consider what they could do to promote their candidate locally, and the question of the DLP began to take on strident party political dimensions as councillors tried to show how their party was doing the best for constituents. The Haddenham councillor, having taken a strategic view that Haddenham was the most sustainable location for more development, sensed the unhappiness in the village. He then began to adopt a more representative role, and attempted to redirect some development out into other smaller villages to reduce the dissent within Haddenham.

Just a couple of years previously, the councillor had helped to orchestrate the relocation into the village of a large spice-processing plant. His stated aim was to increase employment, particularly for some of the ex-council tenants who had been unemployed since an engineering firm had moved away. The new factory had created a deep split through the village between two opposing groups. There were those who objected to the noise and smell that was bound to be generated by the new factory, sited within 100 yards of new and old village housing on land designated as business class, for non-polluting industry only. But there were also those who looked upon the village as a working environment, and supported new jobs for the unemployed. Within two years the split became irrelevant, since the objectors were struggling with the pollution that had resulted from the new factory. Even those formerly in favour of new employment had found that the factory had actually brought very little employment to the village, as the management imported workers from other sites it had closed down. However, the splits that had appeared as 'class divisions' over the factory were not repeated over the new housing, where individuals previously opposed found themselves agreeing. The councillor's support for the factory and for new housing led to accusations from some of the more outspoken villagers that he was 'empire building', or trying to build up the constituency to provide more support for his own political position. It seems more likely, given the political clumsiness with which these manoeuvres were made however, that the politician was trying to reconcile conflicting demands on him to fulfil roles as representative and strategist – roles often diametrically opposed.

Some of the villagers in the protest group (introduced at the beginning of the chapter) suggested to me that the councillor's actions could be explained by his method of interacting with villagers. One evening, after a late meeting of the protest group, I walked home through the village with one of the members, several generations of whose family had long been involved in village politics. I asked him about the councillor, and as we walked past one of the local pubs, he told me that, of course, the councillor got his ideas about what villagers wanted from the old men in the pub. The councillor, he suggested, was easily taken in by a small group of elderly men who sat in the pub in the evening and complained about 'newcomers', lack of employment and rising house prices. That explanation made some sense to me, at least, since the politician's efforts to bring in new employers would certainly seem to appeal to the older, less wealthy residents, since many of the wealthier, newer residents worked outside the village. However, the significant point is that the problem of representation meant that the politician's legitimacy was challenged as too partial, and this is a more general problem in local party politics and protest action. Clearly, despite the representative system of electing local politicians, those people who believed that their own interests or beliefs were not being represented through their elected politicians blamed both the politicians and the democratic system for failing them. They accused the politician of not representing fully enough the various views of villagers. The complaints of the villagers will be considered more fully on pp. 00–00.

Two other significant positions were apparent from politicians within the leading Lib Dem group. Firstly, many believed that the objectors in Haddenham were 'NIMBY'; that is, self-seeking people who were worried about the value of their property more than the welfare of their fellow citizens. This denigration of objectors agrees directly with the planners' moral good of providing houses for people, since anyone who then objects to new housing must, at least indirectly, be depriving someone else of housing. This rather simplistic moral argument was used extremely often and to powerful effect politically to attempt to silence objectors. In a more party-political vein, some Lib Dem councillors, including the then leader of the Council, considered all the objectors from Haddenham to be members of the Conservative opposition, therefore not to be taken seriously, and their arguments to be seen as smokescreens for property interests. As one politician said, 'I know who they are.' This was rather unfortunate, however, since she clearly did not know who they were, given that objectors included both lifelong Liberal campaigners, left-wing Labour voters and council tenants, whereas supporters of development within the village included the most prominent Conservative residents, including the local County Councillor. Conservative support may have been partly in line with Conservative party policy of supporting the building industry, but may also have served personal interests, since some Conservative landowners hoped to sell their own land for profit. Where the idea came from that all objectors were 'Tories' is hard to define, but it may represent a partiality in the perceptions of the other local District Councillors of village society, and the particular perspective on village life of the local politician mentioned above.

In summary, politicians and planners seemed to share a view of the District Plan as a problem to be solved. Houses had to be built, and it was their duty to locate housing development to give the best possible outcome for the whole District. For some politicians, this presented an insoluble problem of conflicting roles, since they were elected to represent their constituents, yet felt obliged to try to cooperate with their party colleagues to develop a strategic view of the whole District. This dilemma occupied a great deal of time during discussions of the plan for many politicians, and the question of what constituted public service became one of the most pressing problems. However, certain prior assumptions as to appropriate places for housing underpinned location decisions, and much of the strategic technical argument elaborated by planners over locating development emerged to justify initial assumptions about concentrating development in 'obvious' locations. This approach notably relied heavily on spatial rather than temporal mapping of the district, beginning from the scenario of the district's physical and social appearance in the present and spatial requirements, rather than any reflection on its historical development.

The Village

Whilst a great deal of objection came from the village to the Council's plans to allow further development there, it would be a mistake to think of the village having a homogeneous opinion on its future, which merely needed to be articulated. Whilst much planning discourse on the use of 'consultation' or 'participation' tends to assume that planners' problems lie in evaluating 'local knowledge', little attention is devoted to the diversity of 'knowledges' with potential relevance to planning. Planners and politicians favour increased consultation on planning issues, despite warnings that soliciting responses to plans may raise as much conflict as consensus (Bruton 1980). However, many responses from the village shared a reference to the recent history of the village. Previous experiences of village expansion informed villagers' various responses to the plans, although not uniformly.

Growth is not new in this village. Throughout the twentieth century in particular, while agriculture has been in decline, the village has seen a rise in population and a growth in housing. The opening of the railway in 1906 brought an important resurgence in population to around 1,400, restoring the population to its level prior to the 1870 agricultural slump. The first council houses were built in the 1930s, followed by 'homes for heroes' shortly after the Second World War, and small developments and 'infilling' of the village's open spaces continued throughout the 1950s and 1960s, including some quite radical architecture (including England's only grade 2* listed 1960s homes). In the late 1970s, a large private estate of 250 houses was built between the then village and the railway line. At the time, this represented an increase of about a quarter of the village's size and proved to be a major trauma for many of the older village families. A new nomenclature developed, of 'old villagers' and 'Sheerstock' (the name of the new estate), overpowering earlier hostilities to the many people who had moved to the earlier developments in the village. Although development had been continuous, this particular develop-ment marked a significant moment of change. I quote from a conversation I had with a couple who moved to the village in the 1960s:

She: 'When Sheerstock came, was it 900 extra people, 200 houses – it was quite a shock to the rest of us. I mean, I don't remember there being any debate about whether it should come or not.'

He: 'No, the shock was afterwards. Because suddenly, you just didn't recognize everybody in the street. It was very strange, you know, you think you know your Haddenham, and suddenly everybody in the queue in front of you at the fête is a stranger. It's rather as if you'd moved.'

As the housing boom continued through the 1980s, local perceptions of change altered. While, generally, post-war housing development had been considered to be necessary to house the increasing population, by the late 1980s and early 1990s, the general population was no longer significantly increasing. The feeling that had characterized earlier building, that the village must modernize and make sacrifices to the success of the national economy, began to weaken. People realized that the growth of the village was not a finite jump from one state to another, but rather a change in condition from one of relative stability to one of continual, inexorable growth. This new perception was that the village would not just be consolidated as a larger, better-served village, but could potentially continue to become a town. This experience of prior growth was central to villagers' diachronic perspectives on the future of the village, in contrast to a technical, problem-solving asynchronous approach taken by planners (see Kohn 1997).

The idea that the village and its surroundings could become urbanized has never been popular. As village historians like to point out, at one time in the village's history it might have become a town. In 1295, Edward I gave the village a charter to hold a weekly market, but the resentment of the already established nearby market town of Thame led the village to give up its weekly market, and it remained a village, retaining only an annual feast and fair to celebrate the relinquished charter.

More recently, however, throughout the flux of post-war migration towards the South East of England, and into many similar rural parts of the Home Counties (those counties surrounding London), people have moved in specifically with the desire to live in the country, in opposition to notions of urban living. For those who commuted into the city this dichotomy was perhaps particularly important, even while they brought the comforts of metropolitan sophistication into what had been something of a rural backwater. The new population also brought a different approach to authority, founding a 'Village Society' dedicated to maintaining high standards of planning and architecture in the village, and participating directly in local government planning activities through membership of councils and through public protest.

Since the 1960s, the village seems to have particularly attracted architects and planners, and awareness of the governance of planning has been high. Over the years, as government planners have placed increasing stress on the importance of consultation over new plans, not only has the general public awareness of planning increased but planning has become a focus in many villages, including Haddenham, for debates over broader local issues about the village environment. The changes in planning law during the early 1990s, which expanded planning from its preoccupation with towns to cover all areas of the country, have furthered this process. Planning has supposedly become more 'participative'. Those who are consulted have come to expect their voices not only to be heard but also acted upon. They expect more favourable decisions, and at the same time they see the failings of the planning system and local government more clearly through their closer involvement in local governmental processes. People are very aware that the housing that is springing up throughout the county, and particularly within the village, is too expensive to accommodate homeless households. Nor is it intended to satisfy need (and certainly not local need), but, according to many villagers, to fulfil demand for luxurious and valuable property and to make profits for landowners and builders of expensive housing for commuters.

I would argue that this constitutes a quite different moral framework in which it is the residents' duty to defend the village against the ravages of untrammelled capitalism (even while many of them work in the City of London). This is not to say that objectors necessarily saw growth as a morally bad thing, in contrast to the sort of ecological protesters described by Berglund, for example (1998: 85). Indeed, I rarely heard anyone suggest that economic growth as the basis of British society was morally questionable, even though many people felt that continued house-building in the South East of England was environmentally and socially untenable. Consequently, many villagers saw the failure of planning law to control the type of house built as undermining the aims of planning – to supply houses for people that need them – that they supported, at least in principle. The failures they perceived, in other words, were attributed to insufficiently expert planning, rather than problems with either the underlying economic conditions or ideas of planning that were being used by the state.

As mentioned, many of the residents who had moved in since the 1960s, including early members of the Village Society, had imagined and experienced the village as a timeless place of long-established families forming a stable core of 'real' community. Rapid immigration to the village had obscured that feeling, described as 'knowing everybody'. As most of the houses that have been built are large and very expensive, there has been very little chance of the children of local families staying in the village. Even so-called 'affordable' housing built in the village is extremely expensive (and out of the range of, say, newly qualified teachers or manual labourers – and certainly of academic contract researchers). New building is designed for, and attracts, further immigration of wealthy professionals, while young people from the village move out to cheaper areas. Suddenly the perceived core of the village began to appear to villagers as a decreasing minority, and the Village Society generation of the 1960s and 1970s felt the old village slipping away. One of the founders of the Village Society described fondly the village dances of those days where, she said:

> literally everybody joined in, danced with everybody else. I mean, I can remember Professor Lady Williams and her husband, Sir William Enrys Williams – he started Penguin Books, and she was actually in those days financial adviser to the government, she was a professor at Birkbeck College – and she would dance with everybody, you know, John Clarke who was the coal man, and you know, everybody, shopkeepers, and it was like that! And now, I mean, for a long time, the past twenty years, it's been two villages. The old people who are feeling increasingly beleaguered, and the new people.

A sense of familiarity is no longer possible in such a large village. One could, feasibly, know 1,000 or 1,500 people, but one cannot know 5,000 people personally when most of them spend little time in the public space of the village, remaining mostly within their own houses. However, more important to the sense of village community than sheer numbers was a perception of potential classlessness. Another member of a very long-established village family suggested the same:

> The thing I quite like about [the village], I suppose, compared that I've lived in Sydney, Toronto, Auckland – big places – is that there doesn't seem to be a great class distinction here. You go to an event, and no matter what you are, you're all in it together, sort of thing, and it doesn't make any difference.

None are naive enough to suggest that there is literally no class distinction, but that such distinctions are not enacted through exclusion from village activities. Whilst divisions were perceptible along obvious lines between council estate and 'executive' closes (culs-de-sac), these differences did not bar participation in communal activities. This was due in part, perhaps, to the importance of the various village churches (Anglican, Baptist, Methodist, Catholic, and various fellowships) which encouraged their parishioners to enact notions of community through cooperation and exchanged services. There was not perfect harmony between church communities, however, with many of the smaller church congregations feeling resentment at the patrician attitude of the Anglican church, and some villagers were unhappy with the new vicar who arrived just as I began fieldwork.

The question of church roles in village life is too large to consider here, but it is worth noting that the land under 'threat' of development was owned by the Church Commissioners, the property-arm of the Church of England. This placed the Anglican church in a rather sensitive position, since its decision to build on the land was seen by some of its parishioners, and others, as 'immoral', as a bowing to capitalism over the interests of both the people and nature. The Church, though, always claimed its need to raise money for other 'good deeds', and maintained a separation between the local church and the Church Commissioners' role as landowners. The local vicar's comment on the development was that he could not object to the prospect of new parishioners arriving in the village. This question was a moot point: few villagers would directly challenge the Church Commissioners' disposal of land, despite their disappointment in the Church's actions which they characterised as those of an 'irresponsible' landowner.

This focus of responsibility on planning rather than on the desires of landowners to realize their capital was not limited to the Church Commissioners. Most, if not all, protest was directed towards the council and, in particular, the planners, rather than the landowners. There is some irony in this practice, since planners can only identify land for development if they have ensured that the landowner is considering selling the land; that is, that the land is 'available' for development. In other words, if a landowner has no intention of selling, the land cannot be identified in the plan, and other sites must be found. In fact, many landowners approach the council to ask to be included in plans, since this allows them to realize enormous profits on the value of the land, as the value for building can be more than a hundred times more than the value at agricultural prices.

This 'blindness' of protesters towards the role of the landowner in development practices is perplexing, and is extremely difficult (and perhaps inappropriate) to 'explain', but we could link it to the assumption mentioned above that no one would quarrel with the good of economic growth. While people did criticize one local politically active landowner for appearing to act in her own property interests, it appeared to be self-evident for most people that given the opportunity for massive financial gain most people would take it, and therefore they could not criticize others for doing so. However, there seemed also to be a fundamental misunderstanding of the planning system, whereby people associated the identification of sites by the Council with an intention to build, even though these two functions are separate in both intention and authorship. The effect of this, as perceived by the protesters, was to transfer moral responsibility for growth from landowners (who, in fact, held the right to choose where to build prior to the introduction of Planning Laws in Britain in 1947) to the state, both local and central, which now effectively chooses between the sites on offer from different landowners. Moreover, this added to the perception that it was planners rather than politicians who made decisions over which sites should be chosen so that local planners who received objections were held responsible for planning decisions as representatives of the technical demands of the central state.

These planning decisions about the use of land were then translated into local arguments about the future of village society. Alongside village perceptions of a loss of familiarity, mentioned previously, was a perceived crime problem and an outcry over increasing vandalism. Some of the young people in the village often met up at the recreation ground, or sat together on the bench by the primary school, or wandered around the village, particularly on summer evenings when there was no other legitimate meeting place for them. A group of two or three boys were drinking and taking drugs, and behaving threateningly. One night, for example, they barged into the village hall where a group of adults were playing badminton, swearing and threatening, and showing off to a couple of equally inebriated girls from another village. This followed a series of incidents where the boys had sprayed racist graffiti on the wall of the village hall, broken windows, destroyed the Christmas tree (provided by the Public Relations department of the new spice factory) and damaged the fence of the primary school. Around the village this was taken as evidence of urban degeneration – the sort of problems normally identified with inner-city neighbourhoods, the kind that forty years ago 'would have been sorted out by the local bobby by a swift thrashing behind the police station'.

The local police were more aware that rural areas have never been exempt from lawlessness, attributing their inability to tackle pervasive drug problems to their general lack of resources. The village policeman did not wish to live in the village, where he would not only be targeted by vandals but would never be able to escape his policeman's role. The lack of police presence, though, dismayed many villagers. This kind of problem did not match a notion of rural living which most of the population had sought when they moved to the village. The threat of more problems which they perceived as 'urban', which they felt would increase inevitably through a further increase in the population, and the inability of such a large population all to 'know' one another, lent weight to the rejection of the plan to build more houses.

These questions of the urban and rural 'character' of settlements reinforced the feelings of many objectors to the plan, since the plan proposed building on as yet unbuilt-on agricultural land. Feelings of antipathy towards urban life that had motivated incoming residents from the outset to village life, rather than life either in London or in small local towns, were directly roused by the idea that the village might become urbanized. This was expressed by many villagers in terms of their unhappiness with the idea of digging up 'yet more of our green countryside' to build homes for profit rather than need. The sentiments of those politicized through their past experiences with the unpopular factory (and previous similar planning disputes), were voiced more readily through the competing claims over the use of the land surrounding the village.

A central paradox to the controversy over the plan was that many of the objections to continued growth in the village addressed the issue of whether 'green fields' should be uprooted. This argument ignored implicit ecological questions over the 'naturalness' of land, which was actually being used for intensive agriculture. However, many actual objections were not specifically concerned with environmental issues but with political problems arising from previous government policies. As such, it was not the actual land that presented a problem but rather the people who would later occupy it. Even then the problem was not with those people personally, but rather with the fact of their numbers. The consequences of that are clear, particularly with the inevitable use of cars (since road congestion was and still is a major political issue in most parts of England) and their use of resources. The local fund-holding GP practice was in debt, and very much under pressure from the increased population. A particular demographic pattern had resulted in overcrowding of some classes at the local primary schools, and the general increase in car use had resulted in what began to appear as town-like traffic through the village. More broadly, the privatization of the water utilities a few years previously had led to a loss of investment in water supply. With increasing development and extravagant use of water throughout the South East, this had led to serious questions over the sufficiency of the water table and general water shortages. The District Council's 'solution' to housing demand was not seen within the village as a solution so long as so many other political, ecological and economic problems were not addressed. For many residents, the expansion of the village took on political dimensions about the long-term future of the region, as well as the short-term future of the village.

Moralities

It is easy to appreciate that there are competing moralities at work here that could be characterized as being concerned with either the physical appearance of the village, its social conditions, or the righteousness of local versus strategic decision-making. By morality, I refer to a form of reasoning about what is considered 'right' (see Howell 1997). Given the generality of the term 'morality', however, it might be more appropriate here to adopt the term 'righteousness', since it is the claims as to what is right and for whom that are in direct competition. The notion of moral difference includes the idea that it is both the method of reaching these righteous conclusions and the search for legitimacy of those methods that differ, and this chapter argues that political debates over planning encompass both competing interests and differing paths of reasoning. Clearly, different righteous arguments are being posed by different parties to the debate over the plan, such as the District Council and the villagers.

But there are also different moral positions and understandings of the world within those broadly characterized stances. Within the District Council there are variations in interpretations of how the environment ought to be considered as a factor affecting all decisions, according to a particular notion of 'sustainable development' promoted by both the former Conservative and the current Labour governments. This philosophy dismisses the absolute moral stance adhered to by many conservationists that any destruction of natural environments is wrong, since this precludes the possibility of ever increasing the use of resources required for constant economic growth. For local councils such as Aylesbury Vale, this notion of sustainability allows them to continue to build on agricultural and undeveloped land and to use increasing resources, in the name of 'balance' and 'responsibility' between economic growth and conservation. The resulting position of the Council, as expressed through its plans (in line with government advice) is that 'green fields' should only be built on if no other derelict sites are available for redevelopment in the most convenient sites. This is environmentalism that retains social and economic primacy, declared by local politicians and planners to be a 'responsible' position. A clearer indication of their moral righteousness would be difficult to assert.

Furthermore, a separate moral context governed councillors' negotiations – that of 'taking fair shares' of development amongst themselves. If councillors rejected outright development allocated to them, they could be accused of being 'NIMBY' (Not In My Back Yard), or selfish and uninterested in the consequences of their own self-interest (a problem identified elsewhere in Europe; see Berglund 1998: 81). To counteract this politicians attempted to demonstrate how their constituencies were taking their 'fair share' of development, either historically or currently. Politicians were also engaged in negotiating political discourses, trying not only to find solutions to problems of District-wide resource allocation, but also to find ways to work within and across political party allegiances. Politicians were also concerned, not surprisingly, with gaining votes, particularly in the run up to the General Election in 1997, since some local politicians also stood for the national parliament. These considerations also applied at a higher level in the strategic planning hierarchy, especially in the way that counties and regions worked on the basis of having to take 'fair shares' of nationally required development. This system of sharing out the evils of modern life had little basis in technical planning solutions, but holds a great importance in the way that planning decisions are made in the UK. Councillors were thus trying to negotiate complex and competing forms of moral reasoning, prioritizing social, environmental, economic, as well as political interests.

Within the village there are also opposing definitions of the 'proper' conduct of villagers, expressed most clearly in a discourse of 'participation' in village life, allied to issues of kinship. When the village expanded in the 1970s, there existed a relatively secure feeling of village familiarity, with easily identified 'old village' families. As the new 'Sheerstock' estate began to be occupied, many villagers reportedly perceived new, unknown residents as 'outsiders' and resented their attempts to become 'involved' in village life. Nonetheless, their gradual incorporation into the village was indicated through an oft-quoted remark made by a 'real old villager'. Mrs M, an influential defender of the 'old village', remarked to a 'newcomer', who had lived in the village for some years, that she, just as many of the old villagers, had formerly been as mistrustful of incomers. But were it not for their participation in running day centres for the village elderly, running children's clubs, WI and church coffee mornings and supporting services, such as the library and health centre, the village would have died a death like so many other nearby depopulated ex-farming villages left without even a bus service. This admission of the old villagers' dependence on the newcomers took nearly twenty years to be stated, and did not deny old villagers' sense of authentic belonging. A passage from my field notes indicates their dilemma:

> Met [Pat] at the 'Friday Coffee Stop' . . . It was only a small village with a population of about 500 when she moved here [in the 1940s]. It was terribly difficult, the locals were very close knit - all the families intermarried. She was saying to a woman the other day, who was from one of what she calls the old village families, 'I've been here 50 years now' and this woman said 'well, I think you can call yourself local now'! Funny! But it's all built up since she moved here. It isn't a village any more, it's not the village she knew. All the old village families say that. But people have got to have somewhere to live. Her mother had three children and each of them needed a house.

Pat's world made sense in terms of the old village, now lost for the sake of housing people – a reason powerful in itself but still painful for those attached to the old village. Her ambivalence about this loss is actually quite representative of older villagers, many of whom feel that current arguments over continued growth are out of step with the changes in the village throughout the century. Had the old families also opposed growth all along, most of the protesters wouldn't live in the village at all. However, there is also a palpable sense of dismay, where many 'old villagers' feel that the destiny of the village is out of their hands. There are rumblings of complaint, and a clear discourse of 'old villagers' needing better representation, but little political mobilization. The parish council, once a stronghold of village 'worthies' (the landowners, the headteacher, the vicar) was by the 1990s equally split between 'old villagers', landowners (farmers rather than landed gentry), Village Society and village protectionists.

Much of the dispute within the village over its future development concerned not whether villagers wanted houses, or in what number, but how to cope with external pressures. One of the main problems with the plan was that it imposed not only solutions but problems generated externally, rather than being a village-centred plan for the future. This translated into comments about who might live in the proposed new housing, such as those of one well-known 'old villager', made on this occasion at yet another coffee morning, though often repeated elsewhere:

> He said it's all right if it's not the wrong kind of people, and [Pat] said yes, we don't want any more yuppies. They don't bother with anything, they don't come in and help run this sort of thing [the coffee morning], they don't want to bother with anything or anybody in the village, they just move into their houses and get on the train to go to work, and they don't want anything to do with anybody. The old village is disappearing because of that. Michael says 'it's fine if it's people like your good self, people who get involved, but those people don't want to be bothered'. 'Their' image of living in the countryside is to move in and close their doors.

His complaint also referred to the use of private cars, which apart from creating pollution also resulted in social isolation: 'Used to be you'd walk down here and it'd be hello Mr [somebody], nice day.' People driving around the village in their cars were isolating themselves from social interactions, polluting the atmosphere and posing a threat to people who chose to walk or cycle. Indeed, according to him, those protesting most about the urbanization of the village were those too lazy or too precious to walk half a mile to the railway station, the school or the church. Within this discourse, those who were protesting over village expansion were characterized as 'people who do nothing for the village until it comes to something that affects them personally' (NIMBYs again). They merely experience the village on a visual or perceptual level, rather than through bodily involvement (see also Rapport 1997).

In contradistinction to their rejection of continued expansion he did not reject the policy to introduce more housing, but would have preferred that housing be 'affordable' to local village families. His attachment to a particular morality of village life that prioritized involvement in communal activity over the mere physical contours of the village was made particularly clear in one conversation we had. He stopped his bicycle to talk to me as I walked through the village one day, and we began yet again to talk about 'all that fuss' over the plan. He complained about those moaning people objecting to new housing, so I asked him whether the village ought therefore to continue growing indefinitely. He said that he thought there was probably a limit to how big the village ought to be, then admitted that that size was probably about its present state, recognizing that this contradicted his argument in favour of building on the fields around the village. His argument, though, was with the protesters' version of the village, not with the question of how big the village ought to be or which land ought to be built on.

Protesters also took different positions as to why development was wrong, and whether any building should be permitted at all. These arguments coalesced around two particular positions. The first stated that the village was 'large enough' already and ought to be prevented from expanding any further into the surrounding countryside. The second position assumed part of the District's strategic discourse about the need to provide housing for increasing numbers of households, as forecast by the government's statistical forecasts (referred to, obliquely, by Pat above in her reference to expanding families needing housing). While the latter group would have strongly preferred the village not to expand further, they were prepared to concede that continued development was inevitable, given the national and regional conditions of increasing households and the thriving and lively character of the village. They took the position that it should be controlled, minimizing the amount and setting design parameters. They therefore accepted the government's formulation of 'housing shortage' and saw the village not as an isolated whole but as part of a broader regional and national context.

The former group rejected the government's and the Council's stance altogether, and argued that the village should not be designated for any large housing estate on 'green fields' (i.e. previously not built on), since the statistics were not to be trusted and had been badly interpreted. They argued that sufficient new housing could be found in existing derelict urban areas and that new developments should not need to be built elsewhere. They accepted that new housing would appear in the village anyway, on planning appeals for small sites ('small' sites for 5–15 houses need not be specified in the District Plan). They felt that this would be more than sufficient to cope with 'indigenous growth', since if previous trends continued the village could expect at least 150 new houses to be built in the plan period, quite apart from any specified designation of new sites. Many of these protesters felt despair at the apparent inaction and apathy of old villagers such as those described above, commenting that 'if it was up to them, the village would be completely destroyed' as builders won the right to construct endless housing estates all around. Even the village pond, one of its most picturesque features, was maintained by 'incomers', albeit long-standing ones. They felt that it was them, not the 'old villagers' with their claims to authenticity, who were the guardians of the village's future. After all, they reasoned that those same 'old villagers' who complained about 'newcomers' running everything were the very people who had sold their land to builders to make profits for themselves in previous years. Here, in contrast to the laying of 'responsibility' for development with the planners in the current case, the landowners were identified as enabling development.

Conclusions

This chapter outlines the variety of approaches to territoriality in one location and illustrates how territory encapsulates a range of beliefs and ways of reasoning about society, nature, ecology, politics, economics, class and development. In this case, a large English village under a great deal of development pressure from the continuing, and increasing, expansion of London exerted a great deal of resistance to plans to build on agricultural land. This resistance became an expression of the feelings of various villagers about land and housing, and represented a variety of competing claims to authenticity of the identity of the village. I have set these within the context of administrative and political perspectives on what is 'most appropriate' for the village, and the struggle for influence over the definition of planning policy. I have chosen not to articulate these explicitly in terms of 'identity', since the different versions of 'who we are' are based on those beliefs and stances of all those described here. Claims about identity and interests have been implicit in the visions of the village discussed. I have also avoided extensive use of the term 'identity' in order to avoid inadvertently creating a scenario where discrete 'identities' are described and individuals allocated to them, since this seems to me to be a flaw easily read into discussions of 'identity'. In common with Hall and others (see, for example, Hall and duGay 1996), I tend to believe that 'identity' does not have independent existence from discursive activity. Identity is therefore a linguistic product of the activity of 'identifying with', of asserting allegiance or imagining ideals (see also Abram 1997).

Crucial in the situation described above, however, is the instrumentalization of the moral or righteous positions and claims of identification. Moralities may have intrinsic interest, but here they also have instrumental consequences – firstly in the linguistic shape of how policies are written into the plan, and then physically in the shape of buildings that are constructed as the plan is implemented. 'Direct action' usually addresses the stage of plan implementation, which is not considered here, but the decisions about what plans will consist of are subject to debate and argument over which form of reasoning will prevail.

For pressure groups to be effective in influencing plans, they must adopt both the moral and technical discourse of the decision-makers; that is, the planners who write policies, the planners who judicially review policies, the politicians and civil servants who set strategic targets centrally (i.e. government) and the politicians who adopt policies at the local level. If all those versions of moral arguments differ, pressure groups clearly have a complex struggle if they are to win concessions towards their points of view. This perspective allows us to appreciate why changing government priorities is so often described as 'steering the supertanker', since there is often a great deal of resistance to new or rapidly changing conditions, making rapid responses from governments difficult. I have written elsewhere how protesters to plans are forced to adopt the discourses, and therefore enter the 'moral worlds' of planning in order to be effective in their protests (Murdoch and Abram 1998; Abram 2001; Abram et al. 1998). In this chapter I have tried to show not only how interests but also how identifications, moralities and futures are central to discussions about land and houses in Britain.

References

Abram, S. (2001), 'Amongst Professionals: Working with Pressure Groups and Local Authorities', in D. Gellner and E. Hirsch (eds), *Ethnographic Research in Industrial and Organisational Settings*, Oxford: Berg, pp. 183–203.

Abram, S. (1997), 'Introduction', in S. Abram, J. Waldren and D. Macleod (eds), *Tourists and Tourism: Identifying with People and Places*, Oxford: Berg.

Abram S, Murdoch, J. and Marsden, T. (1998), 'Planning by Numbers: Migration and Statistical Governance', in P. Boyle and K. Halfacree (eds), *Migration into Rural Areas*, Chichester: Wiley.

Berglund, E. (1998), *Knowing Nature, Knowing Science*, Cambridge: White Horse Press.

Bruton, M. J. (1980) 'Public Participation, Local Planning and Conflicts of Interest', *Policy and Politics*, 8(4): 423–42.

Foucault, M. (1991), 'Governmentality', in G. Burchell, C. Gordon and P. Miller (eds), *The Foucault Effect*, pp. 87–104, Hemel Hempstead: Harvester Wheatsheaf.

Hacking, I. (1990), *The Taming of Chance*, Cambridge: Cambridge University Press.

Hall, S. and duGay, P. (eds) (1996), *Questions of Cultural Identity*, London: Sage.

Howell, S. (ed.) (1997), *The Ethnography of Moralities*, London: Routledge.

Kohn, T. (1997), 'Island Involvement and the Evolving Tourist', in S. Abram, J. Waldren and D. Macleod (eds), *Tourists and Tourism: Identifying with People and Places*, Oxford: Berg.

Murdoch, J. and Abram, S. (1998), 'Defining the Limits of Community Governance', *Journal of Rural Studies*, 14(1): 41–50.

Rapport, N. (1997), 'The Morality of Locality: On the Absolutism of Land-ownership in an English Village', in S. Howell (ed.), *The Ethnography of Moralities*, London: Routledge.

5

Out of Place: Symbolic Domains, Religious Rights and the Cultural Contract[1]

Davina Cooper

This chapter is about the relationship between community and space. More particularly, it is about orthodox Jews' attempts to create communal domains within urban neighbourhoods through the device of the *eruv*. On the sabbath, Jewish law forbids a range of labour. In addition to formal work, these include travelling, spending money, and carrying objects beyond the home. The *eruv* relates to this last injunction. By creating a bounded perimeter which notionally extends the private domain, it provides a way for objects to be carried on the sabbath within a designated area.

Eruvim have become common in large urban districts in Canada, the USA, Australia, and Europe, as well as Israel. Nevertheless, the requirement symbolically to enclose space, including, in many instances, miles of urban city and neighbourhood, and the dwellings of gentiles as well as Jews, has subjected several *eruv* proposals to intense scrutiny. In the USA, the American Civil Liberties Union (ACLU) have been particularly watchful to ensure *eruvim* do not violate the establishment clause of the First Amendment creating a wall between church and state.[2] Excessive entanglement is seen to occur in the level of state involvement, particularly where new structures, such as poles and wire, are needed to complete the boundary. In London, an attempt to establish an *eruv* in the 1990s provoked intensive protest. Opposition centred on the planning permission process, generated by the application to install additional poles and wire to complete the eleven-mile perimeter.

At the fore of the objections expressed were aesthetic and visual concerns. Yet, the environmental harm wrought by eighty additional poles and wire, in a London borough with many thousand, cannot alone explain the depth of emotion. This chapter aims to explore why the London *eruv* proposal generated such a hostile reception in contrast to the relative indifference shown in many other jurisdictions.

My argument draws on my earlier analysis, published elsewhere,[3] which located the *eruv* within a modernist conception of threats to its norms and values. Here, I want to link this threat to relations of belonging, framed in the language of a cultural contract.

I begin by providing more background to the *eruv* issue, and then set out the terms of the cultural contract. The rest of the chapter explores the ways in which this contract appeared to be undermined by the *eruv* project. My analysis draws on field research carried out between 1995–1996, including semi-structured interviews with approximately twelve activists on both sides of the dispute. In particular, I discuss how the *eruv* was seen as territorializing and privatizing space; undermining the public/private divide; and sabotaging the relationship between citizens and the nation-state.

Eruvim in Neighbourhood Space

> Driving under the gateways . . . to enter the Barnet Ghetto would be like entering a concentration camp.[4]

'*Eruv*' literally means 'a mingling', and can take several forms. The one relevant here is the *eruv* that creates a mingling of space, enabling a relaxation of sabbath carrying restrictions. According to Jewish law, Jews are prohibited from transporting objects between domains during the sabbath.[5] The creation of an *eruv* enables transportation to take place by turning the space between private domains into a single private arena.[6] However, the requirements for establishment are extremely complicated,[7] and subject to rabbinical dispute. For instance, what kind of perimeter is acceptable? How large a population can an *eruv* encompass? How should *halakhically* difficult structures such as busy roads and parkland be treated?[8] Past disagreements meant some *eruvim* were only recognized by particular rabbis. In Toronto, the validity of the *eruv* boundary became increasingly disputed, due, in part, to the fact that it encompassed a major highway. In the late 1980s work began on a new perimeter, installed in 1996, in the hope it would prove more widely acceptable.

Although *eruvim* go back many hundreds of years, the modern movement gained force in the 1960s. Since *eruvim* enable prams and wheelchairs to be pushed, interest in their establishment has been linked to a growing orthodoxy amongst young people, the women's liberation movement (in particular, women's interest in participating more fully in religious life)[9] and more recently to demands for disability rights. *Eruvim* also symbolize an increasing confidence amongst orthodox Jews to create the communal structures that improve their quality of life. Much of this confidence draws on the gains of other minority communities, such as African-

Americans – one reason, perhaps, why *eruvim* have proved more acceptable in the USA where there is a stronger tradition of minority cultural entitlement than in Britain.

The Cultural Contract

The concept of the cultural contract, as I am using it, parallels the metaphorical social and sexual contracts developed in liberal and feminist thought respectively. The contract is an *imaginary* settlement to identify the consent of a community to a particular set of cultural, social and governance norms. The notion of a contract is important because of the idea of exchange. This does not mean a real relation of exchange exists, or that there is consent or a clearly delineated agreement. Rather, these elements appear to exist from the perspective of the dominant culture –a perspective which was, in turn, highly influential in shaping the beliefs, norms and values of *eruv* opponents.

In saying this, I do not wish to suggest that *eruv* opponents were simply duped by the ideology of a cultural contract. Despite their broad adoption of this perspective, they nevertheless reshaped it in ways structured by their own experiences. To understand why *eruv* opponents took the position they did, we therefore need to consider who they were. One of the most striking elements of the *eruv* controversy was the leading and active role played by non-orthodox Jews.[10] In the main, these Jewish opponents came from a particular background: over 45, European, and middle class.[11] Their stance towards the *eruv* and commitment to Enlightenment norms replicates a common theme of modern Jewish history. For European Jews who took advantage of nineteenth-century emancipation and assimilated, cultural norms such as a public/private division, civic inclusion and formal equality functioned as both the means of integration as well as personal symbols of its achievement. Thus, many who integrated developed a sense of loyalty towards the cultural contract alongside hostility towards those orthodox Jews who remained visibly Jewish,[12] and 'culturally backward'. The refusal or inability of such orthodox Jews to be accepted as part of the ethno-cultural majority drew attention to assimilated Jews' own roots and precarious sense of belonging.

The cultural contract *eruv* opponents drew on has four main elements. I discuss these further in the rest of the chapter, so I shall briefly outline them here. First, the contract is predicated on an English cultural essentialism. In other words, a history and heritage that is culturally Anglican defines Britain's identity. The cultural contract incorporates a commitment to maintaining this. Second, within this Protestant settlement, minority practices are acceptable if performed privately. However, not all practices are deemed legitimate even where they remain private;

for instance, where they appear non-consensual, against public policy, or entrench 'unacceptable' inequalities. Third, the British public forms a national community based on rational, liberal values. Citizenship identifies an unmediated relationship between member and state; thus, any involvement by citizens with voluntary, private or civil organizations must be uncoerced and consensual. Finally, public space should reflect the values of the cultural contract. It is where the contract is both constituted and lived out.

The rest of this chapter explores the way in which the London *eruv* was seen by opponents as threatening the four elements just outlined. In doing so, my objective is not just to provide a detailed reading of the menace *eruvim* were feared to pose, but, in addition, to use the *eruv* as a prism through which wider questions relating to governance, community and public space can be posed. In the discussion that follows, two aspects of the North London *eruv* are particularly important to bear in mind. First, the fact that it constructs an eleven-mile perimeter around densely populated residential areas; second, its requirement for poles and wire to complete the boundary.

Privatizing Space and Territorial Claims

The starting point for opponents of the London *eruv*, and the argument they returned to again and again, was what they saw as the territorial agenda and practices of *eruv* advocates. 'The religious side is just a ruse . . . They put up poles as a demonstration of their territoriality – they don't need poles' (objector, interview). To emphasize the territorial aspects of the *eruv*, opponents drew on the *halakhic* principle that an *eruv* symbolically privatizes space, evidenced in the notional payment of rent. Adopting a zero-sum formulation of ownership, opponents argued if space now belonged to orthodox Jews it could no longer belong to them. Installing an *eruv* was a strategy for both naming, and fixing, informal Jewish areas as Jewish, and then expanding outwards into non-Jewish areas. '[The *eruv*] identifies a non-Jewish area as a Jewish area. The Jewish area is moving further out, away from Golders Green' (objector, interview). At the heart of this complaint lay the belief that *eruv* proponents were using the *eruv* as a strategic, territory-setting device through which to create their own zone. Feeding off widespread anxieties regarding ultra-orthodox behaviour in Israel, opponents claimed that within an orthodox zone, access, belonging, sanctioned behaviour and social relationships would be constituted according to orthodox Jewish norms rather than the terms of their own cultural contract.

While the fears of opponents seem somewhat overstated, in at least two ways the *eruv* can be seen as having territorial implications. First, as one leading Barnet rabbi did acknowledge, the *eruv* was partly about developing a sense of community 'which has a boundary . . . that comes into play on the sabbath' (interview). Similar claims have been made in the USA, where the establishment of *eruv* perimeters in Miami Beach, St Louis and Baltimore, amongst others, have been linked to the intensification of an orthodox community identity.[13] The authority that emanates from boundary-setting is particularly apparent in cases, such as Toronto, where prior to the 1996 *eruv* boundary, different perimeters were recognized by different rabbis. While this was done ostensibly on technical, *halakhic* grounds, it allowed rabbis to control the demarcation of their own community space. Thus, different congregations would operate according to different imaginaries of the boundaries and interior of belonging.

Second, opponents argued that the installation of a London *eruv* would have demographic consequences. This phenomenon has been noticed in relation to other *eruvim*. For instance, in the American city of Baltimore, the installation of a new larger *eruv* encouraged orthodox Jews to move into the area. The potential demographic effects of establishing an *eruv* in Barnet was for opponents a major concern. The fear of imbalance was summed up in racialized terms by one opponent who declared the area's historic stability 'would be harmed if the proportion of Jews increased . . . It is a matter of the right proportions and balance in the community.'[14] Opponents did not see this population shift as an incidental effect; rather they perceived the *eruv* as a deliberate strategy to increase the strength and numbers of orthodox Jews within the neighbourhood.[15] 'They want to demo-graphically alter the population of the area . . . to deliberately move Jewish people into the area to live together' (objector, interview). Opponents drew attention to the fact that property advertisements in the *Jewish Chronicle*, a weekly newspaper, already referred to properties as being within the boundary of the proposed *eruv*. More than one interviewee suggested that this would have a distortive impact on market values.

Assimilated Jews and gentile opponents thus perceived themselves as becoming the new dispossessed. The cultural and demographic incursion and entrenchment of orthodox Jewish space threatened to leave them out of place: their cultural norms and values replaced by those of the religious *shtetl*. As one opponent stated, 'People feel they've taken over. This isn't my area anymore' (interview). Yet, the position for secular and liberal Jews was also more complicated than simply feeling alienated by the *eruv* proposal. While, on the one hand, they saw orthodox Judaism as exclusionary, arrogant and presumptuous in its expectations, at the same time they felt equally angry at the prospect of being labelled as belonging within 'backward' Jewish space.

Public Expression of Minority Beliefs

So far I have argued that opponents saw the *eruv* as territorializing public space. I want now to consider the way in which opposition focused on the publicizing, as well as privatizing, qualities of the *eruv*. The public aspect of the *eruv*, critics claimed, undermined the cultural contract in three primary ways. First, the *eruv* transgressed the requirement that minority expression be contained within the private domain. Second, the *eruv* attacked and reconstituted the relationship between soil and cultural identity. Third, the *eruv* was a further downward step on the slippery slope of multicultural pluralism and relativism.

The Public/Private Divide

Opponents perceived the *eruv* as transgressing the public/private divide largely through its identity as a spatial perimeter. In this way, the *eruv* was compared unfavourably to religious structures such as a church or mosque. According to one objector: 'A building is a discrete, enclosed, limited thing' (objector, interview). Within church or mosque walls, only participants know what is taking place. With the doors closed, others are protected from having to view rituals they may find offensive. In contrast, an *eruv*, criticized for privatizing public space, was seen, at the same time, as also transgressing the divide by bringing inappropriate expressions of religious faith into the public domain.

This publicization had three effects. First, it posed the prospect of tainting space seen as belonging to and enjoyed by the whole community. Interviewees placed stress on the quality and significance of the urban space involved. This was particularly apparent in relation to one neighbourhood enclosed by the proposed *eruv* boundary: Hampstead Garden Suburb. A highly regarded example of the early garden suburb movement, residents perceived Hampstead Garden Suburb as almost 'sacred', modern space (a view somewhat disparaged by other *eruv* opponents). Given the special quality of the area as aesthetically 'pure' and socially harmonious, it would be unforgivable to impose an *eruv* upon it.

Second, the *eruv* was perceived as inappropriately visible; yet this was largely the result of the publicity and media interest generated by opponents. In most cities where *eruvim* exist few residents other than those who observe the boundaries can identify where they lie. Indeed, this was a factor in the US courts permitting *eruvim* to be established. In *ACLU of New Jersey v. City of Long Branch et al.*,[16] the district judge stated that the largely invisible character of the *eruv* boundary (combined with the secularism of its physical form) meant residents would not have a religion imposed upon them.

Third, opponents claimed that enabling orthodox Jews to carry outside of their homes on the sabbath would enable private 'differences' to be expressed in public. Yet there is a contradiction here. While it is probably true that an *eruv* means more orthodox Jews are visible on the streets between Friday and Saturday sundown, at the same time the *eruv* normalizes orthodox Jews by allowing them to behave more like the majority.

Cultural Identity and Soil

As well as breaching the public/private divide, opponents argued that the construction of the *eruv*, particularly the installation of poles, would attack and
rearticulate the relationship between soil and cultural identity. The *eruv*, it was
claimed, 'disfigured' the land because it does not belong. In a sense, we can see it
functioning, within the vision of opponents, metaphorically, like an inverted
circumcision; where a circumcision cuts away, the *eruv* implants. Through the
installation of poles, alien, deeply rooted markers are embedded within the soil.
Paralleling those who criticize circumcision for disfiguring the body, here implanting
both assaults and disregards existing forms of belonging. This perception came to
the surface in one instance, in particular, in relation to a Church of England school,
the playground of which formed part of the *eruv* boundary.[17] Here, the prior, explicit
ethnicization of the soil was seen to make the concept of a 'Jewish boundary line'
particularly inappropriate.[18]

Opponents characterized orthodox Jews, during interviews, as intensely arrogant
in their disregard for existing spatial meanings, and in their assumption that they
could legitimately appropriate Christian designated space. Their association of
orthodox neighbourhoods with cultural and social outsiderness highlights the
embarrassment of more assimilated Jews towards an orthodox 'kin' who fail to
understand the relationship between soil and belonging. Underlying such discomfort
is a particular vision of orthodox Jews: that they are so absorbed in their own
narrow 'lost' world that they do not know where they are; more particularly, that
they are somewhere else. Their vision always turned to the past, orthodox Jews
remain forgetful of the ways in which diaspora territory and space is both
meaningful, and already 'taken'. In other words, it is not vacant space that can be
inscribed from scratch.

Indeed, one of the paradoxes of the *eruv* is that despite being criticized for
giving public space a religious façade, its actual relationship to land is arbitrary;
although it entails a spatial marking, inscription relates to current demography
rather than pre-existing physical or cultural geography. An *eruv* can be stretched
across almost any soil where a Jewish community exists. It is intrinsically a structure
for a nomadic or diaspora people – a private domain they can take with them
anywhere.

The Slippery Slope

The third problem, opponents identified, concerned the 'floodgates' opening. The
establishment of a 'special' structure for orthodox Jews would lead other minorities
to demand similar entitlements. 'It would be a slippery slope of ethnic minorities
asking for things, wanting special facilities' (objecting councillor, interview). '[A]ny

minority will see it as a green light for their own particular view to be expressed'.[19] Opponents saw the advent of a north London *eruv* as assisting *eruv* proposals elsewhere in Britain. Indeed, in the USA, where many *eruvim* exist, orthodox communities, in some instances, are driven to establish them for fear of losing congregants to areas where *eruvim* are already in place.[20] While this is scarcely yet a problem for Britain, opponents of the *eruv* saw it as legitimizing the demands of other minorities for public expression.

In this regard, interviewees revealed a degree of consistency in their opposition to supporting minority interests. Most of those I asked opposed state funding for minority ethnic provision, such as 'mother-tongue' classes, and expressed concern at the widespread emergence of minority religious structures with public visibility. In part, this concerned the role of government. *Eruv* opponents tended to argue that the state should only involve itself in universalist forms of provision. It also concerned the status of minority faiths in a nation with an established Church, as I go on to explore. However, linked to the assertion of heritage rights was a concern to protect the 'rational', and to maintain a hierarchy of cultural sense. Thus, the slippery slope climaxed, for several interviewees, with the vision of totem poles on Hampstead Heath, the horror of the premodern and uncivilized intensely apparent in this repeated racist image.

A Question of Harm

So far I have discussed some of the ways in which the *eruv* functioned, both as a privatizing and also as a public, symbolic structure. Opponents identified a range of harms that would transpire from this development. First, public status would force otherness on the general public without their consent; second, installation threatened to bring violence into the community; third, the *eruv*'s communalism jeopardized a universal, national citizenship; and, fourth, it threatened a disorder that would transcend the *eruv* boundaries.

Forcing otherness onto the general public undermined a key element of the cultural contract: the right to be protected from minorities. There are clearly parallels here with the opposition expressed towards public expressions of homosexuality. Heterosexual demonstrations are so naturalized they remain unapparent – wearing wedding or engagement rings, talking about marriage or honeymoons or dating, kissing or holding hands in public places. However, analogous signifiers of sexuality by lesbians and gay men, lacking a naturalized status, remain highly visible and are construed as flaunting. In an analogous manner, one woman I interviewed, an active opponent of the *eruv*, while vaguely content with public installation of Christian symbols, expressed her concern at the public display of minority, religious symbols, such as large *menorahs* attached to lampposts along the high street. Yet, it would be misleading to see her opposition as simply a generic hostility towards non-Christian faiths. For, in contrast, she spoke positively about occasions when her neighbour had brought around pastries baked to celebrate an Islamic festival. The difference about the latter was not only that it occurred within the 'privacy' of her home, but as well the related fact that it was grounded in consent. For this interviewee, it was largely the lack of active consent – the forced viewing of minority culture – which made her feel displaced and out of control.

One consequence of such feelings – a second danger of public, minority symbols – was the threat of violence. 'Anglicized Jews felt [the *eruv*] broke the rules of the game. They saw it as unBritish . . . The *eruv* fulfils the Jewish stereotype of pushy and aggressive' (objector, interview). Such violence threatened not only orthodox Jews but others who also became identified with the anti-Semitic vision of an aggressive, grasping other. As one councillor, opposed to the *eruv*, stated, 'A minority of the community having staked out and identified its precise territory leaves the whole Jewish community open to attack, abuse and vandalism.'[21] Equated with their orthodox kin, liberal Jews felt they would be punished for their inability to remain culturally invisible, even though this move was unwillingly taken. The *eruv* proposal 'outed' them, and much of their anger seemed to relate to this. Several interviewees living in Hampstead Garden Suburb recounted how, as a result of the *eruv* controversy, questions of individual religious identification came up at local parties and gatherings. What had previously been of little interest and unknown was now forced to speak its name.

Opponents argued that the harm resulting from defining people by their religious background, and responding to them on those terms, would be amplified by the *eruv*'s actual installation. Its establishment would generate anti-Jewish feeling amongst local residents who had 'never previously had an anti-Semitic thought' (objector interview). In other words, several opponents, including Jewish ones, identified anti-Semitism as a potentially rational response from an alienated *majority*. Yet, while one opponent suggested he knew several middle-class residents who would undermine the boundary's integrity, in the main physical violence was identified with 'elsewhere' (working-class bigots entering the borough, bringing with them the race hatred of London's East End).

In response, proponents dismissed the likelihood of violence, suggesting that opponents were raising it for purely rhetorical purposes. (There was also some suggestion that if violence or vandalism did occur, opponents would be largely to blame, either as the perpetrators or for whipping up hostility to the *eruv* proposal.) Yet while some opponents may have intentionally exaggerated the threat of violence, their arguments reflected wider fears of religious and ethnic brutality. In this respect the *eruv* was seen as a provocation, or, at best, a careless indifference to the world-wide hatred and strife ethnic communal claims generated.

This fear of more widespread disorder and hostility highlights two further issues. First, opponents saw the *eruv* as contributing to the jeopardizing of a universal, national citizenship. The terms of the cultural contract require difference to remain private so that people can come together in the public domain as fellow citizens, albeit in hegemonically coded ways (see next section). If difference can be contained within the private domain it can be safely expressed without Britain fragmenting into a series of disparate peoples or nations. 'Ghettos', by representing a restructuring[22] or refusal to privatize difference, threaten a common citizenship. A post-modern interpretation that marks them as interesting places of intense cultural expression and diversity is, I was told, dangerously naive. Ghettos represent troubled symbols of cultural ill-health and disequilibrium. Several interviewees cited the USA, where the capacity of cultural minorities to form local majorities enabled them, it was argued, to remain outside of, and thereby undermine, universal(izing) citizenship identities.[23]

The dangers, opponents believed, went beyond local anti-Semitism; for ghettos cannot be contained. While Barnet's *eruv* might appear to offer a container for difference, enclosing a large proportion of London Jewry within a single, symbolic perimeter, this perimeter is always in danger of splitting – literally and figuratively – and contaminating the surrounding area. At one level, such contamination relates to the premodern norms with which the *eruv* is associated; at another, the contamination concerns the expression of modern, subnational territorialism. Thus, the slippery slope extends beyond totem poles on Hampstead Heath to the threat or fear of a Rwanda or Yugoslavia: symbols of nations and even supranational regions contaminated and fragmented by a racialized out-of-controlness.

Christian Hegemony and Religious Law

For the last 30 years, my wife and I have every Christmas put a very large tree in the front bay window of our house. This has, I venture to suggest, given a great deal of pleasure to the community . . .[24] The *eruv* will, I think, create exactly the reverse effect.[25]

So far I have talked about the importance of difference remaining within the private domain without making particularly explicit what difference I refer to. However, it is clear in this context that it is *minority* faiths that are expected to remain private. The dominant faith – Christianity – can legitimately be expressed within the public domain. Indeed, Christianity's expression within the public sphere is seen as playing a crucial role in the reproduction of traditional forms of belonging and national identification. The maintenance of Britain's Christian heritage was affirmed by *eruv* opponents, even Jewish ones. According to one objector, 'Christianity is fundamental to our culture and 95 per cent of the population' (interview).

The special place of Christianity needs to be kept in mind in considering *eruv* opponents' valuing of secularism. Secularism is usually taken to mean religion's location within the private rather than public sphere.[26] It also signifies the rejection of religion as a foundation for policy-making or political decision.[27] Within Britain, however, the impact of secularism on different religions is clearly uneven. Not only does secularism coincide with an established Church of England but Christianity is also less disadvantaged by the political subordination of religious bases for action than other faiths. Like heterosexuality, Christian space 'has an air of neutrality . . . the epitome of rational abstraction . . . [because it] has already been the focus of past processes whose traces are not always evident in the landscape'.[28]

Thus, when *eruv* opponents object to religion functioning as a criterion for action, their target is non-Christian faiths. One woman I interviewed proffered an analogy: 'Suppose you have a wonderful bush at the end of your garden, but the person living behind you, who shares the bush, believes it represents evil; do you have to remove the bush just to comply with their religious beliefs?' While this raises generally interesting ethical questions regarding religion's status as a basis for action, equally significant was the specific illustrative context: a person from the Caribbean who believes in voodoo. Thus, at the heart of this analogy is a criticism of action to accommodate 'irrational', *non-establishment* belief systems. And there is fear. If 'irrational' beliefs can legitimately demand action simply on the ground of being a belief, does any basis for distinction remain? This question reverberates with 'cultural relativism' anxieties; it echoes, for instance, recent British attacks on multi-faith teaching for refusal normatively to privilege Christianity as the superior faith framework.

Competing Governance

As I mentioned at the start, a key aspect of the cultural contract is the relationship between individual and state. This has several components. First, it takes a monist rather than pluralist view of law, seeing citizens as subject to the law of the state rather than to the laws of their subnational community. Indeed, as I discuss below, the very *legal* character of such subnational normative systems is itself placed in doubt. Second, it means that citizens are governed directly by the state rather than through the mediation of civil structures. Third, while civil forms of governance are permitted, these must function voluntarily and by agreed membership. Fourth, the unmediated, singular relationship between citizen and state (sovereign) is crucial to the sustenance of the liberal nation-state.

Legal Pluralism and the Cultural Contract

While opponents tended to treat minority faiths as irrational and potentially dangerous unless contained within the private domain, Protestantism was, by contrast, cool and level-headed. Within the discourse of the cultural contract, Protestantism fulfilled the appropriate role for religion: to supplement and complement social life, not to provide a competing structure or set of norms. In the case of Britain, Christianity is needed to provide the cement of national belonging. Any absence or deterioration will leave a gap.

This defining of the legitimate realm for religion, based on the role played by Anglicanism in a nation where the Church of England is the established faith, defines other faiths as hazardous. Judaism, for instance, has historically borne accusations that it fails to facilitate nation-state belonging, being at best neutral and at worst counter-productive in its demands for 'special' treatment and its extra-national loyalties. In addition, critics have perceived its legalistic form as threatening a monist, hierarchical notion of law.

In the context of the *eruv* controversy, opponents refused to accept that Jewish law was law. They did not simply treat *halakha* as subordinate to secular, domestic law,[29] but dismissed its very legal status. (This rejection carries particular significance if law is seen as the expression and projection of community identity.) Jewish law was denied legal status for several reasons. First, it could not be law since law was perceived to operate according to a singular state hierarchy of legislation and case law. Second, drawing upon Christian imagery, the role played by God in the construction of Jewish law meant that religious laws were not laws but matters of faith and spirituality. According to one leading *eruv* proponent, opponents proved so unwilling and unable to comprehend *halakha* that they gave up trying to explain:

> Jewish law is very complicated, we were aware of trying to explain it to people who hadn't a clue . . . It's hard to find ways of expressing the idea of the *eruv* . . . Eventually we said we can't explain it or you'll never believe it . . . We presented it as a facility the community needs, to explain why we need it is our business. We just want you to respect the fact we understand it (proponent, interview).

As a consequence of being perceived as not real law, opponents portrayed Jewish law as voluntary – grounded in choice and consent rather than obligation; and as indeterminate – lacking the fixity and clear meanings of proper law. At the same time, Jewish law was characterized as rigid and obscure in opposition to the mercy, forgiveness, and accessibility perceived as emanating from the Christian tradition. This depiction of Jewish law produced two main responses to the *eruv*. First, the reduction of *halakha* to voluntary belief and closed principles meant one either believed in the singular, underlying purpose – here, not carrying on the sabbath - (and complied) or one did not.[30] One of the most repeated accusations thrown at the *eruv* was hypocrisy: 'It allows people of a certain persuasion to break the law' (objector, interview). This criticism was reinforced by pointing to sections of the ultra-orthodox community who had publicly repudiated the *eruv* proposal.[31] Asserting *halakha*'s interpretive closure, opponents claimed if the ultra-orthodox did not accept the *eruv*, then this must be the best 'right' position (interviews by author). They rejected the possibility of equally valid competing interpretations of *halakha*, a recognition that would undermine law's hierarchy, internal and external.

At the same time, the perception of Jewish law as technically obscure and disputed (as well as voluntary) meant *eruv* requirements were deemed entirely plastic. In other words, opponents declared that an *eruv* could be constructed according to any measurement that suited both users and the wider community. For instance, several interviewees suggested an *eruv* might be more acceptable if it embraced the entire British mainland. When I replied that an *eruv* could only be of a limited size, enclosing a limited population, I was met with a shrug and rejoinder that since the whole thing was ridiculous, it was pointless to look for 'rational' rules. More broadly, *eruv* opponents approached the subject of Jewish law with the view that people should do what they want – carry if you want, don't carry if you don't. But they refused to accept that the decision whether or not to carry might be a legal one or one that could be legally enabled through highly detailed, open textured, legal provisions.

Civil Governance

As I said above, opponents perceived the installation of the *eruv* as undermining the direct relationship between citizen and state. In this way, the *eruv* functioned anachronistically, reverting to premodern forms of Jewish governance which brokered and mediated the relationship between community and nation. In addition, they claimed, the *eruv* would inappropriately structure the lives of people who had not consented to incorporation. As one objector put it: '[W]ithin those physical boundaries around 80,000 people will be enclosed, the vast majority of whom have no desire at all to live within a private Jewish domain.'[32]

Territorial

The final aspect of the *eruv* to threaten the relationship between state and people, according to the terms of the cultural contract, concerned its territorial character. The articulation of space to a community perceived by the cultural majority as

insular and clannish symbolically constituted the *eruv* as threatening the repro-
ductive work required to sustain the nation-state. I have already discussed some of
the demographic aspects of this undermining. However, a key element concerned
the *eruv*'s emphasis on borders. Borders are important because they allow a discrete
territory to be imagined – crucial to the production and reproduction of nationhood.
According to Balibar (1991: 95), external frontiers of the state have to be constantly
imagined as a 'projection . . . of an internal collective personality, which . . . enables
us to inhabit the space of the state as a place where we have always been – and
always will be – "at home"'. In addition, borders function as a boundary that
regulates entry and exit. A leading *eruv* proponent described these boundaries as
vitally important to an internal sense of community. On the sabbath, he suggested,
it was vital that orthodox Jews knew where the boundaries of their community lay,
and functioned within them. This restriction on observant Jews is more than
symbolic since if they are carrying objects on the sabbath they cannot convey them
beyond the *eruv* perimeter.

But will the boundary impact upon anyone else? Clearly, opponents perceived
the *eruv* perimeter as a symbolic wall that would keep the non-orthodox unwelcome
and excluded. Anxiety that the *eruv* would constitute a form of 'home rule' within
its borders was given added fuel when the main local newspaper, the well-respected
Hampstead and Highgate Express, claimed to have received minutes from a group
of Jewish zealots who planned to patrol the perimeter to ensure its sabbath
integrity.[33] These minutes were subsequently dismissed by the Jewish Board of
Deputies as a hoax;[34] however, their production and effectiveness both built upon
and reproduced images of a Jewish militarized nation – a fortified, turbulent,
Middle-Eastern Israel within suburban, staid, conservative, north-west London.

But does this perception contradict other anxieties that the *eruv* would con-
taminate surrounding areas? Can the *eruv* be both a highly militarized stronghold
and a locus of disintegration? These two images may be compatible if we see
fragmentation as threatening the British nation-state, while localized Jewish
governance solidifies, drawing for its strength on modern coercive techniques. At
the same time, we might see the *eruv* not as threatening the *possibility* of a British
nation-state so much as its current identity. What it means to be British or English
– the emphasis on a single sovereign, legal system, citizenship and public faith –
is challenged by the governmentality an *eruv* is seen as posing. At the heart of
British opposition to the *eruv* is a fear of change – that the British nation-state will
be transformed into the American model of opponents' imaginations. But it is
also a fear that there is no essential British identity. In other words, it is a fear that
Britain *can* live with an *eruv*, that Britain's national identity may organically change
without crisis or rupture.

Conclusion

In this chapter I have addressed the question: why did the application to install eighty poles and some thin, high, invisible wire to complete an *eruv* boundary in London in the mid-1990s generate such acute fear, hostility and distress amongst local residents? My argument draws on my earlier exploration of the relationship between the *eruv* and modernist, liberal norms. Here, I explored the extent to which these norms were articulated to a cultural contract according to which hegemonic forms of British belonging were constituted. In exploring the way in which the *eruv* breached this contract, I have focused on four 'transgressions'. First, the *eruv* was seen as privatizing space that belonged to a wider public. Second, it flaunted minority beliefs, practices and loyalties in a way that provocatively disregarded the liberal public/private divide. Third, it resited religious law within public decision-making, and constituted religious law as a legitimate basis for public action. Finally, it troubled modernist forms of nation-state governance.

Above all, and at its most simple, opponents saw the *eruv* as a form of territorialism or 'taking' that would transform their neighbourhoods along both premodern and post-modern lines.[35] Yet their fear that existing residents would be displaced, and British nation-work obstructed, has to be located within the context of modern anti-Semitism. Analogous initiatives by other minority faiths may well have engendered similar levels of hostility. However, the specific character of what happened here is rooted in the orthodox Jewish nature of the *eruv* enterprise within a residential area with a significant Anglo-Jewish population and identity.

Thus, one of the most interesting, but not necessarily surprising, aspects of the conflict was the role played by non-orthodox Jews. Having said that, it is important not to forget the many opponents who were not Jewish; Christian and secular residents also opposed the *eruv*, and much of the public displays of opposition came from local Church figures. However, the opposition of non-orthodox Jews was a distinctive aspect of the conflict. In considering the specific motivations that gave their response such intensity, I would suggest a key factor was displacement. Here, I do not simply, or primarily, mean physical alienation; rather, the *eruv* proposal extracted secular Jews from assimilation, and relocated them in a wasteland of non-belonging: neither at home with observant Jewry nor part (any longer) of a universal citizenry. Their membership and loyalties recast as ambiguous, we can read their intensive, arduous opposition to the *eruv* as necessary Jewish labour, fulfilling their commitments and obligations within the prevailing cultural economy.

Notes

1. This chapter is a slightly revised version of *Governing Out of Order: Space, Law and the Politics of Belonging*, London, Rivers Oram, 1998, Chapter six. I would like to thank the local residents and politicians of Barnet, North London who agreed to be interviewed, providing me with much of the material for this chapter, and to the British Economic and Social Research Council for their funding of the research (award no. R221591). I would also like to thank Beth Widdowson and Wendy Ball for their excellent research assistance and intellectual feedback, as well as Edward Black, Ken Foster, Michael Freeman, Hillel Furstenberg, Didi Herman, Bernard Jackson, Shauna Van Praagh, Michael Saltman and Carl Stychin for their comments and suggestions.
2. See *ACLU of New Jersey* v. *City of Long Branch* 670 F. Supp. 1293 (D.N.J. 1987).
3. D. Cooper, (1996).
4. Outline of Mr Lush and Ms Popper argument (objectors), quoted from Inspector's Report, para. 4.41, 10 January 1994.
5. In Jewish law or *halakha*, the public domain bears a particularly narrow, restrictive interpretation. The prohibition on carrying or pushing was thus extended by rabbinic law to a *carmelit*, a domain that is neither public nor private. Most public areas outside of Central London are probably carmelits. However, since they were identified as 'public' within the Barnet *eruv* debate, I will do likewise, although strictly speaking within Jewish law they are not public; indeed, if they were it is doubtful whether they could become part of a private domain by means of an *eruv*; see Metzger (1989: 68).
6. This only applies to articles that can already be carried within the home. It does not for instance allow cars to be driven.
7. See *Phoenix New Times*, 9 May 1996; insurance difficulties have also been a problem; see *The Washington Post*, 14 January 1980.
8. Problems arose in Miami Beach regarding the golf course and waterways. These were treated as recreational and therefore as residential; see *The Record*, 20 September 1994.
9. There is a growing literature on the changing and often contradictory approach of Jewish orthodoxy to women.
10. Most of the opponents I interviewed identified themselves as Jewish. One woman refused to disclose her identity, and two identified themselves as non-Jewish.

    Many non-Jews opposed the *eruv*, including high profile figures such as Lord McGregor and Lord Soper; however, some non-Jews expressed ambivalence about becoming publicly active in the campaign, in case they appeared anti-Semitic. According to one leading Barnet councillor, 'Jewish

objectors were needed by non-Jews, so it would be legitimate to criticize'
(interview).

11. See also M. Bunting, *The Guardian*, 14 December 1993.

12. Z. Bauman (1988–9).

13. See *The Record*, 20 September 1992; *The Baltimore Sun*, 28 January 1995; *The Sun (Baltimore)*, 25 September 1994, 5 March 1995; *St. Louis Post-Dispatch*, 20 November 1994.

14. Outline of Mr Thomas's argument, Inspector's Report, para. 4.67.

15. See outline of Mr Max's objections, Inspector's Report, para. 4.52.

16. 670 F. Supp. 1293 (D.N.J. 1987).

17. A similar argument is made by Barnet *Eruv* Objectors Group, Inspector's Report, para. 4.12, regarding parishioners who have to pass under the *eruv* wires to attend church.

18. See Inspector's Report, para. 5.36. For judicial rejection of the argument that an *eruv* imposes religious beliefs on non-participants within it, see *ACLU of New Jersey* v. *City of Long Branch* 670 F. Supp. 1293 (D.N.J. 1987).

19. Collective letter sent to councillors from opponents, 2 October 1992.

20. In relation to New York's Upper West Side, see *The New York Times*, 29 May 1994.

21. Cllr Frank Davis, letter, *Hampstead and Highgate Express*, 4 December 1992.

22. Thanks to Carl Stychin for this point. Areas defined as lesbian and gay ghettos provide a similar example as the division between public and private expression of homosexuality is redrawn rather than rejected.

23. See also *The Independent Magazine*, 16 January 1993.

24. Formally, the tree is in the private sphere of the home; however, its public visibility highlights some of the limitations of a simple public/private divide. Do passers-by who find sight of the tree offensive have any right/legitimate basis for complaint?

25. D. White, letter, *Hampstead and Highgate Express*, 16 October 1992.

26. Turner (1991: 9).

27. This opposition, paradoxically, enables religion to retain its importance as a rationalization for opposing religious-based, political developments.

28. H. Lefebvre (1976).

29. This is not to suggest that Jewish law and British state law *should* be analogized; rather I am interested in the implications of defining Jewish law as Other.

30. An alternative approach would be that refusing to carry or push prams is no longer necessary to fulfil the underlying injunction to rest/not work on the sabbath. Thanks to Bernard Jackson for this suggestion.

31. See *Hampstead and Highgate Express*, 5 February 1993.

32. Jacobs, Witness Statement, p. 2.

33. 'Jewish Zealots: We'll Patrol Eruv', *Hampstead and Highgate Express*, 15 January 1993.
34. See letters in the *Hampstead and Highgate Express*, 22 January 1993.
35. The *eruv* was not simply portrayed as a form of religious communalism, but also as constructing a consumerist relationship to space in which symbols could be arbitrarily installed regardless of pre-existing meanings and identifications.

References

Alderman, G. (1995), 'English Jews or Jews of the English Persuasion', in P. Birnbaum and I. Katznelson (eds), *Paths of Emancipation*, Princeton, N.J.: Princeton University Press.

Agnew J. and Corbridge, S. (1995), *Mastering Space: Hegemony, Territory and International Political Economy*, London: Routledge.

Ashburn, D. (1994), 'Appealing to a Higher Authority', *Detroit Mercy Law Review*, 71.

Audi, R. (1989), 'The Separation of Church and State and the Obligations of Citizenship', *Philosophy and Public Affairs*, 18.

Balibar, E. (1995), *Race, Nation, Class*, London: Verso.

Bauman, Z. (1988–9), 'Strangers: The Social Construction of Universality and Particularity', *Telos*, 78.

Birnbaum, P. and Katznelson, I. (eds) (1995), *Paths of Emancipation*, Princeton, N.J.: Princeton University Press.

Bradney, A. (1993), *Religions, Rights and Laws*, Leicester: Leicester University Press.

Connolly, W. (1993), 'Democracy and Territoriality', in M. Ringrose and A. Lerner (eds), *Reimagining the Nation*, Buckingham: Open University.

Connor, M. C. (1995), 'The Constitutionality of Religious Symbols on Government Property: A Suggested Approach', *Journal of Church and State*, 37.

Cooper, D. (1995), 'Defiance and Non-Compliance: Religious Education and the Implementation Problem', *Current Legal Problems 1995*, 48.

—— (1996), 'Talmudic Territory? Space, Law and Modernist Discourse', *Journal of Law and Society*, 23.

Davidman, L. (1990), 'Accommodation and Resistance to Modernity: A Comparison of Two Contemporary Orthodox Groups', *Sociological Analysis*, 51.

Diner, H. (1994), 'Jewish Self-Governance, American Style', *American Jewish History*, 81.

Encyclopedia *Judaica* (1971), Vol. 6: 849–50.

Etzioni, A. (1993), *The Spirit of Community: The Reinvention of American Society*, New York: Touchstone.

Howard, E. (1945) *Garden Cities of Tomorrow*, London: Faber and Faber.

Judd, D. (1995), 'The Rise of the New Walled Cities', in H. Liggett and D. C. Perry (eds), *Spatial Practices*, London: Sage.

Kunin, S. (1994), 'Judaism', in J. Holm with J. Bowker (eds), *Sacred Place*, London: Pinter Publishers.

Lefebvre, H. (1976), 'Reflections on the Politics of Space', *Antipode*, 8.

MacFadyen, D. (1933), *Sir Ebenezer Howard and the Town Planning Movement*, Manchester: Manchester University Press.

Metzger, J. (1989), 'The Eruv: Can Government Constitutionally Permit Jews to Build a Fictional Wall without Breaking the Wall between Church and State', *National Jewish Law Review*, 4.

Miller, M. and Gray, A. (1992), *Hampstead Garden Suburb*, Chichester, Sussex: Phillimore.

Mosse, G. (1993), *Confronting the Nation: Jewish and Western Nationalism*, Hanover: Brandeis University Press.

Pateman, C. (1988), *The Sexual Contract*, Cambridge: Polity.

Pfeffer, L. and Pfeffer, A. (1989), 'The Agunah in American Secular Law', *Journal of Church and State*, 31.

Sachs, J. (1992), *Crisis and Covenant: Jewish Thought after the Holocaust*, Manchester: Manchester University Press.

Shapiro, M. and Neubauer, D. (1989), 'Spatiality and Policy Discourse: Reading the Global City', *Alternatives*, 14.

Sharot, S. (1991), 'Judaism and the Secularization Debate', *Sociological Analysis*, 52.

Stone, S. (1993), 'In Pursuit of the Counter-text: The Turn to the Jewish Legal Model in Contemporary American Legal Theory', *Harvard Law Review*, 106.

Turner, B. (1991), *Religion and Social Theory*, London: Sage.

Walzer, M. (1984), 'Liberalism and the Art of Separation', *Political Theory*, 12.

Zarrow, J. (1985), 'Of Crosses and Creches: The Establishment Clause and Publicly Sponsored Displays of Religious Symbols', *The American University Law Review*, 35.

6

Ritual, Distances, Territorial Divisions: Land, Power and Identity in Central Nepal

Joanna Pfaff-Czarnecka

The late German artist Joseph Bouys suggested that we may perceive of societies as of sculptures. This idea serves as a useful metaphor for imagining and conveying the picture of social relations in time and space. A three-dimensional image emerges highlighting social orders presented through inequalities and status distinctions by their linkage with territorial divisions. Such social sculptures come about through dynamic processes within societies, their members negotiating constantly over mutually conflicting projects to be ordered in space and time. Struggles occur through attempts to maintain and to challenge the existing societal divisions. They relate directly to the quest to negotiate identities, to (temporarily) define the general character of the social body, to define one's place within the given order, to put highly valued notions forward and to struggle for them.

This chapter recalls a fierce ritual battle fought simultaneously over status, territorial allegiance, patterns of land distribution and power differentials. It occurred in Nepal in 1986. In fact, we may simply say that the battle was fought over the patterns of landownership and over land entitlements because all dimensions of the social life related to it. Until five decades ago, the issue of landownership was not just a question of which plot of land you tended and how much of it, but also whose land it was – because until then almost all land in Nepal was owned by absentee landlords. Ownership and entitlement did not merely pertain to the nature of economic transactions since the category of land one tended defined the administrative regulation of respective rights and duties between the owner and the tender. This circumstance again impinged upon rights and privileges, as well as political status, within the local society. On the other hand, categories of landownership related partly to status within the Hindu hierarchy because members of particular caste groups could receive land on the grounds of particular merits and entitlements given through the caste membership. The spatial distribution of land, furthermore, determined not only the quality of a particular plot but also the forms of living distance within the local societies.

At the heart of this presentation stands an event: the great annual festival of the Durga Puja. Its celebration in 1986 in the central Nepalese village of Belkot is of a special interest here because a particular conflict situation relating to territoriality and land exerted a lasting effect upon the festivities. To return to the metaphor of a social sculpture, the occasion of the celebrations presented a picture of local society with most of the wind and the life-juices squeezed out of the social body. What happened? The members of one ethnic group, called Tamang, who lived in this locality and who had just recently risen to power, deliberately spoiled the annual ritual celebrations on the grounds that this particular festival was a symbol of their oppression. They said it commemorated their low status in the local polity, reflected especially in the patterns of land distribution.

Durga Puja, also known as 'Dasai', as celebrated in Belkot in the second half of the twentieth century, consists of an elaborate ritual sequence. Specialists act as the protagonists in the majority of the rituals, and local power-holders play the major role on the last day of the festivities. By and large, Belkot's festivities conform to the broader pan-Indian tradition of Durga Puja celebrations.[1] But they include some local peculiarities, along with specific 'local meanings' added to this model.[2] By now, Dasai has evolved into a trial of strength among hostile village factions. Thus, in the last decade the Tamang community (in Belkot accounting for more than half of the population) has refused to participate in the festivities any longer, claiming, as noted, that Dasai commemorates Tamang subjugation to the central rulers and their local high caste representatives. The most influential group in this endeavour consists of Tamang politicians who, on that occasion, managed to persuade the entire local Tamang community to boycott the communal celebrations, and not to perform animal sacrifices at the village's main Devi temple.

The narration of this event will allow us to analyse the causes of the ethnic conflict as well as the identity politics that is involved in the process of identity formation. Three interrelated issues are at the centre of this account. First, by going back to the historical formation of this polity, it becomes obvious how thoroughly the patterns of landownership and territorial divisions have shaped the social body of Belkot – the central Nepalese locality where this ritual battle (see Pfaff-Czarnecka 1998) took place. Second, it is to show how specific events, such as ritual occasions, provide special opportunities for negotiating status and identity. Third, it is my aim here to put forward the idea that landownership and territorial divisions as such are not necessarily identity markers, unless certain groups of people dispose of ideas of how they are owned by the lands they dwell on. However, it becomes obvious that the memories of how landownership and territorial allegiances have made groups of people relate to and negotiate with one another provide highly fertile grounds for identity formation. To understand these developments we need to look back at Belkot's history.

The Local Society in the Making

The ritual of Durga Puja – commemorating the Goddess Durga's victory over the demon Mahisasura – as it is celebrated in Nepal today goes back to the military conquests initiated by the king Prithvi Narayan Shah in 1744 that eventually resulted in the unification of Nepal in its present size (see e.g. Pfaff-Czarnecka 1993). Long before military unification various rulers within the present Nepalese territory worshipped the Goddess and counted upon her divine protection. In the middle of the eighteenth century the Goddess apparently answered the prayers of Prthwi Narayan Shah, then the ruler of the rather small and economically weak principality of Gorkha. He was able to establish the foundations of a polity which is known today as the Kingdom of Nepal.

In the course of their military conquests the Gorkhalis extended their rule over comparatively vast territories, declaring the soil as 'the entire possessions of the King of Gorkha' (Burghart 1984: 103), and establishing the king's ritual authority over the realm. With their newly acquired wealth the rulers were able to promote religious cults at various religious sites throughout the kingdom. In so doing they succeeded in linking their political power to the spiritual power of the Goddess formerly worshipped in her different manifestations by the ruling houses they had conquered. Durga Puja emerged in Belkot as a ritual of power by virtue of two interrelated processes: the central rulers' cultural measures to consolidate their power, and the mediation of these by societal processes at the local level. The complex socio-political processes at the local level had a substantial impact upon the way the central rulers' message reached the local population, both in general and on the specific occasion of Durga Puja. In Belkot the communal Durga Puja celebrations are reported to have been a political battleground among competing local elites (belonging mainly to high Hindu castes) during the period of Rana rule (1846-1951).

By promoting the Durga Puja at various sites of the country, as was the case in Belkot after unification, the central rulers strove to legitimate their rule (Burghart 1984; Unbescheid 1986). However, their legitimizing endeavours differed significantly from those required in other political systems. Instead of seeking popular consent as in the democratic model, the rulers sought to substantiate and demonstrate[3] their powerful position by linking their worldly power with divine power. By promoting the local cult in Belkot the rulers expressed their religious feelings and at the same time conveyed a message substantiating their worldly power. The local population was expected to acknowledge this fact by displaying their deference. Confronted with a specific symbol of the emerging political culture shaped by central rulers, the local elites (holders of administrative offices, priests, influential families) took the opportunity to express their loyalty, but also sought to confirm, in turn, their power or elevated status by linking their prerogatives to symbols related to the central rulers. The local population, subject to the central rulers and to the local elites, was made to witness such endeavours. They were compelled, rather than invited, to attend, to bring tributes, to bow, and to watch. By showing obedience they formed part of the festive background. Their presence served to assert the importance of those who were able to establish themselves as the focus of the celebrations.

Belkot, situated less than two days' walking distance from Kathmandu, has been constantly affected by various measures imposed on it by central elites. Its history reflects major trends of societal processes at the national level, such as changing relations of production (Pfaff-Czarnecka 1991), centralization of the administrative apparatus (e.g. Regmi 1978b) and significant migratory movements within the emerging polity. Throughout the nineteenth and twentieth centuries the ongoing processes at the local level have been reflecting broader processes at the 'national' level in various ways. Belkot was a society in the making during the unification and consolidation process. None of the local families today performing Dasai ritual functions lived there when Prthwi Narayan Shah's troops conquered the place.[4] Only a few of the local landowning high-caste families that were clients of the central elites and political leaders lived there at that time. Some local families later appointed as office holders by central elites (see pp. 00–00) moved here only in the first decades of the twentieth century. Several high-caste families (Upadhyaya and Jaisi Brahmins, Chetris) moved here from the west of Nepal during the 1920s and 1930s when what are now the most fertile lands on the valley bottom were cleared for cultivation – which became possible thanks to the eradication of malaria. Two of the newcomer families managed to acquire the post of headmen (*thari*) of small local administrative units (*taluk*), when the clearing of new plots of land required additional administrative tasks.

In the administrative sense, until the 1950s local society was far from unified. It was divided not only by various forms of landownership patterns and revenue collection but also by differing forms of subordination. While some local political leaders could claim durable links to central elites (especially to the royal family), an increasing number of office holders were appointed by the state on a yearly renewable basis. On the occasion of Durga Puja celebrations, fierce battles were fought since it was the only annual occasion when their respective ranking could be expressed. Among those competing were various office holders below the rank of the headman; for example, men in charge of collecting taxes and of employing 'free labour'. The many political leaders and office holders did not fail to display and to dispute their relative statuses. With these symbolic endeavours the local elites aimed, like the central rulers, at substantiating claims to power and status and at marking socio-political distances, rather than seeking approval from their subjects. In this sense their ritual message corresponded to local cultural forms and values (such as clear displays of the ritual hierarchy). Even the Tamangs, the section of the local population least exposed to the Sanskritic tradition, were able to understand the message. As they admit nowadays, they used to 'read' it as the expression of their political subjugation. Local informants from the various castes and ethnic groups living in Belkot today (see Table 6.1) say that the majority of the peoples living there now (Brahmins, Chetris, Magars, Tamangs, Kamis) were represented by their forefathers already before the unification, but many families, including those that are now the ritual specialists, came only later.

Table 6.1 Caste and Ethnic Groups of Belkot (Vertically Ordered According to the Status Granted to them within the Hindu Hierarchy)

Brahmins	Twice-born
Chetri (Kshatriya)	
Newar	
Magar	Alcohol-drinking
Tamang	
Damai	Low-caste (untouchable)
Kami	
Sarki	

During the course of the nineteenth century and in the first half of the twentieth a substantial part of Belkot's forests was cleared and turned into agricultural land. The fertile soil attracted the attention of Kathmandu elites in addition to locally powerful families. During the period in question Belkot's land was distributed among various landholders under a variety of tenures. Several informants estimated that at the beginning of the twentieth century local land was held under different forms of land tenure (see Table 6.2) in the following proportions. About 70 per cent of the land was *birta* (that is, given to individual families on a hereditary basis); about 7 per cent was under *jagir* (a form of pay on a temporary basis) belonging to two army units as well as to the eastern commander-in-chief;[5] about 5 per cent was under *raikar* (directly taxable) tenure belonging mainly to those serving as *hulaki*, namely to transport goods in relays (gradually *birta* and *jagir* have been turned into *raikar*); and about 15 per cent of the land is reported to have

Table 6.2 Landownership (Five Categories of Land)

Category	Owners or Holders
Birta	Brahmins, members of the royal family
Jagir	The army
Raikar	Individual local owners
Guthi	The temple and ritual specialists
Kipat	Some Tamang collectivities

Table 6.3 Functions in Relation to Land

Dware (the administrative head of the village)

Nine *mukhiyas* (in charge of nine village subdivisions, divided into five *tharis* – usually recruited from twice-born castes and the Magars – and four *taluks* – usually recruited from among the Tamangs – all in charge of maintaining law and order, as well as revenue collection on *birta* lands)

Revenue collectors on *raikar* lands (*jimmawal)* and on *jagir* lands (*dhokre*)

Persons in charge of organizing transportation of goods in relays (*hulaki mukhiyas*)

Ritual specialists with titles to *birta* and *guthi* lands

been used as *guthi* (tax-free religious land held by various families in connection with ritual duties around the Niranjana temple) (Table 6.3).[6]

The Durga puja in Belkot: Ritual Expressions of the Local Polity

Having introduced briefly the local society of Belkot we can now turn to the ritual celebrations of local power, ownership and land. But first some remarks upon the nature of power rituals are necessary. Any important cultural event can turn into a political symbol in no time. Political rituals are especially prone to contestation when members of political units start to perceive cleavages among themselves where cohesion prevailed before. Established ritual orders can become both devices to 'celebrate the perpetuation of social values and self-knowledge' (Baumann 1992: 99) as well as symbols of oppression. In consequence, rituals of power can eventually become battlegrounds where meanings are negotiated. Different sections within a local society can answer the question: Does a particular ritual order express divine grace (which emanates through the ruler from the top to the bottom of the society), or is the ritual meant to cement and to substantiate the subordination of wide sections of a given society?

Political rituals are often centred on a text commemorating a mythical event, and they are embodied: during the subsequent ritual sequences people gather and segregate according to the ritual orders which, more often than not, correspond to the existing societal divisions. The central idea of this argument runs as follows. Rituals 'are not just expressive of abstract ideas but do things, have effect on the world' (Parkin 1992: 14). Both the ritual texts and the ritual action underlie a constant process of reinterpretation which renders power rituals ambiguous. It endorses Parkin's idea to highlight the performative character of the ritual occasions which reflect and affect the social relationships (so power rituals are not just contested but provide contestation grounds). In this sense this position runs counter to Maurice Bloch's notion of a non-correspondence between the ritual ranking and the actual distribution of power. This position neglects the seemingly self-evident idea that power rituals relating to religious complexes are about power.

In his most fascinating article on the disconnection between power and rank in Madagascar, Bloch showed how a turbulent state was based on unscrupulous exploitation by a small ruling minority of a large ruled majority; and how, at the same time, this order was misrepresented as a harmonious system of fine gradation of rank free of sharp social breaks (1982: 321). Bloch argues that

> this cultural mystification is . . . more than just a veil over the eyes of the actors; by hiding the reality of exploitation and transforming it into an ideology which stresses the beneficent effect of the presence of the ruler it serves to preserve the power of the rule, to facilitate its acceptance and thereby to maintain it . . . The non-correspondence [between the system of the political-economic ranking and its ideological manifestation . . . is one of the innermost mechanisms of the reproduction of the political system ([1977] 1982: 321).

In our example a very different situation obtained. Instead of disguising their dominant position, those in power strove to accentuate inequality, among other things by recourse to ritual means. Local political leaders sought to present themselves as especially close to the Goddess whose divine protection emanated through and from the king. Generally I am inclined to believe that in political systems drawing upon religious legitimacy, disguising the actual power relations has not been a concern. Bloch's (1987) account of the ritual bath itself provides a fascinating illustration of this point. On the contrary: Durga Puja as a ritual event is a power display; substantiating ranks, divisions, directly highlighting the established order. Ernest Gellner remarks rightly that '[a]mong the higher strata of agro-literate society [such as Nepal's] it is clearly advantageous to stress, sharpen and accentuate the diacritical, differential, and monopolizable traits of the privileged groups' (1983: 10–11).

Since rituals are meant 'to do things', meanings can be instrumentalized, according to the agendas of the various actors who seek to affect directional change.[7] When ritual occasions comprise 'competing constituencies' (Baumann 1992), those who compete usually do so to acquire supremacy within a certain given ritual context derived from a mythological event. They seek to mobilize its central elements for their own endeavours – thereby creating a powerful link between the myth and the ritual action. The opposite option is to withdraw from the celebrations altogether, aiming to deprive the others of a strong political tool. In relation to our case it is important to stress, furthermore, that power rituals in complex societies pertain to specific socio-political orders and to the authority of those in focal political positions within these orders. They not only express and dramatize social realities, but also, more specifically, organize social groups by relating them with one another. One important element in relating social groups is the establishment of symbolic means for expressing the supremacy of one group and the subordination of others. However, there always remains wide scope for ambiguity (Kertzer 1988: 11) and for disagreement to exist between various participants who may attach multiple meanings to a religious celebration at different ritual levels (Lukes 1977: 206; Humphrey and Laidlaw 1994: *passim*).

Let us go back to the ritual itself. The Durga Puja, as celebrated in Belkot until the second half of the twentieth century, consists of an elaborate ritual sequence, with ritual specialists acting as the protagonists in the majority of the rituals and with local power-holders playing the major role on the last day of the festivities. By and large Belkot's festivities conform to the broader pan-Indian tradition of Durga Puja celebrations. They contain some local peculiarities, however, along with specific 'local meanings' added to this model. In Nepal also the term 'Dasai' is synonymously used for 'Durga Puja'. The celebrations start on the first day of the waxing lunar fortnight of the month *aswin* (September–October). On that day two men, the Dasai priest, a Brahmin, and the *upasye*, a Magar, install themselves in the Dasai house which is situated a few metres below the Devi temple. Besides fasting with the Dasai priest inside the house, the *upasye*, another ritual specialist is supposed to perform several duties outside the Dasai house, and he has to sacrifice animals and to carry a sword on the procession of the seventh day. The Dasai priest and the *upasye* stay in the house together through the entire period, fasting, performing rituals assigned to them, reading and/or listening to the Devi-Mahatmya. They are assisted by the temple priest who has to perform rituals inside and outside the house. On the first day the Goddess is invoked by the planting of barley seeds and by the establishment of a water vessel. Throughout the day Brahmins arrive at the temple and read from the holy Devi-Mahatmya text. The

Damai orchestra assembles in the morning and in the evening, as it does throughout the year.

From the second to the sixth day Dasai activities are confined to the inner area of the Dasai house. Every day the ritual objects symbolizing the Goddess are worshipped, the Dasai priest and the *upasye* continue with their fast (that is, they eat only once a day after sunset), and they listen to Brahmins who come occasionally to the house and read the Devi-Mahatmya. Towards the end of the sixth day several preparatory activities are carried out: the sacrificial ground next to the Dasai house is repaired and ritually purified by the *pujari* (a Brahmin temple priest) who is assisted by the *naike* (a village servant who is a Newar). Towards the sixth day some eatables are collected that will be put on one of the plates on which the barley plant is growing. The Goddess's weapons are cleaned and put into the Dasai house.

On the seventh day, known as *phulpati*, Dasai activities are carried out in three places simultaneously. While the Goddess and the weapons are being worshipped in the Dasai house, the *naike* purifies with cow-dung a spot about 200 metres down the slope (a *deurali*, 'place of worship')[8] where also a bel (*Aegle marmelos*) twig is planted. A third party, consisting of two Magars, goes down to collect the *phulpati* ('flowers offered in worship'). In the afternoon the *kalas* (holy vessel) and the plate containing the *jamaro* (barley offshoots) and nine offerings to the Goddess are taken out of the Dasai-house. A procession is formed with the Damai orchestra in front. It is followed by the village servant, then by the temple priest who carries the *jamaro* plate, his helper (no special name) who carries the *kalas*, the *pandit*, and two men (a relative of the Magar official and a political office holder of lower rank) each carrying a sword. The procession reaches the sacred spot (*deurali*) at the same time as the two men who carry the *phulpati* from the valley. After everybody has arrived (a large crowd accompanies the ritual specialists), the *pandit* worships the bel twig, the sacrificial knife, and a pumpkin. A he-goat is sacrificed at the spot and its blood is shed onto the twig, which will remain there. Subsequently, the procession climbs back towards the Dasai house where the ritual objects are put into place. Two more he-goats are sacrificed, one in the Dasai house and one in the grounds in front of it; the *phulpati* is distributed as blessing among the people.

The eighth day is relatively quiet. Rituals are performed inside the Dasai house. Many private persons visit the temple and the premises of the Dasai house on this day, sacrifice their own animals, and listen to the Brahmins' recitations. Towards evening the sacrificial ground is purified with cow-dung by the *naike*. It is only in the evening that the sacrifices start. The night sacrifice starts with the worship and sacrifice of a pumpkin and is succeeded by the sacrifice, first of buffaloes and then of goats (a small procession goes to the spot where they meet the main sacrificial buffalo and accompany it to the sacrificial ground). The sacrifices continue on the ninth day. After the sacrifices the meat of the animals (which until three decades ago were said to be provided by the royal brothers, i.e. by the tenants among the local population) is distributed as a religious blessing (*prasad*) to local people.

On the tenth day the last goat is sacrificed in the morning. Its head is put on a leaf-plate and placed in the Dasai house. Outside Brahmins gather and they read from the Devi-Mahatmya. A crowd gradually assembles in and around the sacrificial ground. Inside the Dasai house the Dasai priest worships the objects which symbolize the Goddess. Shortly before he gives a sign for exchanging *tika* (a ritual marker put on the forehead) outside, he distributes three *tika* inside the house: the first *tika* goes to the king of Nepal, the second to the God Vishnu, and the third goes to his own lineage deity. After the ritual objects, including the last goat's head, are brought and arranged outside the Dasai house, the Dasai priest gives the first *tika* (with some *jamaro*) to the political village head, the second to the *upasye*, and the third to the *pujari*; all receive it with a bow. The *upasye* and *pujari* give a tika to the priest in turn; however, he does not reciprocate the bow. Subsequently all ritual specialists distribute *tika* and the barley plant to the gathered crowd.

Before the Pancayat reform the celebrations on the tenth day are reported to have been preceded by fierce disputes which carried over onto the ritual ground. More precisely, the battles occurred during the week-long preparations of the celebrations. The actual festivities were the outcome of the preceding negotiations among the powerful and the office holders. According to several former political leaders of the village, the highest ranks did not compete in this. It was mainly the various tax collectors and the *hulaki mukhiya*, as well as the different clients of central elite families who disputed through ritual. Unfortunately, informants could not agree on any issue – which again may indicate how much local perceptions of the celebrations differ.

Observations of the festival in 1986 and accounts of how the tenth day was celebrated until three decades ago differ significantly. In 1986 the new political head of Belkot did not attend Durga puja festivities at any stage because he, a Tamang, opposed their communal performance. The 'political power' was represented by the village secretary who was a Chetri. This was a departure from Durga Puja celebrations during the preceding period when the village head was always a member from the twice-born castes. Though the villagers were not obliged to deliver any tokens (foodstuffs) to the village headman in the Pancayat period anymore, many felt compelled to appear on the tenth day and to bow in front of him. No status rivalries have been reported from this time.

It is noticeable that the Tamangs opposed Durga Puja immediately after they came to power, so this was already the fourth year in a row with this kind of conflict. Originally this opposition came especially from young, dynamic leaders of the Tamang community who had a radical vision of change in Nepalese society. Gradually they came to be supported in their opposition against the public displays of hierarchical relations on Durga Puja by a very large proportion of the Tamang community. In the view of many Tamangs, nowadays actively expressed mainly by the younger generation, Durga Puja is an expression of the dominance of the Nepalese political system under the rule of the king, and the dominance of his clients who belonged to the twice-born castes. Otherwise, during the local Durga Puja celebrations the twice-born office holders liked to present themselves in the focus of the celebrations as if they were *dware*.

Status, Subordination and Ambiguity of Meanings: Ritual Contestations during Durga Puja

The Durga Puja celebrations in Belkot consist of many patterns structuring the relationships, and express a variety of meanings which can be differently interpreted by various actors. The Brahmanic knowledge and values attached to Durga Puja celebrations are shared by the population to differing extents. The sanctity of the text, the idea of restoration of the cosmic order and the concept of divine kingship, and the symbolism of holiness and prosperity through specific Vedic notions are surely less accessible to some sections of the society than to the Brahmins.[9] However, even those within Belkot's population who have been scarcely exposed to Brahmanic values are conscious of at least some of its most general elements. These included force and bravery attached to divine power (with some sharing in it and others being subjected), ritual purity (with some ranking higher and others ranking lower within the hierarchy), the notion of plenty (with some partaking in it and others watching them doing so), and auspiciousness (again, enjoyed to varying extent by different people).

All the more scope exists for various meanings to be attached, given that specific actors play more or less visible roles within different ritual sequences that vary in symbolic meaning:

1. During the first six days: the purity and the secrecy of Brahminic rites.
2. On the seventh day: the connection with power centres (Gorkha, Nuwakot and Kathmandu), divine power, and the display of cooperation of all ritual specialists in a public context (e.g. this is the occasion when the Damai orchestra is very prominent).
3. On the occasion of the sacrifices of the eighth and ninth day, ritual power is evoked and created, and the benevolence of the Goddess who accepts the sacrifices is stressed.

4. Finally, the tenth day focuses on the (worldly) display of evoked (divine) power. Note that on this occasion ascribed and achieved statuses complement each other, and compete.

Many actors involved share in their common preoccupation to express the importance of the place on the occasion of Durga Puja. Belkot as a locality bearing a sacred site is distinguished by a ritual donation of land (now lost) – in this case an unambiguous indicator of royal assent. Members of the local society strive to augment local importance still more: the villagers mark the shrine's connection to other far more important holy places by worshipping stones which represent other manifestations of the Goddess. The importance of Belkot is further stressed by the ritual specialists who claim that the *phulpati* is sent from Gorkha. By this, Belkot is presented as inferior to Gorkha but as having a strong ritual link to this key origin place of the present royal dynasty.[10] The Brahmins in charge of the ceremony maintain that until a few decades ago a *tika* was sent to the royal palace in Kathmandu on the tenth day. The importance of Belkot is also seen in the story mentioned above that the local temple was destroyed and rebuilt by the Gorkhali army. The ritual weapons displayed on the occasion of Durga Puja are meant to commemorate the battle. Also, the spot where the *phulpati* sacrifice takes place is deemed a historic site. Durga Puja is the only ritual occasion when Belkot's importance during the unification period can be communally displayed.

Once the ritual significance of the place, hence of the local polity is established, individuals and groups try to take advantage of its amassed importance. Among the most striking features here is the way in which the major Durga Puja priest connects his lineage deity with the king of Nepal and the god Vishnu by giving three *tika* just before leaving the Dasai house on *dasami*. Though this measure is largely unknown to the villagers, it has great importance for the priest in question, who strives to bring the village under his ritual auspices. Similarly the members of the Magar ethnic group attach great importance to their prominent role throughout the festivities. In their view, their active role symbolizes their bravery in the course of the unification (though they have in fact lost some of their former prerogatives; however, economic and political decline may make the Magars cling to ritual prerogatives and historical connections all the more), and their previously prominent role as local chiefs before their defeat. Carrying the sword is connected with the royal power. This is a privilege of the Magar that nobody would contest. The majority of the high-caste Hindus in the village hold the *upasye* in high regard.

At the communal level there are differing notions of unity and division which become apparent during Durga Puja. From the point of view of Belkot being a sacred site, unity is symbolized by a hierarchical order that accords specific ritual tasks to hierarchical ranks. In this holistic perspective most of status groups living in Belkot are represented by some of their members. In this way the Brahmins, the Magars, the Newars, and the Damais are represented, and they all play indispensable roles in the festivities. Several Chetris perform within this complex the role of the 'powerful', along with some Brahmin leaders. The local Kamis and Sarkis are not represented. This is surprising, especially in the case of the former, since the Kamis play an important role in producing or at least sharpening the weapons that are displayed.[11]

The numerically most important group of the village, the Tamangs, are not represented as performing any ritual tasks at all, not even by their political leaders, who under the Ranas had to travel to Kathmandu on this occasion. In the capital the Tamang *mukhiya* had to bring tribute and bow before their immediate superiors. No data could be collected on this issue; probably the Tamang leaders were asked to go to Kathmandu so that they might be brought under direct control of their superiors. Their presence in Belkot during the Durga Puja festivities would have added to the *dware*'s importance. Where a common belonging of some local status groups was expressed in the holistic idiom of Hindu hierarchy (representatives of the local castes and ethnic groups cooperate ritually, having tasks assigned to them which correspond to their hierarchical caste ranks), the Tamangs, Kamis and Sarkis had to remain outside the order.

Whereas the publicly displayed ritual order was ambiguous, excluding some and binding others together, the political order expressed itself in a clear-cut way. On the tenth day, ideally, all had to be present (more precisely, members of every household had to appear at the fortress – namely the 'fortress' where the Devi temple was situated, with the Dasai house slightly below). By appearing in front of the *dware* everybody was compelled to acknowledge his supremacy. In this sense all villagers were actors. At the same time, the majority of the villagers were also spectators: they were witnesses to the strategic games of the 'powerful'. As discussed above, among various officials – some having had durable links with central elites, some having been appointed annually – political ranking used to be fiercely negotiated as every Dasai approached. We note that appointments to and removals from office occurred before Dasai. Therefore, the struggles in connection with the tenth day referred rather to the relative importance of functions. Apart from this festival the various ranks and duties were not well defined in relation to one another. Unlike other ritual occasions celebrated at the local level,[12] the power display at the tenth day was the only occasion when the office holders felt compelled to appear in a hierarchical order. The first man who received a *tika* from the *dware* appeared to be more important than his successor. In front of the villagers, the officers not only endeavour to outdo their political rivals but also to create the greatest possible distance between the spectators and themselves by striving to be closer to 'power' than the others.

The case of the Tamangs indicates that even if everybody seemed to be participating in a ritual and to be sharing its values, under the surface of the mere display conflicting values and interpretations were hidden, even though – despite the claims by the politicized Tamangs of Belkot – we cannot be sure that under the Ranas the Tamangs resented the Dasai celebrations as much as they do today. All Tamangs, with the exception of their local leaders, were compelled to appear on the tenth day, and to display their inferiority towards the *dware* as well as towards the other villagers since they were allowed to approach him towards the end of festivities only, just ahead of the low-caste people.

The Tamang rejection can be interpreted in the light of Scott's argument on the 'moral economy of the peasant'. In his influential book Scott argues that people display compliance because external circumstances force them to do so. Much that passes as deference is in fact a strategy to please those in power. 'There may be in fact a large disparity between this constrained behaviour and the behaviour that would occur if constraints were lifted' (1976: 232).[13] The present case fits well with this argument – all the more so as the Tamang leaders and their followers ceased attending and supporting the Dasai celebrations as soon as their faction won the local elections.

However, by supporting Scott's argument I do not wish to suggest that ritual behaviour and connected values are merely displayed by all actors. This would be missing the point entirely. In the case of Belkot some sections of the local population certainly share the central meanings, but we cannot conclude that all who partake in a ritual of power share the same values. There is scope for everybody to attach more importance to some elements than to others, and some participants are likely to attach unexpected meanings to the Dasai celebrations – namely, resentment. An important feature of power rituals is that some of the participants gladly appear in the focus of the rites and are able to exercise power over some others by compelling them to participate and to witness the display of their importance.

Conclusion

This narration was meant to highlight the connections between territoriality, land, ethnicity, and identity displayed during the ritual negotiations, which reflect the relations within the local society. Since these are the major elements of this volume, let me conclude with several inferences pertaining especially to them.

Territoriality

Two aspects of territoriality stand out in this account. First, territoriality refers to establishing borders within landscapes; second, it highlights significant sites that eventually may become objects or centres of contestations. In Belkot, the territorial divisions give rise, among other things, to a multiplication of functions, since, until about five decades ago different territorial units defined by the categories of landholdings were managed by different types of office holders. The territorial divisions fragmented local society, and reorganized it according to the administrative requirements; namely, the establishment of law and order and tax collection. In this process new functions, hence new bases for status, came about. Therefore, the multiplication of functions that follow the territorial divisions may enhance the political negotiations between different office holders, which eventually may turn into symbolic contestations – as was the case in Belkot. The territoriality in the sense of significant spots linking symbols to landscape is present throughout the Durga Puja. This ritual enables the inhabitants of Belkot to locate themselves within the realm (i.e., the religiously defined and legitimized polity) and to place Belkot within the ritual geography when ritual sites linking the local deity to the other places of worship are especially displayed on this occasion.

Land

Land is of interest here as the major commodity available in Belkot. This feature has become evident in a variety of relations: in the rulers' interest in land and in local people's efforts to receive land titles and to acquire, maintain, and display political power closely relating to landownership. The conflict described here is a case of a collective power struggle; therefore, it was introduced through the metaphor of a social sculpture linking land and territory to societal divisions. We saw that titles to land (not necessary ownership) are one thing, but it is something else to assess what kind of functions, duties, and privileges are attached to land. The example of the conflict created by the Tamangs shows that the quantity of land naturally provides the material basis for human existence. But certain elements of status and power relate to factors other than just an entitlement: to the question whose land it is one tends, what kinds of allegiances come about, and the forms defining how duties are to be performed.

Ethnicity

Ethnicity makes for clear-cut divisions in the everyday life. It defines – here through the notion of the Hindu hierarchy – the ritual distances, even though there are no clear-cut barriers. Distances, however, do not presuppose complete avoidance. On the contrary: the Durga Puja celebrations evince a large degree of cooperation, hence contact, through the ritual division of labour. On the other hand, the ritual division of labour on Durga Puja reinforces ranks. The ritual division of labour corresponds to the local caste division, comprising not only the Hindus but also members of ethnic groups to whom hierarchical ranks – below the so-called 'twice-born' castes and above the so-called 'untouchables' – have been accorded. At the communal level there are differing notions of unity and division which become apparent during Durga Puja. From the point of view of Belkot being a sacred site, unity is symbolized by a hierarchical order that accords specific ritual tasks to hierarchical ranks. In this holistic perspective the majority of status groups living in Belkot are represented by some of their members. In this way the Brahmins, the Magars, the Newars and the Damais are represented and they all play indispensable roles in the festivities. However, the numerically most important group of the village, the Tamangs, are not represented as performing any ritual tasks at all, not even by their political leaders, who until the 1950s had to travel to Kathmandu on this occasion. In the capital, the Tamang *mukhiya* had to bring tribute and bow before their immediate superiors. The Tamangs were excluded from the celebrations.

Identity

Let us, therefore, finally consider the issue of identity from the Tamang perspective. I have tried to demonstrate how one of the major Hindu rituals, the Durga Puja, has become subject to contestations in a minor historic site in Nepal, the last Hindu kingdom. The political conflict carried out at the ritual ground relates directly to ethnic mobilization in this area. After over two centuries under the rule of high-caste Hindus and their supporters, members of the various ethnic Nepalese communities all over the country started fiercely to oppose the existing societal order embraced by the Hindu ideology. Contesting a major Hindu ritual, as in our case, turns against the ritualization of subordination.

Within the local social hierarchy the Tamangs have been outside (if not at the bottom of) the order. No representative of theirs plays any specialist role during the celebrations. Furthermore, since their political leaders do not participate in the *tika*-distribution on *dasami* (where they would rank high – although no one can say how high), the only role they can play is that of mute subjects who must attend, deliver tributes, and bow. Paradoxically, in the course of the recent political development the Tamangs of Belkot have assumed an active role in the celebrations by publicly contesting it. By contesting Durga Puja's importance at the communal level, they compel political activists who are eager to retain the political character of the celebrations to mobilize their fellow villagers – while the ritual specialists continue to perform the religious rites as ever. Durga Puja, shaped over many decades as a power ritual, became an institutionalized means to convey particular messages between the ruling and the ruled. Regarding the dynamic properties of power rituals discussed before, I believe I have demonstrated how the Durga Puja has been continuously adapted according to the various participants' objectives.

Those at the apex of the local hierarchy and those striving to attain it could take advantage of the existing ambiguities in the ritual celebrations and contribute to what Lewis (1980) and Parkin (1992) have described as 'ruling'. There probably was consensus among those in power that enlarging the ritual complex would enhance the means of emphasizing one's own significance.

While the high-caste members of the local community strove to make the festivities a resource to affirm their importance, the members of a hitherto low-ranking (by Hindu standards) ethnic community, the Tamangs, moved to stop the Durga Puja celebrations altogether after they acquired political power. The Tamangs in Belkot made a conscious choice not to endorse the central values of the ritual even though, having attained political power, they could have celebrated themselves at the focus of the ritual order. Claiming, however, that the Durga Puja ritual not only commemorated their political subjugation but also symbolized their ritual inferiority within the Hindu hierarchy, the Tamang leaders chose to boycott the entire complex. One could claim that Tamangs, being – by the local standards – partly outsiders in the Hindu order, did not grasp the meaning of the festivities. I suggest that they did, and utilized this powerful symbolic means to make a forceful political statement: the Tamangs chose to 'read' Durga Puja as a symbol of their oppression within the Hindu realm. It is remarkable that after more than two centuries of apparent accommodation within the ritual complex they decided to break with the past. Instead of using the ritual ground to display their newly acquired power by embodying it in the ritual space, and hence to endorse the existing order, the Tamang leaders decided to contest the Durga Puja's meaning. Apparently, Durga Puja's powerful symbolism has rendered 'ruling'[14] playing with fire. The new political alternative is to shake at the ritual's very rules.

Notes

1. See Dirks (1987), Fuller (1992), Kane (1958), Levy and Rajopadhyaya (1990), Unbescheid (1986).
2. The 'ethnographic present' relates to 1986.
3. Geertz's (1980) model of the theatre state in nineteenth-century Bali provides important insights for our case.
4. This holds for the Brahmin and Magar ritual specialists as well as for the Damai musicians. According to members of each family in question none of them has been living in Belkot for more than eight generations.
5. The *jagir* belonging to the army units was converted into *raikar* at the beginning of the twentieth century.

6. Several Tamangs stated that the local Tamang chiefs held *kipat* lands that
    were granted to them with their offices. It is questionable whether *kipat* tenure
    really existed in Belkot – especially since this statement shows a clear
    misconception of the notion *kipat* (communally owned land, held as of right,
    not in return for services).
7. For important discussions on the ritual dynamics, see, Bloch ([1977]1982),
    Lewis (1980) and Turner (1992).
8. According to some informants, this particular site is where an important battle
    was fought during the unification process.
9. The uniformity of the religious rites performed throughout the South Asian
    sub-continent during Durga Puja can first be attributed to religious practice
    rather than state intervention. The performance of the ritual sequence is
    codified in religious texts, and the ritual specialists, the Brahmins, usually
    learn at religious centres remote from their villages. The most important
    Brahmin priests of Belkot have studied in various Indian cities, the major
    one being Varanasi (Willke 1993).
10. We cannot be sure that *phulpati* was never in fact brought from Gorkha.
    Unbescheid (1986) provides many examples of various villages being
    compelled to send small tokens to Gorkha. Even though Belkot is not
    mentioned, it is probable that in former times something was sent to Gorkha,
    and something was brought back.
11. In Bandipur (West Nepal) the Kamis play a very important role during Durga
    Puja celebrations (personal communication from S. Mikesell).
12. *Sagun sankranti, candi purnima, cait Dasai.*
13. This said, the problem emerges at a different level that we cannot discuss in
    detail. We are confronted here with Hinduism which 'is' a religion as well
    as a specific form of social organization. Concerning the religious aspect of
    the ritual, it is difficult to make out when observance is genuine and when
    not. At the religious level this seems to be a false problem. However, at the
    level of the socio-political organization, how emotionally deeply a ritual is
    experienced pertains to the legitimacy issue.
14. 'Ruling' is a term introduced by Lewis (1980) in reference to situations where
    there are no precise rules governing rituals.

References

Abercrombie, N., Hill, S. and Turner, B. S. (1980), *The Dominant Ideology Thesis*, London:
    Allen & Unwin.
Baumann, G. (1992), 'Ritual implicates "Others": Rereading Durkheim in a Plural Society',
    in D. de Coppet (ed.), *Understanding Rituals*, London & New York: Routledge.
Bennett, L. (1983), *Dangerous Wives and Sacred Sisters*, New York: Columbia University
    Press.

Bloch, M. ([1977]1982), 'The Disconnection Between Power and Rank as a Process: An Outline of the Development of Kingdoms in Central Madagascar', in J. Friedman and M. J. Rowlands (eds), *The Evolution of Social Systems*, London: Duckworth.

Bloch, M. (1987), 'The Ritual of the Royal Bath in Madagascar: The Dissolution of Death, Birth and Fertility into Authority', in D. Cannadine and S. Price (eds), *Rituals of Royalty: Power and Ceremonial in Traditional Societies*, Cambridge: Cambridge University Press.

Burghart, R. (1984), 'The Formation of the Concept of Nation-State in Nepal', *Journal of Asian Studies*, 64(1): 101–25.

de Coppet, D. (1992), 'Introduction', in D. de Coppet (ed.), *Understanding Rituals*, London & New York: Routledge.

Devi-Mahatmya (1975), *Celebration de la Grande Déesse*, (translated by J. Varenne), Paris: Société d'Edition Les Belles Lettres.

Dirks, N. B. (1987), *The Hollow Crown: Ethnohistory of an Indian Kingdom*, Cambridge: Cambridge University Press.

Dumont, L. ([1966]1979), *Homo Hierarchicus: Le système des castes et ses implications*, Paris: Gallimard.

Dumont, L. (1962), 'Kingship in Ancient India', *Contributions to Indian Sociology*, 6: 48–77.

Durkheim, E. (1915), *The Elementary Forms of the Religious Life: A Study in Religious Sociology*, London: Allen and Unwin.

Fuller, C. (1992), *The Camphor Flame: Popular Hinduism and Society in India*, Princeton, N.J.: Princeton University Press.

Geertz, C. (1980), *Negara: The Theatre State in Nineteenth-Century Bali*. Princeton, N.J.: Princeton University Press.

Gellner, D. (1992), *Monk, Householder, and Tantric Priest: Newar Buddhism and Its Hierarchy of Ritual*, Cambridge: Cambridge University Press.

Gellner, E. (1983), *Nations and Nationalism*, Oxford: Blackwell.

Habermas, J. ([1962]1990), *Strukturwandel der Öffentlichkeit*, Frankfurt: Suhrkamp.

Hasrat, B. J. (1970), *History of Nepal: As Told by Its Own and Contemporary Chroniclers*, Hoshiarpur: V.V. Research Institute Press.

Heesterman, J. C. (1985), 'Power, Priesthood, and Authority', in J. C. Heesterman (ed.), *The Inner Conflict of Tradition: Essays in Indian Ritual, Kingship, and Society*, Chicago: University of Chicago Press.

Hobsbawm, E. and Ranger T. (eds) (1983), *Invention of Tradition*, Cambridge: Cambridge University Press.

Höfer, A. (1979), 'The Caste Hierarchy and the State in Nepal: A Study of the Muluki Ain of 1854', in *Khumbu Himal*, Innsbruck: Universitätsverlag Wagner.

Höfer, A. (1986), 'Wieso hinduisieren sich die Tamang?', in B. Kölver (ed.), *Formen kulturellen Wandels und andere Beiträge zur Erforschung des Himalaya*, Sankt Augustin: VGH Wissenschaftsverlag.

Holmberg, D. H. (1989), *Order in Paradox: Myth, Ritual, and Exchange among Nepal's Tamang*, Ithaca, N.Y. and London: Cornell University Press.

Inden, R. (1978), 'Ritual, Authority and Cyclic Time in Hindu Kingship', in J. F. Richards (ed.), *Kingship and Authority in South Asia*, Madison: University of Wisconsin Press.

Inden, R. and Nicholas, R. (1977), *Kinship in Bengali Culture*, Chicago: The University of Chicago Press.

Kane, M. P. V. (1958), *History of Dharmasastra*, Vol. V, Pt. I, Poona: Bhandarkar Oriental Research Institute.

Kertzer, D. I. (1988), *Ritual, Politics, and Power*, New Haven, Conn. and London: Yale University Press.

Kirkpatrick, C. ([1811]1969), *An Account of the Kingdom of Nepal*, New Delhi.

Lévi, S. (1905), *Le Népal: Etude historique d'un royaume hindou*, Vols. 1 & 2, Paris: Toit du Monde.

Levy, R. I. and Rajopadhyaya, K.R. (1990), *Mesocosm: Hinduism and the Organisation of a Traditional Newar City in Nepal*, Berkeley, Los Angeles, Calif. and Oxford: University of California Press.

Lewis, G. (1980), *Day of Shining Red: An Essay in Understanding Ritual*, Cambridge: Cambridge University Press.

Lukes, S. 1977 'Political Ritual and Social Integration', in S. Lukes (ed.), *Essays in Social Theory*, London and Basingstoke: Macmillan.

Michaels, A. (1997), 'The King and Cow: On a Crucial Symbol of Hinduization in Nepal', in D. Gellner, J. Pfaff-Czarnecka and J. Whelpton (eds), *Nationalism and Ethnicity in a Hindu Kingdom: The Politics of Culture in Contemporary Nepal*, Amsterdam: Harwood Academic Publishers.

Parkin, D. (1992), 'Ritual as Spatial Direction and Bodily Division', in D. de Coppet (ed.), *Understanding Rituals*, London & New York: Routledge.

Paul, R. A. (1989), *The Sherpas of Nepal in the Tibetan Cultural Context*, Delhi: Motilal Banarsidass Publishers.

Pfaff-Czarnecka, J. (1989), *Macht und Rituelle Reinheit: Hinduistisches Kastenwesen und Ethnische Beziehungen im Entwicklungsprozess Nepals*, Gruesch: Ruegger-Verlag.

—— (1991), 'State and Community: Changing Relations of Production after the Unification of Nepal', in H. J. M. Claessen and P. v. d. Velde (eds), *Early State Economics*, Political and Legal Anthropology, Vol. 8, New Brunswick and London: Transaction Publishers.

—— (1993), 'The Nepalese Durgapuja Festival, or: Displaying Political Supremacy on Ritual Occasions', in C. Ramble and M. Brauen (eds), *Anthropology of Tibet and the Himalaya*, Zurich: Ethnologische Schriftenreihe 12.

—— (1998), 'A Battle of Meanings: Commemorating Goddess Durgan's Victory Over Demon Mahisaa as a Political Act', *Asiatische Studien*, 52(2): 575–610. (Asia in Swiss Anthropology – Asien in der Schweizer Ethnologic, Hrsg. J. Helbling.)

Ramirez, P. (1996), 'Luttes d'influence dans l'empire de la Déesse', in G. Krauskopff and M. Lecomte-Tilouine (eds), *Célébrer le pouvoir: Dasai, une fête royale au Népal*, Paris: CNRS.

Regmi, M. C. ([1963–8]1978), *Land Tenure and Taxation in Nepal. Bibliotheca Himalayica*, Series 1, Vol. 26, Kathmandu: Ratna Pustak Bhandar.

Regmi, M. C. (1978b), *Thatched Huts and Stucco Palaces: Peasants and Landlords in the 19th Century Nepal*, New Delhi: Vikas Publishing House.

Scott, J. C. (1976), *The Moral Economy of the Peasant: Rebellion and Subsistence in Southeast Asia*, New Haven, Conn. and London: Yale University Press.

Stiller, L. F. (1968), *Prithwinarayan Shah in the Light of Dibya Upadesh*, Ranchi: Catholic Press.

Stone, L. (1977), *Illness, Hierarchy and Food Symbolism in Hindu Nepal*, Ann Arbor, Mich.: Human Relation Area Files.

Turner, V. W. (1982), *From Ritual to Theatre: The Human Seriousness of Play*, New York: Performing Arts Journal Publications.

—— (1992) *The Ritual Process*, New York: Walter de Gruyter.

Unbescheid, G. (1986), 'Göttliche Könige und Königliche Götter: Entwurf zur Organisation von Kulten in Gorkha und Jumla', in B. Kölver (ed.), *Formen kulturellen Wandels und andere Beiträge zur Erforschung des Himalaya*, Sankt Augustin: VGH Wissenschaftsverlag.

Vajracarya, D. and Shrestha, T. (1975), *Nuwakotko Eitihasik Rupreka* [The History of Nuwakot], Kirtipur: Centre for Nepalese and Asian Studies.

Willke, A. (1993), 'Durga-Puja in Benares', Berne: Berne University Press.

7

Imitating Ethnicity: Land, Territoriality and Identity in a Swazi Zionist Christian Church

Fiona Armitage

Abstract and Theory

'Territoriality' is a term which has hitherto been used mainly in analyses of 'nationalism' and in anthropological studies of primate behaviour. In this article I explore the term in relation to a religious group or association. I propose that land or space is a necessary base for territoriality, temporary or permanent, and that territoriality is one of several expressions of ethnicity or separate identity. I use a particular case study, that of a religious association, to demonstrate that with any kind of space there can be territoriality but that land-based territoriality is a particularly potent expression of it. It is proposed that various forms of territoriality contribute towards the separate identity of the religious or other symbolic association. Territoriality is one among several possible expressions of group identity or ethnicity. It can be a temporary as well as a permanent state. Its expression can be achieved through intangible agents, such as noise and ritual – in nature the beautiful variants of the blackbird's song are not only enjoyed by the singer but used also to establish territory. So it is with the singing or noise-making member of the Zionist Church. By extension it proposes that the relationship between identity and territorial expression exists as much in religious associations as in tribal or kinship associations, and that ethnicity of a religious association is similarly linked to a multi-layered experience of land, partly shared with other groups and partly peculiar to itself. Ownership is not a necessary precondition of territoriality, however. Members of the religious association being discussed have not, until recent years, owned much land, and women have had no property rights over land or cattle in customary law (Levin 1997)[1] until a new law for women was introduced in 1999.

The religious group used for illustration is the Swazi Christian Church (SCC) in Zion of South Africa, a Swazi association of churches formed in 1942, whose members have, until recent years, been predominantly semi-literate and from rural areas. An increasing number of members are now urban-based and a few have reached university level education. Their churches have, however, retained a separate identity.

Introduction

This Church is a federation, a symbolic association made visible by the wearing of a uniform. It has an identity demonstrably separate from other groups, while encompassing a variety of form and practice within itself. It ordinarily uses land for livelihood as well as having ontological attitudes to it. It does not conform to many of the definitions of kin, clan or race, being polyethnic, and is not contained within formal political boundaries. It 'imitates ethnicity', however, and meets some of the criteria of an ethnic group suggested by anthropologists like Barth (1969: 1–38), Obeyesekere (1975) and Cohen (1954) who have defined 'ethnicity' or an 'ethnic group' with greater or lesser emphasis on clan, narratives of descent and origin, distinctive cultural attributes, geographical boundaries and functions for the wider society, or as having, in the words of Cohen, 'symbolic association'. As a 'symbolic association' the Church can have access to people of power and even influence them, assisted by its identity as a group with a particular church and protected living space.

The relationship between identity and territoriality, explored elsewhere in this volume in a variety of regional and cultural contexts, suggests a number of traits in common with the SCC in Zion. Among them is the evidence of spiritual ontological and social roles, as well as economic roles for land or space. This is particularly true in rural communities, and less overtly among people who have a more commercial and material concept of land and territoriality. Invariably, formal political boundaries, whether in the Caribbean, Canada, Kenya or Swaziland, bear little relation to the way in which some local communities regard land and the non-economic dimension of their lives. In most examples discussed, including the English village, there is a sense of preserving space from invasion by outside forces and of asserting, if not flaunting, an independent ethnic identity. It is not uncommon for a mythical or spiritual world to coexist with the changing and pragmatic world – in a sense it is a source of survival in the midst of hostile forces.

The relationship to land of a religious association, as a dimension of the particular ethnic identity of the group, may be seen more broadly as part of the dynamic interdependence between power relationships and symbolic action in complex society (Cohen 1974).[2] The Zionist churches of the SCC have their own system of power relationships and territoriality which, to some extent, compensates for their members' exclusion from both traditional and state political systems of power. Land and topography are frequently the material of symbols and spiritual forces, while the religious practices in relation to landscape are both invented and transformed from a traditional to a Christian framework.

Church History

The SCC in Zion of South Africa is the title of an association of mainly Swazi Zionist churches, the outcome of a resolution in 1942 by the League of African Churches in Swaziland, King Sobhuza II and the British Resident Commissioner to bring 'all the various groups of the Zion Church in Swaziland under the auspices of one organisation'. In effect it was an attempt to reduce the potential for the growth of multiple and conflicting ethnicities into one all-encompassing association which shared general attributes, including use of the land.

The Zionist Church movement, as a whole, began in Swaziland *circa* 1915, with the arrival of Zionist prophets from South Africa, and included Zulu as well as Swazi Zionist churches. Their origins are ultimately traceable to Alexander Dowie of Zion City, USA. All were marked by a tendency towards fissiparousness – due to leadership contests, dreams or migration. Some South African Zionist churches may have claimed membership of the SCC in Zion to avoid registration as separate churches, since the official restriction on the introduction of new churches came in at this time.

The present Swazi Zionist Church was originally divided into two main divisions founded by two contenders to the leadership – one having had more years of schooling than the other.[3] Further presidents were appointed within these divisions. All churches had between 20 and 100 branches and each branch 20 branches, accounting for about 7,600 congregations or more. From the 1920s the King of Swaziland encouraged the leaders and bishops to obtain training for the priests and ensure that the children went to school. This ran counter to the mystique of the uneducated man or woman favoured by the Zulu leader, Daniel Nkonyane, who introduced his Zionist church from South Africa in about 1915, and whose church still baptizes members of the Swazi royal family.

Prior to the Zionist churches in Swaziland were the breakaway Methodist churches – the African Methodist Episcopal Church in 1904 and the Independent Methodist Church, with African-American origins, in 1906. The absence of Ethiopian churches may have been due to the control of the religious life of the nation by the Swazi royal family, especially Queen Mothers such as Labotsibeni, mother of Mswati II.

The Role of Topography, Ethnicity and Territoriality in the SCC

There is some degree of correlation between the location of Zionist churches and 'biblical' landscapes in Swaziland, insofar as they cluster in areas of fertility near royal residences, in mountainous areas, near rivers and waterfalls, and even in dry areas in the vicinity of mountains or sources of water.

The land systems of Swaziland are part of the dendritic landscape of south-eastern Africa. Twenty-five land systems have been identified by land surveyors[4] and cartographers, of which three systems are of particular interest in the case of the Zionist churches of the SCC in Zion. These are the Lobamba land system, the most fertile, which lies in scattered 5-10 square mile acreages in the south-east and centre of the country, bordering the Kildonan and Havelock high veld to the west.

Clusters of Zionist churches, communities and royal residences coincide in the Lobamba systems which contain red kaolinitic soil on the valley sides, on plateaux and interfluves, as well as clay or red loam on rock outcrops. Such soils are used in healing by both traditional Swazi and Swazi Zionists. These have been natural areas for the settlement of royal representatives, communities, and churches. In biblical terms the Lobamba system may be said to be 'the land of milk and honey', with its gently undulating plateaux and moist upland tree grassveld. Members have helped, or been obliged by custom to help the chiefs, in the cultivation and cattle raising of such areas. Close to churches and settlement ancestral graves are to be found, as at Mahlanya, infusing a spiritual dimension to the land. The Zionist priest and the local chief exercise power over people in the area – the former having moral authority and attracting voluntary membership, the chief having coercive powers. This has led to tensions between the two representatives. Although these have eased over the years, and certain chiefs have attended Zionist services, the ruling that there should be only one Zionist church in an area may have served not only the purpose of minimizing conflict between churches but also of securing the local political power of the chief.

Other clusters of SCC churches are to be found in the mainly Kildonan, Wagontree and Havelock mountain systems in the western region of Swaziland, before it dips down to the high veld plateaux of the Transvaal. The mountainous terrain is a larger area of mountains, waterfalls, springs and rivers, an area thus used to symbolize 'the kingdom of God', in biblical terms, and containing many instances of the Holy Spirit in the form of rain, wind and lightning. The high veld systems continue (under South African names) into Vryheid, Durban and Natal, where the SCC in Zion also has branches.

Important sites in the low veld also have their Zionist churches: from Tshaneni, near the northern border with South Africa's Northern Province, to Big Bend, a major sugar- and cotton-growing area in the centre of Lavumisa where Zionists are among those employed. Apart from the irrigated areas, this area comes closest to the biblical description of desert and wilderness. To the east, however, is the Lubombo range of mountains, frequented by representatives of both the traditional religion and Zionist churches. A Big Bend Zionist congregation is near enough to the mountains and forest to hold its services at a higher altitude. It would serve as a refuge for those who are relative strangers to the area.

Water from the Usutu river in the centre, Great Umbuluzi in the north, and the Ingwavuma river flows over much of their respective regions and so is potentially present for religious or ritual cleansing purposes. The Mnyame and Palata rivers flow from the Lubombo into Mozambique, ensuring a distribution of SCC in Zion churches to the coast (see Figure 7.1).

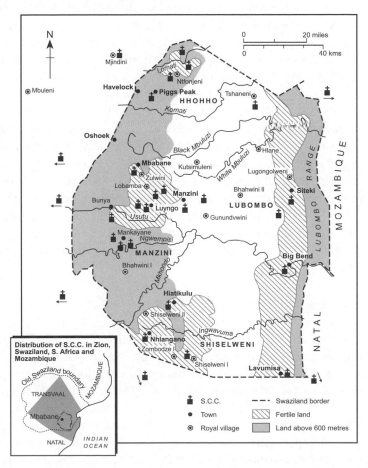

Figure 7.1 *SCC in Zion of South Africa (est. 1942) in relation to landscape, most fertile land and royal villages, past and present.*

The Nature of Ethnicity and its Relationship to Land

As mentioned, the SCC in Zion churches are polyethnic and do not conform to many of the characteristics of kin, clan or race which define other ethnic groups; neither are they confined to formal political boundaries or a geographical area.

For the purposes of this chapter the land and 'landscape' dimensions of ethnicity in the SCC in Zion are taken to mean not only the aesthetic and physical properties of 'land' but also its 'scope' in having spiritual meaning and functional properties for human beings. There are layers of meaning and historical memories, often missed by developers, which affect the behaviour and psyche of individuals. The SCC in Zion illustrates how in peasant and urban communities the sense of land and place is made up of memories, ancestors and spirits – all above and beyond physical properties. Industrial societies and developers have to some extent lost this sense, but an attachment to place is still very important and is a source of social stability.

The SCC derives its membership not only from a large number of clans and chiefdoms which have recognized spheres of influence throughout Swaziland, but also from South Africa, Lesotho, Botswana and Mozambique. Consequently, the land, to which they relate, transcends political boundaries. This is not only on account of Swazi tradition, or at least the dominant royal clan's way of viewing areas of land as spheres of influence rather than as rigidly demarcated areas of ownership, but is also due to the Swazi Zionist Christian way of viewing topography as having biblical parallels and significance regardless of boundaries. Such biblical landscape is to be found in all the surrounding territories, as well as in Swaziland itself, and is represented by mountains, rivers, waterfalls, pools and lakes; it is affected by climatic factors such as winds, storms, thunder and lightning. These are signs of the traditional God, Mkulumkande, as well as symbols of the Christian God and Holy Spirit.

Territoriality in the SCC

The SCC in Zion churches experience land and modes of territoriality at several levels. The latter are specific to the churches and arise in opposition to the agents of traditional religion, while the other modes are shared with such ethnic groups as Swazi descent, class and denominational groups. The territoriality specific to the churches of the SCC is present in the perceived sacred nature of the church space itself, and the second is the area in and around Zionist members' houses protected from witchcraft by particular substances like sea pebbles or sand, and the accompanying ritual. Another symbol of territoriality protecting Zionist members is the flag flying from the roof of a Zionist house, appliquéd with a dream-inspired design (such as a crescent moon and star). The flag, as it flutters in the wind, is interpreted to be the Holy Spirit being active in its protective and healing work. A fourth, and temporary or shifting mode of territoriality, is, I suggest, the 'noise' made by SCC in Zion members in their services and in processions outside the churches. For a while this intrudes on space shared with other groups and excites the hostility of outsiders. The subject is dealt with further in the section on territorial aspects of cultural practices in the Zionist churches (see pp. 150–53). Thus new symbols have been invented to link members with a society aspiring to change in order to protect them from traditional jealousies and restraints. Traditional concepts of land ownership and territoriality, promoted by the King of Swaziland and dominant clans, have not hitherto promoted individual ownership, which I have suggested is not crucial to expressions of territoriality, although rights of access to spheres of influence have been encouraged in return for labour on a chief's land. Zionists, other churches and individuals are now buying land which has boundaries in areas where territoriality can more clearly be rationalized. A new law will soon extend the right to women as well as men.[5]

The sacred nature of church space in the churches of the SCC protects from hostile influences, and reinforces the separate identity or ethnicity of their Zionist members. They have a core identity related to the church that they regularly attend, and then a broader identity related to their association of the SCC. The greatest protection from hostile forces is afforded by the space of the local church which they regularly attend. Within this space regalia like crosses or *sondeza* can be secured from sorcery. Within the church the priest occupies a space at the edge of a circle; disgraced people, frequently young women who have become pregnant before marriage, have to sit near the door. The centre of the circle is the arena of prophets, possession, prophesying and healing, this latter by a combination of laying on of hands and shaking by the shoulders – a feature of numerous spirit possession cults around the world.

Church space in SCC churches is at once inviting and exclusive, welcoming and protecting for those who want to participate, but excluding for those who wish to cause harm or break church rules. This can be illustrated by the way the church is used to express approval and disapproval in matters of childbirth, marriage, pregnancy and witchcraft. It is a microcosm of the outside world, where every aspect of life can be scrutinized and afforded order and solutions. Whether the structure of the church be stone or brick bought from congregation funds, or made of rural materials (branches, leaves or straw), the space they surround is believed, except possibly in the case of violent spirit possession, to be a safe one. A priest's or congregation's aspirations to build a more solid structure show how the modern scene of towns, industry or company estates is infiltrating the minds of the believers and furnishing them with another layer of symbols of association with the capitalist and industrial world. These may include table-knives, chains, tablespoons and forks hung round members' necks (especially true of the Jeriko Church) and transformed for religious purposes. Considerable self-expression is allowed to members within this framework, orchestrated and conducted by the priest to refrains of loud 'Amens' – in stark contrast to the mission churches which are characterized by the one-way communication of priest to congregation.

In these ways the Zionists, like people of all religious groups, take control and impose their mark on part of the landscape. It is not merely a background to their activities, as the poet W. II. Auden would describe it. The landscape, and particular spaces within it, is inextricably involved in the spiritual journey from life to death regardless of particular conventions of land ownership. As with the Australian Aborigines who still view land or landscape as the 'dreamtime', the sacred ground of their ancestors, the land is not simply material to be exploited for profit.[6] It is without formal boundaries and is imbued with symbolic meaning. For a Swazi Zionist church, some of whose members need to use the land in order to feed themselves, the landscape is not only a source of profit and sustenance but also a source of symbols which sustain its particular idea of itself, its ethnic identity. These symbols are accorded power and authenticity through their treatment and reflection in biblical narratives.[7] For Zionists it is a biblical landscape and home of the ancestors; for other groups it is a landscape of the traditional god and spirits, and also of the ancestors who are treated as spirits to be praised and propitiated; for developers and investors, or the cattle ranchers in competition with the Aborigines in north-eastern Australia, it is the basis for production and profit.

Politically Arranged Landscape

Beyond the internal space of SCC churches, and the surrounding space of Zionist homesteads, there is the politically arranged background to all the work of churches and members as well as the geographical scene of mountains, rivers, pools, plains and waterfalls within which church activities take place. Reflecting the landscapes involved in the Bible, these reinforce the members' sense of having a Christian or particular religious identity. The land or landscape is, moreover, a source of substances for symbolic activities and healing. It is also a source of continuity with the traditional past and the unfolding future, in which ancestral graves confirm the spiritual connection with the land of all Swazi people.

The politically divided landscape is shared with other groups and categories of people. Swazi Zionist churches are mainly located on Swazi Nation land under the authority of a chief, but today are increasingly to be found on purchased land in or near towns.

The land connection of the SCC churches in Swaziland has differed, I suggest, from Zionist churches in South Africa. This is due in part to the historical and political circumstances of the former that linked them with the land of the Swazi

Nation and partly as a consequence of their bearing allegiance to the King of Swaziland, formerly Sobhuza II and now, less favourably, Mswati III. Having a role as unofficial advisers and prophets to Sobhuza II elevated them from their largely rural and lowly status. Leadership struggles currently taking place in the SCC at Mahlanya and Manzini, however, may have transferred influence to the representatives of the League of African Churches. In South Africa, Zionist churches have been largely established on tribal lands, and, as Jean Comaroff suggests, this may have compensated members for relative absence of political representation, resources and state support.[8] At the same time they made themselves more acceptable to the dominant community through the outward symbols of religious association.

The territory of Swaziland, the size of Wales, is mainly a product of the colonial period (Funnel 1996). So many Swazi people, and such people as the Tsonga owing allegiance to them, have been stranded across its borders in South Africa and Mozambique, and even in the southern part of Zimbabwe.[9] These have provided further opportunities for extending church links across borders. Some of its shape and composition is due to disputes between African kingdoms in the eighteenth and nineteenth centuries, during which the Ndwandwe defeated the Ngwani. Land grants to Wesleyan missionaries from King Sobhuza I encouraged the entry of numerous white missions, followed in the twentieth century by Independent Methodist churches, and Swazi and South African Zionist churches. An early President of the SCC in Zion was asked by the Queen Mother, Joanna Nxumalo, an African Independent Methodist church member, to leave this church to join the Zionists where his mad behaviour would be better understood.

In the Anglo-Boer land partition of 1907 only 39 per cent of the area was left for the exclusive use of the Swazi. The rest was allocated as Title Deed land for the use of outsiders or whites, and 4 per cent was Crown land. Today 70 per cent is in Swazi ownership and 6 per cent in private ownership.[10] The potential for Zionist church territorial acquisition and stability has increased. It has provided members with economic and educational status; this, in turn, has enabled them to buy and maintain land so that noisy services do not irritate neighbours.

The internal land distribution is a potential basis for conflict between the 'haves' and 'have nots', especially as the population increasingly outstrips the availability of land. Royal and dominant clans continue to have the most control over it, and labour migration and seasonal patterns of farming are disrupted by new immigration restrictions in neighbouring South Africa.

Other Church Landscapes

Superimposed on land partition along Swazi private and commercial lines, there is also partition of land according to church influence, 'mission' and indigenous church spheres of operation. In the twentieth century there have been at least three attempts to restrict the growth of such churches.

In 1911 a meeting of white church leaders agreed that Swaziland, with over forty foreign mission churches, should be divided into several areas so that 'no new work be undertaken by any missionary society within effective range of an existing mission station'. In order to similarly limit the growth of new African churches, the Swazi National Council and Resident Commissioner passed a resolution, in 1936, to limit the number of Zionist churches to one in each chief's area. Neither group reckoned, however, with the spontaneity and arbitrariness of how the Holy Spirit works in the Zionist churches, and they continued to grow and proliferate.

In 1955 John J. Nququ, the king's representative, tried yet again to restrict the number of churches forming in Swaziland by means of instituting a United Church of Africa. It would seem that a division of the church was seen, essentially, as not only unhealthy for the Christian Church but also as a form of ethnic division, which had increasing implications for the division of land.

The SCC in Zion leaders have had the same rights as other church leaders to acquire land from chiefs for church use and subsistence. Only fairly recently have they purchased plots in the towns. Early mission churches were given land by kings Sobhuza I and II, both in the town and country, to pursue their work.

Biblical Meaning of the Swazi Landscape for the SCC

Medieval churches in Europe had visual images of Bible stories depicted in stained glass windows for the many people who could not read. The rich and varied scenery of Swaziland, along with oral testimony, has been used to bring biblical experience to life in the SCC in Zion churches.

In many ways Swaziland and the surrounding regions are replicas of biblical landscapes. Many of the mountain settings and rivers are used for religious dramas and reflect the images and symbols so important for folk memory in the Bible. Swaziland's mountains, the Lubombo in the east and the high veld in the west, with the dry, hot 'wilderness' or plain in between, substitute for those of biblical Palestine and Egypt as settings for revelations, prophesies and dreams. Spectacularly so, it might be added, for the leader of the Amajeriko branch, Revd Elias Vilakati, recently deceased, who reported visions of brightly robed Old Testament prophets and multi-headed beasts on the mountains. Whether he saw these beasts as the representation of Rome and its provinces as symbolized in the Book of Revelations is still open to question.[11]

Water, fire and wind are at the same time part of the Swazi landscape, part of Zionist church ritual and important biblical symbols of the Holy Spirit. Swazi Zionist church members are identified by outsiders as *Abakamoya* (people of the Spirit) from the Xhosa word *moya* or 'breeze', or *Amajoyini* (members of the churches), or in Botswana as 'People of the Water'.[12]

Landscape as a Source of Continuity with the Traditional Past and the Unfolding Future

The SCC in Zion churches demonstrate some continuity with traditional religion in their relationship with and use of the landscape – although Zionists emphasize they are transformed in the service of a Christian God. The same land similarly predominates in the symbols and schooling of the practitioners of the traditional religion; namely, the *tinyanga* and the *isangoma*. For both these representatives of continuing traditional culture, prophets and members of the SCC, the control of the landscape differs in concept and practice from the way control is managed by the technical agents of commercial agriculture or industry. Landscape, for the former, contains many spiritual forces for both good and evil. The SCC congregations perceive themselves as controlling these forces for the good, against manipulation by external forces for evil. Swazi individuals can choose, however, between continuing within traditional or within Zionist associations in order to solve their problems. They often seek help from the Zionist churches, as SCC conversion histories show, because they do not charge money for healing and often seem to them to be more effective than the 'inyanga' or Western-style hospital.

In these ways, Zionists are physically close to and in constant spiritual tension with the world of the traditional witch doctor, their professed differences often serving to release individuals from being controlled by traditional beliefs and practices. While asserting that they do not use the same techniques and medicines as the witch doctors they frequently perform a role as witch finders, and women are often accused, as in traditional witch-finding, of being the cause of another person's illness. This witch finding role occasioned social disturbance and violence in the 1930s, and again recently, and has given some outsiders a negative image of the Zionist churches.

At Zionist homesteads, territoriality in defence against witchcraft or sorcery is expressed by ringing houses with ribbons of sand and pebbles. The activity is often inspired by fears of jealousy or evil spirits and is a magic-encircling phenomenon, recorded for other, especially pre-Christian, cultures in Europe. For the SCC members the sand represents the power of the Holy Spirit, which outweighs that of the wizard or sorcerer, *batsakatsi*.

Ancestral graves on the other hand are common to Zionists and traditionalists, so when they are disturbed, in the building of a road or railway for example, both categories of people would expect some manifestation of anger from the ancestors.[13]

Zionists claim, however, that while they recognize that ancestors still have influence among the living, they no longer worship them.

Land and Nature: Sources of Symbolic Substance and Separate Identity

Traditional and Zionist rituals of cleansing use similar or identical substances – a red mud (*manzana*, *litombonkala* or *libovu*) from slow-moving streams is used in *siwasho* (Zionist cleansing substances) and in traditional Swazi rituals of purification after death and before marriage. It might be used in the treatment of a family afflicted by successive deaths of children, attributed to sorcery (*imfelwa*) or during a post-funeral ceremony for laying the spirit of the dead (*inzilo*); this takes place after two months in the Zionist churches, roughly equivalant to traditonal *inzilo* for ending a period of long mourning.

The substance and site of a small hill *isiduli* is used in prescriptions of Swazi Zionist healers, as well as by traditional healing cults in Swaziland and elsewhere in Africa.

Conversion histories of SCC in Zion members frequently mention ash or *siwasho* being used in healing. It is sanctified by Christian prayer, which contrasts with the substances and words used by the witch doctors. *Siwasho* may consist of ash, chalk, red mud, urine or a combination of substances derived from local soil types. It is a generic term for remedies, which are much more varied, innovative and strange than simple 'ash' would imply. In Zionist understanding they are distinguishable from traditional remedies by their church context and association with Holy Spirit.

Mud, sand, water, ash and clay are not the only land-derived natural substances marking territory and supporting the symbolic world of the SCC in Zion churches. Zionists fashion instruments, inspired by biblical precedent and mission church example, to control spiritual forces. The most potent of these is the *sondeza* (cross or rod,[14] as it is often referred to in translations of the Old Testament). *Sondeza*, carried by the priest and other senior members of the Zionist churches, are made of wood or metal, and among priests may be topped by horse brasses or other decorative insignia. Thus the brasses are transformed from another culture to serve a new purpose as a result of dreams or 'prophesy'. (Sometimes aesthetics, not dreams, govern the choice of insignia as when I was asked to send horse brasses from the UK on my return from Swaziland.)

Water, mountains and other elements of the wild are frequently mentioned together in 'prophecies' for healing. For example, a ten-year-old child is advised to fetch water from a waterfall; to find a chicken with which to pray for the water; and then to go to the mountains where the grandmother will dig a hill (*isiduli*) and bury the sacrificed chicken in whose blood the child has been washed – a practice abandoned in some SCC branches. From here the child has to go, without looking back – a subliminal recollection perhaps from Genesis in which Lot's wife is told not to look back but does so, and is turned into a pillar of salt. Swazi people also traditionally believe that disaster befalls a person who looks back.

In another oral history, a SCC church founder recalls a dream in which he was standing in a pool of water preaching and people came from all directions to hear him. He interpreted this to mean he was full of God's power, like John the Baptist with whom Zionist preachers easily identify as baptizers of new converts. In using the purifying agent of water, he is also engaging another manifestation of the Holy Spirit.[15]

Waterfalls, also, are used to pound and wash away the demons believed to afflict a person.

Both flora and fauna are enlisted as symbols in the spirit world. Animals are believed to be part of the spiritual world of both Zionists and traditionalists. Certain animals must be kept away from Zionist territory. They may be blamed for miscarriages in cattle or people, or used in healing. Baboons and snakes, believed to be the familiars or incarnations of sorcerers or *batsakatsi*, are sought out in people's homes by the Zionists. The unfortunate iguana, for example, normally low in the scale of value accorded to living things, acquires a special role as an object of sacrifice and a source of healing.[16] In situations of church poverty, trees substitute for church buildings; eucalyptus leaves and branches for church walls.

Linguistic Clues

Linguistic clues as to how features of landscape and climatic factors serve the needs of the SCC in Zion are contained in names. *Abakamoya* denotes their association with the Holy spirit or possession by ancestral spirits; *Inyoni* simultaneously means lightning, bird, and spirit (Kuper 1947); *moya* carries the connotation of a 'breeze' or 'wind'. The Zionists' alternative identity as *umoya oyincwele* from the Xhosa *ngcwele*; meaning clear (as in clear or pure water), indicates their frequent association with water. This is transformed in meaning from the traditional idea of water spirits, or the biblical idea of water as a manifestation of the Holy Spirit. In Swaziland, the Komati, Usutu, Umbuluzi and Ingwavuma rivers supply the water requirements of the Zionist churches just as they supplied the subsistence, settlement and purification needs of the Ngwani and Ndwandwe nations in the nineteenth century.

The predominance of water in SCC rituals is matched by similar use of water in religious rituals world-wide. In Africa it is true for the Aladura churches and traditional religions in West Africa, South Africa and Botswana, where the Zion churches have been called 'people of the water' or 'water churches', due to the water used in baptism, infant blessing and purification. For the Tshidi Zionists, who live in an area short of water, pools of water hold terrors, so baptism is a terrifying experience for new members (Comaroff 1985). This does not appear to be the case for those church members of the SCC, whom I have observed dancing and singing down to a river prior to baptism, the ceremony being conducted quietly without signs of terror.[17] A non-Zionist commented that some spaces by rivers were no-go areas, because they were specifically used by Zionists for healing and baptism. Innocent meddling with objects of healing there could lead to violent unnatural experiences. Adults and children might expect to see monsters in the rivers at these places. It is conceivable, however, that this is part of outsider mythology about unfamiliar religious practices.

Land, Church and Livelihood

Land identified with subsistence is common to Zionist and non-Zionist. It involves a degree of territoriality, varying from portions of land allocated to Zionists by chiefs for farming, trading or resettlement farms. Christian Zionist livelihoods are sustained from vegetable growing and cattle herding in the middle veld, to small-scale cotton and sugar cane growing in the low veld, or intermediary services like retail stores.

Not all Zionist members are farmers. Occupations vary from casual labourer, bricklayer, baker, factory worker (pineapple canning), employment with the Royal Swazi police, potter, to prison warden. There is a clear admixture of rural and urban occupations.

Zionist farmers have often been singled out by technical officers from other farmers because they were seen to be keen to improve their farming, seeking success and unafraid of outdoing their neighbours. They are often the owners of modern utilities such as fridges or cars. I attribute this to the feeling of safety from sorcery, by means of which jealous neighbours might want to penalize their success. This safety is often ensured by symbolic ritual to protect space or territory.

When they are not helping with weeding in the field and cooking food for their families, women of the SCC extend their traditional use of landscape in homestead and farm to set up as small traders selling homegrown fruit, craft work, vegetables on roadside stalls or in custom-built markets. The younger women of the SCC are typically schoolgirls or tend their father's cattle until they are free and have funds to go back to school. (Older women are not permitted by Zionists, nor by traditional Swazi, to tend cattle, which are a symbol of wealth, and must avoid them if in mourning.) Other young women work as domestic servants in Swazi, English and Afrikaner households – a likely influence towards changed aspirations. Three-quarters of the members of one SCC church I interviewed had entered skilled and semi-skilled occupations within the urban districts. Sustenance was mediated through cash as well as subsistence crops. A potter and young prophet referred to himself as a 'scientist', thus identifying himself with the new technical age.

That Zionists enter the occupations of the cash or urban economy is partly a reflection of land shortage and the trusteeship of a large proportion of land by the King of Swaziland and his henchmen, and partly to ensure that their children can go to school and learn the necessary skills to earn a living. Territoriality for subsistence is thus restricted for Zionist church leaders and members – not only by custom but also by economic circumstances. Population increase brings in its wake the reduction of land available for subsistence farming.

Presidents of the SCC (Bishops Mcina, Zwane, Motsa, Vilakati, Lushaba) have been farmers and have encouraged their members to farm, though this has not excluded other occupations such as taxi driving, the occupation of one SCC president's sons. Elias Vilakati, recently deceased leader of the Jeriko church ('denomination', as he called it), owned a tractor and ran a farmer's cooperative where he supplied milling and fertilizer distribution services. Another Jeriko church leader worked for an irrigation company, but as a diviner or *isangoma* on certain afternoons (a practice observed by Daneel [1971] among the Shona Zionists). In the manner of a chief, Vilakati received tithes of mealies (maize), goats, cows, wheat, nuts and chickens; a practice supported by Leviticus 27: 30–4; Deuteronomy 26: 1–14 and Malachi 3: 7–12.

Biblical Derivations of SCC Identity and Territoriality

The Holy Spirit, a biblical concept, has a territorial dimension in that it is believed to ward off hostile forces from spaces associated with Zionist churches and their members. (Zionist Church members are known as *Abakamoya* or 'people of the Spirit'.) It has several manifestations, not only in water, wind and fire but also in the form of possession, common to traditional diviners. It is confirmed as different and as having a biblical identity by its mention in passages of the Old and New Testaments. These manifestations support traditional Swazi Zionist concepts of Spirit as power and as a gift or quality of personality. At the same time they support Zionists' use of Swazi concepts for Christian purposes in Luke 24: 29, Acts 1: 8, and as Spirit directly bestowed by Jesus in John 20: 22: 'he breathed on the disciples and sayeth unto them, Receive ye the Holy Ghost'. In Isaiah 63: 11–14 the Holy Spirit leads the prophets to both anger and rest. In Joel 2: 28 the Holy Spirit is revealed in dreams and visions: 'and it shall come to pass afterward that I will pour out my spirit upon all flesh; and your sons and daughters shall prophesy, your men shall dream dreams, your young men shall see visions'. In Joel there is mention of coming miracles and the promise of deliverance for 'whosoever shall call on the name of the Lord . . . for in Mount Zion and in Jerusalem shall be deliverance'. Thus particular places and parts of the landscape are symbolic of, and identified with, the Kingdom of God. Swazi mountains are treated as being close to God.

Charismatic gifts, contained in Corinthians 1: 14, refer mainly to the Holy Spirit manifest in character and behaviour, and are very important in the Zionist churches. The call to 'follow after charity and desire spiritual gifts, but rather that ye may prophesy' is a key sentence for Zionists. It supports the idea of a scale of spiritual progress in a member in whom possession and speaking in tongues may only be a beginning. Overall the outward manifestation of the members' belief in these qualities of the Holy Spirit is identified by outsiders and insiders as the primary way in which the SCC manifests itself as a coherent group. Another way is their association with features of landscape such as mountains, water and forests.

Healing activities, too, have a spatial 'landscape' as well as a biblical referent. Their pattern is ordained in the sacred confines of the Church, and is concluded in pools, rivers, waterfalls or on mountains and may be assisted by the ash from a tree struck by lightning. They are justified for Zionists by reference to Mark 16: 15–16 about preaching the gospel to every creature; baptism, casting out devils and spirits; speaking in tongues; 'taking up serpents'; immunity from poison; laying hands on the sick. The reference to safety from snakes in this passage is important to Swazi people whose culture holds that ancestors appear and do harm in the form of snakes (Kuper 1947; Snook 1973). The Jeriko church is criticized for using snake symbols in church ritual. A Jeriko member would not feel it incongruous for God to convey a message through a snake medium, or to appear as a snake, even though traditional belief holds they frequently denote the presence of witchcraft. In the Book of Isaiah, God commands Moses to catch a snake by the tail; it turns into a sacred 'rod' or 'staff', thus providing biblical precedent.

Whether SCC leaders are literate or non-literate, their knowledge of the Bible is important symbolically for the members. They can help to make sense of biblical phenomena by referring to, and acting in, similar features of local landscape. On the wing of the church seemingly closest to the traditional religion, the Jeriko church, the founder Elias Vilakati (d. 1997) supported his conversion history at every point with, sometimes inaccurate, biblical references. Landscape features were as common in his account as they are in the Bible, with Mt Zion, Mt Sinai and the story of Moses. Vilakati occasionally cited passages incorrectly when he described receiving the Spirit, being told by God to repent and to become a preacher throughout the land. He received visions and messages from the Holy Spirit while on the mountain where he lived and established his headquarters.

Territorial Dimensions in Cultural Practices of the SCC in Zion

Members of the SCC in Zion are clearly identified by their uniforms – white coats for men, blue or green uniforms and white collars for the women. Jeriko Church members wear red, in breach of the formal constitution of the SCC in Zion. (Red is a colour worn by choirboys of the Church of England, but it is traditionally associated with danger in Swaziland.) Blue and green are connected with the natural environment, with water and fertility, while white is the colour of the Holy Spirit and purity. There is a territorial dimension to the uniform in that it is appropriate for a particular territory and ritual, has to be protected from contamination by hostile forces, and must not be touched by animals such as frogs. King Sobhuza II persuaded the chiefs to let Zionists wear Western clothes if they wished at traditional ceremonies, but Zionists are not rigid in their rejection of traditional dress and rituals. At the Easter ceremony, the *Igoodi* held at the Lobamba Royal Kraal especially inaugurated for the Zionist and other African churches, they can wear their own uniforms. Zionists officially maintain a critical attitude to Western clothing – from bell-bottomed trousers to skirts above the knee – one priest saying that such clothing reveals that 'although a man is a believer, there is more to him than that'. Modest Western dress is considered part of mutual respect and good manners among Zionist people. Such an attitude would set Zionist Christians apart from many Swazi, who have happily adopted Western styles of clothing while adding new designs and interpretations of their own.

The tension between traditional Swazi culture and the relatively new culture of the Christians is played out in the tensions between chiefs and Zionist priests. These are of cultural identity, such as dress codes and religious beliefs, as well as those of territoriality and claims to people's allegiance. In earlier decades the prominent role of Zionist priests was seen as a threat to the power of chiefs. The priests played an advisory and healing role for their grateful members, which potentially could undermine that of chiefs on Swazi Nation land. By the 1970s the tensions between these alternative cultures had eased with chiefs sometimes attending Zionist churches. Church and chief were encouraged by King Sobhuza II to cooperate in maintaining harmony in the community. One priest, knowing that a few Zionist leaders have assumed almost chiefly powers, tried to express their proper role thus: 'The role of the chief in the community is different from that of the priests. The chief has authority over the area in which the chief operates and the people he is working with, while the priest has authority in church.'

Some tension is generated by the work ethic promoted in many SCC in Zion congregations, confirming once again the connection Weber saw between religion, hard work and the rise of capitalism. The hard work has often been connected to land, but its success has depended on the symbolic control of hostile forces supposedly opposing that ethic by agents of the traditional culture. Zionist members who ask for prayers to bring them money are told that this will be done on condition they work hard. The son of Andrew Zwane, a founding leader of the SCC in Zion of South Africa and president from 1942, said his father used to encourage members to farm: 'He used to do this both in church and outside it because God bade all people work hard for their living. Other preachers encourage their members in the same way because Bishop Andrew Zwane did, and because farming is beneficial. Money can be obtained from it' (Joseph Zwane 1971, interview).

The SCC in Zion churches are generally recognized as healing churches, but in a manner and within a Christian set of beliefs that distinguish them from traditional healers – *isangoma* (herbalists) or *tinyanga*. Their healing activities involve both temporary and permanent expressions of territoriality, the latter being those which take place in the sacred space of the church and which tend to be diagnostic as well as instrumental. The temporary expressions appropriate space and resources outside the church to implement the directions from 'prophecy' or diagnosis. Bathing of the 'patient', for example, might be done by women in the protected confines of a Zionist homestead. I suggest, therefore, that there is an important territorial aspect, as well as symbolic difference from Western and traditional procedures, in the healing rituals of the SCC in Zion churches. Although some priests are not rigid in the view, Zionists are urged to keep out of the modern hospital territory in which many Zionists believe patients risk certain death. A former secretary of the Zwane division of the SCC in Zion said: 'Most people come to this church because of ailments which have resisted the cures of doctors, herbalists and diviners.' He cited Mark 16: 15–18 as the biblical sanction for the healing activities of the Zionist priests and prophets: 'And these signs shall follow them that believe; in my name shall they cast out devils; they shall speak with new tongues; they shall take up serpents; and if they drink any deadly thing, it shall not hurt them; they shall lay hands on the sick, and they shall recover.'

It was suggested earlier that the making of noise is one of the intangible, but nevertheless intrusive, ways of expressing territoriality. A separate identity can also be reinforced by the manner of the noise, singing and dancing which might be distinguishable from the absence or presence of noise in other groups. Noise made by a group is associated with either temporary or permanent appropriation of space; the assumption of the right to make noise beyond the normal confines of a building is also a temporary assumption of territory which intrudes on others' assumption of rights to the same territory. Outsiders frequently perceive the Zionist Christians as 'noisy', singing and dancing all night long and depriving people of sleep; processions are accompanied by drumming, with its resonance of traditional culture and witchcraft. Drumming for Zionists discourages the approach of witchcraft and evil spirits, especially in night-time processions and services. The noise irritates and causes disdain among outsiders. For the Zionists noise is part of the energy and enthusiasm needed to awaken the Holy Spirit in the prophets. It is a concomitant of the healing process as explained by a young prophet:

> The Zionists expect that if they make a lot of noise the Spirit will stir, in at least one
> person, the ability to divine that another person is suffering from a certain illness; in the

same way a doctor can diagnose that you have an illness without you telling him what it is. The noise acts as a stimulus to the Spirits of the Prophets.

Thus, Zionist churches provide an example of how noise can be used to control space, but also how it can build up hostility among outsiders and give rise to something like ethnic conflict.

Childbirth customs in the SCC churches demonstrate how the territory of the church is used as a mediator of values and particular beliefs about purity and danger in giving birth. These differ from traditional customs, and differ between the various Zionist churches. The initial focus, in a SCC Zionist church, is on the family in which the child has been born, for whom an all-night thanksgiving service is held. And then the child is taken to the church. At one SCC church headquarters (Ekuphumuleni Zion) babies up to one month old are considered unclean and dangerous and only permitted into church after this time. Not all Zionist denominations accept this custom, nor does it reflect Swazi custom which holds that a baby born naturally is not dangerous. In another church a girl baby is brought to the church to be blessed after one month and a boy after six weeks. Thus the concept of the church as inviolable territory is maintained. If a child dies before it is blessed, however, it is still given a normal Christian burial.

A mother of a new baby, on the other hand, is considered unclean. She has to be confined indoors for seven days after giving birth. The baby is kept out of the church for the same period but is not in itself considered unclean.

Marriage customs also provide another window on how church space can be used to show approval and disapproval in ways which separate Zionist methods from those of the traditional religion. Zionist marriage not only differs from the traditional in not following the complicated ceremonial initiation, but also in not accepting polygyny except for new members from polygynous homes. They also usually do not follow the customs of the levirate and sororate. Of polygyny, an SCC Zionist priest in the Transvaal said that the rules of the SCC were as follows:

> you are a believer and you come to join us . . . being a polygamist we allow you in and welcome you. We do not have a right to make a man forsake his children and wives. If we did that God would punish us. If on the other hand, you join this church having one wife only, the rule is that you remain a monogamist and with your original wife. If you marry a second wife, we punish you and make you sit by the door of the church, because the constitution of this Church does not allow polygyny. Your punishment might last for six months or even a year and you will be persuaded to reject the second wife because otherwise you will foul the Church of God so that tomorrow's people will say 'The Church of so and so is a church of polygamists.'

A similar use of church space is when a girl becomes pregnant out of wedlock. An SCC Zionist priest explained the procedure, which might include sitting by the door during services, rather than at the centre of activity:

> Should a girl become pregnant while a member we usually suspend her from attending services for six months. If the boyfriend pays the damages she is then reinstated. This is constitutional. If the girl is about due and the damages have still not been paid, we don't suspend her in case she dies during childbirth in the midst of her suspension. We just wait until she gives birth and start all over again. We encourage the two parties concerned to get married (Interviews 1973).

In reality, boyfriends often leave without compensating the girl (often they cannot raise enough animals or cash for *lobola* — marriage exchange), which is symptomatic of the way in which the interdependence of kin is being replaced by less stable and varied economic and social options. Many non-Zionist women have said that in spite of having children they preferred not to get married. The Zionist churches, while acquiring a reputation for unorthodoxy, especially among the youth, provide some means of preserving the rules, precepts and views of previous generations, albeit with public exposure of transgression and token punishment.

Services are not generally held in the home, as reported to be the case with the Full Apostolic Holy Church (Comaroff 1985). Priests of the SCC, and Bishop Mncina, felt it was important to have a separate space or church for religious services, even if this were close to the living area. This was explained as discouraging aberration and unchristian practices, which could arise in the private domain of the homestead.

One of the clearest examples of territoriality in the SCC in Zion churches is in their measures to combat *batsakatsi* (sorcery), often aided by *tinyanga* (witch doctors). This differs from the use of space to maintain values in behaviour, to demonstrate the central role of healing, or to accord respect to the Zionist priest. The SCC in Zion churches have a social role in combating anti-social witchcraft and sorcery, and in providing an alternative system of belief. Witches and sorcerers are believed to operate as a permanent group organized within a hierarchy based on their evil achievements. They operate at night but are conscious by day of their nocturnal activities, their actions being evoked by specific situations for which they obtain the assistance of *tinyanga* to afflict an enemy (Kuper 1946).

The Zionists depend on the divining and diagnostic power of the Holy Spirit to combat the activities of the sorcerers (*batsakatsi*) which threaten homes or success in work. Thereafter they use not only counter-magical techniques, but offer forgiveness. If the forgiveness is desired and accepted by the offending party, then a ceremony of healing and cleansing for all the people affected will follow. Medicines of the sorcerer or *inyanga* are burned to symbolize his forsaking the old for a new way of life in which the Holy Spirit has been demonstrated to be more powerful.

The traditional system, by contrast, is unforgiving. It uses retaliative medicine (*Lizekwa*) to destroy a person believed to have deliberately caused a death. It would be considered quite ethical to afflict a thief with swollen joints and to punish an adulterer with a wasting disease.

One of the headquarters of the SCC in Zion, Ekuphumuleni Zion, illustrates this opposition of practice and belief and the consequential struggle for territoriality. Not only is it close to ancestral graves through which a railway line has been driven, but is central to an area of herbalists, sorcerers, diviners and people who have left the churches. It consists of a considerable number of Jeriko households and two Jeriko churches that are known to be involved in various forms of witchcraft. While witch doctors (*tinyanga*) are busy in June and July collecting their medicines, the Zionists are alerted to collect their counter-medicines of sand, salt and beach water. They also gather *manzana* (mud from the geysers and hot springs), which they sprinkle round their homes to protect them from the evil plans of the witch doctors, sorcerers and their clients. Typically sorcerers or their assistants try to breach the territoriality of people's homes by planting medicines in or near them. In addition they would be attributed with causing cars to overturn, physical illness, and electric shocks. Zionists of the SCC in Zion believe that a person going into the home of a witch doctor could fall down dead on entering, but that a Zionist prophet is immune and can divine where all the medicines are hidden, whether in the house or the grounds.

Conclusion

Land or space has been proposed above as the primary basis for territoriality, temporary or permanent, or in intangible forms such as 'noise'. It is also proposed that territoriality is one of several expressions of a symbolic association or separate identity. Analysis of the SCC in Zion suggests that territoriality can be expressed temporarily or permanently by the symbolic allocation of space to different actors, or through the ritual use of substances that protect people and their activities in a particular area. Through religious association it can be free of physical boundaries. The SCC in Zion is guided by biblical example – territoriality is expressed within and outside churches, in and around homesteads. These are, through symbolic action, turned into sacred spaces hostile to evil forces. Territoriality is manifest in sites regularly used for cleansing and baptism, such as waterfalls and mountains. It is marked by types of house or church, by flags with identifiable Zionist designs that fly from the roofs of Zionist homesteads to blow away hostile spirits.

Shared with other groups, however, is the politically arranged background to all the work of churches and members. Within that system it has, until recently, used land at the behest of chiefs. Landscape or topography, as distinct from land as a resource, is also part of Zionist Christian identity as the overall and essential scene of mountains, rivers and pools, plains and waterfalls within which church activities take place. It is a reflection of biblical landscapes which reinforces members' sense of having a Christian identity. It is a source of substances for symbolic activities and healing, as well as being a source of continuity with the traditional past and the unfolding future.

Members of the SCC in Zion of South Africa may not have a conscious political agenda, and may have forgotten the historical origins of their practices, but many of their beliefs and activities seem to have been motivated by a spirit of distaste for the restraints of both traditional custom and the excesses of the capitalist lifestyle. Their sense of an independent identity may partially substitute for the absence of formal political power. It may even guide and influence the powerful, but it also derives from a reaction to a society which appears to be losing moral direction and descending into violence, not least of which is that caused by excessive drinking of modern alcoholic drinks. The landscape, meanwhile, is a material and historically layered background which reinforces their sense of identity. It is also a source of symbols, which enables the SCC in Zion and member churches to perform as a distinctive, innovative, largely life-enhancing, compensatory movement for the aspiring poor.

Notes

1. This study finds a link between the minimal land rights of the majority of Swazis, especially women, and the territorial control of the central Dlamini clan. In Levin's view, Hilda Kuper's anthropological study of the Swazi aristocracy legitimized and reinforced its control over land and other resources. But it is likely to have helped rather than hindered the Zionist churches whose greater tolerance of Swazi traditions found favour with King Sobhuza II and the Queen Mother (Indlovokati)
2. Along with Cohen's other works, this explores the ethnic character of religious groups, including relationship to place.
3. Steven Mavimbela and Andrew Zwane were the rivals for the overall presidency, but it is said that Steven Mavimbela (with more schooling) yielded precedence to Zwane. Within the SCC other presidents were attracting the following and respect given to chiefs. (e.g. Luke Lushaba, Ephraim Motsa, Elias Vilakati).

4. Murdoch *et al.* (1971). These maps derive from a study of geological formations and associated soil and vegetation types. In my chapter, a link is also found between these features, the highest concentration of rural population, the presence of royal residences and Zionist churches. Murdoch also mapped approximate clan areas in the 1950s, which are currently being brought up to date.

5. Announcement by Swaziland's Prime Minister to the Swaziland Society on UK visit, September 1998.

6. Strang (1997) illustrates admirably how completely different views of land can form the basis of conflict, but in this case eventually lead to an interchange of skills and softening of the profit motive among the cattle rangers.

7. Swaziland has mountains, pools and rivers which are essential to rituals of cleansing and baptism. In the Bible the mountain is a symbol of God's kingdom; water, fire and wind are symbols of the Holy Spirit, and, therefore, present in many Swazi Zionist rituals and religious expression.

8. This is a dominant message in Comaroff (1985), though it refers to Tshidi churches in South Africa.

9. Funnel (1996).

10. Funnel (1991).

11. Vilakati's visions were especially inspired by Old Testament prophets like Isaiah, and by Revelations. Whether or not he saw beyond the superficial statements, the mountain features strongly in his vision and experience. A mountain symbolism features in Isaiah 2: 2 'And it shall come to pass in the last days, that the mountains shall be established in the top of the mountains and shall be exalted above the hills; and all nations shall flow unto it.' In scriptural symbolism a mountain means a kingdom (see also Daniel 2: 35; Revelations 13; 17: 9–11). A reference in Revelation 13: 1 to a beast with seven heads and ten horns, bearing ten crowns, refers to ten kings, and the last form a Gentile world power; a ten-kingdom empire covering the sphere of authority of ancient Rome. Revelations 13: 1–3 refers to the ten-kingdom empire; verses 4–10 to the emperor, who is the beast. This can be construed as a political statement.

12. Water, fire, wind and speaking in tongues are symbols of the Holy Spirit described in Acts 2–4, 'and there came a sound from heaven as of a rushing, mighty wind, and it filled all the house where they were sitting' . . . 'cloven tongues as of fire, and it sat upon each of them' . . . 'they were all filled with the Holy Ghost, and began to speak with mother tongues, as the Spirit gave them utterance'. After Pentecost the Spirit was imparted to the Jews who believed in the laying on of hands (another Zionist church practice); when Peter opened the kingdom to Gentiles, the Holy Spirit was given to all who believed.

13. Information from a prophet of Ekuphumuleni Zion – an area troubled a lot by sorcery and witchcraft and close to an area where a railway line runs through ancestral graves.

14. In the Old Testament Aaron's rod is taken to symbolize Christ raised from the dead because it budded, blossomed and yielded almonds, where those of the tribe-heads (authors of other religions) remained dead. Several references are made to a rod with miraculous powers in Exodus 4: a serpent turned into a rod (4: 4); the rod used to make signs (4: 17); and reference to 'the rod of God' (4: 20) in the hand of Moses.

15. Waterfalls are also used to clear a person of evil or malevolent spirits.

16. In the Bible animals are also given negative or positive ritual significance, the negative often deriving from health and practical considerations.

17. Comaroff)1985: 200–1) discusses the symbolism of water both for the indigenous symbolic system and for the Zionist scheme, where identities are redrawn, a unity of spirit is established and 'thirst' is quenched through the symbolism of water.

References

Banks, M. (1996), *Ethnicity: Anthropological Constructions*, London: Routledge.

Barth, F. (1969), *Ethnic Groups and Boundaries*, Boston, Mass.: Little Brown.

Bonner, P. (1983), *Kings, Commoners and Concessionaires*, Cambridge: Cambridge University Press.

Cohen, A. (1974), *Two Dimensional Man*, London: Oxford University Press.

Comaroff, J. (1985), *Body of Power: Spirit of Resistance*, Chicago: Chicago University Press.

Daneel, U. L. (n.d.), *Old and New in Southern Shona Independent Churches 1971/74*, Leiden.

Doveton, D. (1977), *The Human Geography of Swaziland*, New York: AMF Press.

Funnel, D. C. (1991), *Under the Shadow of Apartheid*, Aldershot: Avebury.

—— (1996) *The Swazi Land Deal*, Aldershot: African Affairs.

Hobsbawm, E. and Ranger, T. (1993), *The Invention of Tradition*, Cambridge: Cambridge University Press.

Kuper, H. (1947), *An African Aristocracy: Rank among the Swazi*, Oxford: Oxford University Press.

Levin, R. (1997), *When the Sleeping Grass Awakens: Land and Power in Swaziland*, Johannesburg: Witwatessrand University Press.

Murdoch, G. Webster, R. and Lawrance, C. J. (1971) *Atlas of Land Systems in Swaziland*, Christchurch, UK: University of Oxford.

Obeyeskere, G. (1995) 'Sinhalese-Buddhist Identity in Ceylon', in De Vos and Romanucci-Ross (eds), *Ethnic Identity Creation, Conflict and Accommodation*, Palo Alto, Calif.: Mayfield.

Snook, J. (1973), *African Snake Stories*, London: Macdonald and James.

Strang, G. (1997), *Landscapes, Values and the Environment*, Oxford: Berg.

8

From Cattle Herding to Cultivation — from Territoriality to Land

Michael Saltman

This chapter refers specifically to the connection between ethnicity, on the one hand, and land and territoriality on the other. The case study is not one of a conflict situation over the issue of land between opposed ethnic groups. No group is being rallied, on the basis of its ethnicity, to identify with a political cause. It is, rather, an issue of how a people were obliged to reassess their attitudes towards territoriality and land as a consequence of changing socio-economic conditions. The problem, as such, becomes that of a legal issue, by means of which individual rights in land had to be defined. Prior to these changes, it was the whole society that held collective rights over a territory.

Law is one integral component of a people's culture. The particular way in which people resolve their disputes is a part of the shared understandings of the members of that society. Even if people cannot always comprehend the complexities of the law, they have a mutual comprehension, together with others, of what is right and wrong, what is just and what is unjust. Their culture and their social structure define, to a considerable extent, the very nature of the disputes that they have to resolve in their everyday lives. Many legal scholars do not equate these shared understandings with the law, but this chapter is not designed to enter the battles of legal theory on this issue. Rather, it is designed to illustrate how a people have employed their shared understandings in order to adapt to a radically changing situation involving land, territoriality and identity. Changing historical circumstances, and particularly changes in the economy, require a redefinition both of the problems leading to disputes and the shared understandings employed to resolve them.

A brief, initial delineation of the problem is as follows. The Kipsigis of south-western Kenya were, in the past, cattle herders. The circumstances created by the onset of British colonial rule in East Africa towards the end of the nineteenth century forced the Kipsigis to live in reserves. The economy more or less imposed upon them by the colonial authorities was that of maize cultivation, reducing cattle herding to a secondary occupation within the resultant mixed agriculture. This caused two major changes in the Kipsigis' perceptions of space and attitudes towards land. In the first place, land in itself has no intrinsic value for cattle herders. It contains resources that are of value – grass and water – but the space itself is not necessarily an owned commodity and is very often merely moved over in migratory passage. It is perceived as 'territory' that belongs to the society at large, rather than as 'land' which belongs to defined groups or individuals that make up the society. But under conditions of cultivation, the concept of land ownership becomes a real one. In the Kipsigis case the transformation was a particularly acute one, for they insisted on maintaining their herds at the same time as they cultivated. From the very outset of the establishment of the Kipsigis reserves by the British, the subsequent adoption of maize cultivation and, later, other cash crops, land had to be fenced off to protect against the incursions of the cattle. And yet there were no legal precedents or standards that could offer solutions to the disputes that inevitably derive from the concept of the private ownership of land.

Selected historical variables, assumed relevant for the arguments of this chapter, are as follows. Pre-colonial history, as detailed by Langat (1969), Peristiany (1939) and Orchardson (1961), indicates a long period of migration southwards from an undetermined area in the Sudan. By the end of the seventeenth century the Kipsigis had arrived at the northernmost border of their presently occupied territory and had achieved the final conquest of the whole area by the middle of the nineteenth century. Initially, the Kipsigis drove out or killed the indigenous inhabitants, known as the Sirikwa. But to establish control over the territory, more serious fighting took place between the Kipsigis and the neighbouring Gusii, the decisive outcome of this fighting being a Kipsigis victory at Chemoiben in the middle of the eighteenth century.

The successful conquest of territory does not necessarily mean that the Kipsigis possessed an efficient military machine controlled by a centralized polity. Political and military activity should rather be more appropriately viewed within the politically acephalous nature of the society. Kipsigis military organization was far from efficient. There were originally four named 'regiments' (*poriosiek*), recruitment into which was organized through the age sets. Each regiment was associated with a given territorial area and fought independently of the others, often giving rise to a weak and sometimes conflicting strategy. The Kipsigis suffered resounding defeats in the late nineteenth century – first against the Gusii in the battle of Ngoina, which Langat dates at the middle of the century, and second against a combined force of Gusii, Watende, Luo and Kuria at the battle of Mogori, *circa* 1890. The basic political unit in Kipsigis society is a local territorial grouping, known as a *kokwet*. There are no wider political units above this level. Each *kokwet* is autonomous in handling its own affairs.

The salient features of Kipsigis pre-colonial history that ultimately bear reference to Kipsigis 'legal thinking' are, in the first place, a long period of migration during which it is reasonable to assume that cattle played the most important role in their economy. Second, the acephalous nature of the Kipsigis polity was reflected both in its military organization and in the high degree of local autonomy at the level of the *kokwet*. These two factors will be referred to below, as case material is being analysed. The factor of cattle relates to the nature of disputes, while the factor of a non-centralized polity bears a direct relationship to the logic of Kipsigis legal thinking.

For the same purpose of analysis, two other factors are isolated from the colonial context. The British established their rule over the Kipsigis within a relatively short time-span of seventeen years. The economic effects of this have been discussed by Manners (1967) and Pilgrim (1961). From the outset it was clear that an underlying tenet of British policy towards the Kipsigis was the transformation of the predominantly pastoral economy to one of 'peasant' cultivation. The British appropriated Kipsigis grazing lands, granting them to white settlers, ostensibly to form buffer zones between the Kipsigis and the neighbouring tribes. The justification, as always, was the imposition of the *Pax Britannica*. The Kipsigis were confined to a 'reserve', but insisted on maintaining their herds. Administrations, everywhere, prefer settled cultivators to independent cattle herders constantly on the move. The size of the herds became a point of contention between the administration and the Kipsigis to the extent that the Governor of Kenya, Belfield, wrote to Harcourt of the Colonial Office complaining of the Kipsigis' pernicious pastoral proclivity.[1]

The second historical factor that bears even more directly on Kipsigis 'legal thinking' was the imposition of English law on the territory. In addition to the establishment of a system of courts, the British recognized a principle of indirect rule by means of which they would not get over-involved in disputes between natives. This law stated: 'In all cases civil and criminal *to which Africans are parties*, every court shall be guided by African customary law so far as it is applicable and is not repugnant to justice and morality or inconsistent with an Order in Council or any written law' (my italics).[2] The significance of this provision is that, theoretically at least, a case decided on the basis of customary law could be appealed up to the highest courts in the land and even to the Privy Council. But what was perhaps even more important was that the magistrate's court, in dealing with a civil matter between Africans, would, *de facto*, require a prior hearing at the level of the jurisdiction of the customary law. This in turn means that customary law, falling within the above definition, was now state-sanctioned; the implications of this will be discussed below (see pp. 164–65).

A brief and selective reference will be made to the salient features of Kipsigis social organization, again on the basis of what is considered relevant to the parameters of this chapter's arguments. Descent is agnatic, marriage is polygynous and exogamous, and residence is neolocal. Thus, family structure is based on neolocal patrilineages that are further organized within a wider group of totemic patriclans. The factor of neolocality disperses and weakens the patrilineage, both as an economic and a political unit, one of the consequences of which is that a plaintiff or a defendant presses his case as an individual, rather than appearing with representation and a show of force from the patrilineage. The patrilineage is non-corporate, and plots of land are owned by individuals.

Kipsigis live in territorial units known as a *kokwet*. It would be a misnomer to translate that word into the notion of a 'village'. The typical *kokwet* is dispersed along the ridge of a hill, some distance being maintained between the households. Natural boundaries (e.g. streams, lines of trees) mark the beginning and the end of a *kokwet* and the *kokwet* has a name. People who live in the vicinity of a boundary of the *kokwet* may also feel a sense of belonging to the neighbouring *kokwet*. There is no characteristic size to a *kokwet*. I worked in three *kokwotinwek*,[3] the smallest being twenty-one households comprising 121 persons in an area of some three square miles. The second site contained fifty-five households and 335 persons distributed over four square miles. The most densely populated of the three was again within four square miles, but included within it 130 households and 762 individuals. The layout of a *kokwet* in the area of the former 'reserve' is a random layout, plots of different sizes in their natural topographical contours. Land, formerly owned by white settlers, that has been redistributed to the Kipsigis within the framework of Settlement Schemes, takes the form of neatly parcelled rectangular plots. While the term *kokwet* denotes a territorial unit, it can have two other contextual meanings. It can refer to a group of people, within the territorial unit, who come together for some act of economic cooperation. It is also the group of men that meets in order to resolve a dispute.

Politically, the *kokwet* is autonomous. There are no traditional wider political groupings of a hierarchical nature. There are no defined political authorities. There are, however, 'civil service' chiefs (rather than indigenous ones) who operate together with other functionaries within the state's administrative institutions, to which the Kipsigis are, of course, subject. But the relative autonomy of the *kokwet* is based on the existence of age sets, which accord significant, political influence to those who are senior. There is a cyclical rotation of seven named age sets. An age set is opened up for a period of fifteen years, during which time all those initiated annually are received into that set. A new set is then opened for the next fifteen years. At any given point of time there will normally be representatives of four age sets in a *kokwet*, although it is theoretically possible that five age sets might be represented. The members of the senior age sets are the bearers of political influence in the society. This fact ties up with the third meaning of the concept *kokwet* in its judicial capacity, as mentioned above. For the most senior members present at such a forum will ultimately formulate the decision, unanimously handed down by all present.

In order to understand Kipsigis legal thought, it is necessary to remind the reader that this is an acephalous society, in which there are no institutions that can enforce *kokwet* decisions through coercive sanctions. At the very best, there are informal sanctions that involve ostracism or supernatural sanctions. Ultimately, the absence of coercive sanctions converts the judicial process into one of arbitration rather than adjudication. Compromises resolve disputes more effectively than unilateral decisions. Three indigenous concepts make up the basis of what might be termed Kipsigis jurisprudence. The Kipsigis word for 'law' is *pitet,* that, in a different contextual sentence, could also mean 'nature'. The word describing 'law-breaking' is *sogorge.* Informants were asked to supply sentences using this word, and one such sentence employed *sogorge* to describe a cow that eats meat. If law reflects the natural order of things, then an event of its transgression is unnatural. The third relevant concept is *chupge,* which means to 'curse oneself'. This natural automatic curse is reinforced in some instances, especially in the case of witchcraft, by the public curse, pronounced by an elder (Orchardson, 1961: 18–19).

An apt illustration of these three principles is given in the following case. A plot of land in the vicinity of Kiplelji had been traditionally used by the people of Kiplelji for common grazing. The earth on this particular plot had a high salt content, which was considered beneficial for the cattle. Arap Temuge, an ex-'civil service chief' who lived in Kiplelji, laid claim to this plot of land and fenced it off for his own use. He based his claim on the fact that he had planted black wattle trees on this land some twenty-five years previously and thus had (what may be termed) usufructuary rights over his trees and the land on which he planted them. The people of Kiplelji, ignoring the fences that now enclosed the plot, continued to bring their cattle to graze and use the salt lick. In response to this, Arap Temuge's son, Joshua, placed thorns at strategic points on the plot in order to cause injury to the feet of the cattle. A number of complaints were sounded against Joshua and he was summoned to a meeting of the *kokwet* to answer for his action. But Joshua refused to attend. Given his absence, the meeting of the *kokwet* produced no practical result. Although the opportunity for cursing Joshua at this meeting was a real one, it did not happen. It was rumoured, however, that a number of old men cursed Joshua privately. A few months later, Joshua was killed in an accident.

The above account of this case is a condensation of the main elements of verbatim accounts given by three informants. In these accounts all the informants employed the concepts of *pitet, sogorge* and *chupge,* or derivatives of them, referring respectively to the status of the common grazing land, Joshua's act of spreading the thorns and injuring cattle and, finally, the ultimate cause of Joshua's sudden demise.

It is of particular interest to note the actual sequence of events that took place in this instance. The act of fencing off the field was of little concern to the people. They merely broke down the fence at a certain place in order to gain entry to the plot. Joshua's actions caused a great deal of resentment, but no effective action was taken against him apart from the rumoured curses. Joshua, in taking note of the public opinion against him, did not place any additional thorns on the plot, which now reverted to its traditional usage. As soon as the original state of affairs had been restored, the impression gained was that nothing had really happened at all. The news of Joshua's accident was accepted calmly, most people saying, with a quiet sense of satisfaction, that he had brought it upon himself. No specific rules had been invoked throughout the incident, and from, admittedly, a highly impressionistic point of view the whole sequence of events was perceived as something quite natural (Saltman 1977).

The actual procedure for resolving disputes is straightforward. The case is always held at the place where the events under deliberation took place. The group of people that gather, the *kokwet*, in its judicial sense, usually comprises a core of senior age-set members that invariably take part in these proceedings. But the number of people attending varies considerably, depending on the gravity of the issue and its relevance for the community at large. The complainant states his case briefly, and likewise the defendant replies. The two of them are then sent away to a spot a few hundred metres away within hailing distance. Witnesses are then asked to give evidence and are questioned by the gathering. Occasionally, one or both of the litigants are recalled to be questioned. The *kokwet* then begins its discussion of the matter, the senior representatives rendering their opinions first until a consensus is reached. The litigants are then recalled and are asked if they accept the decision. If the answer is in the affirmative, then the matter is closed. If not, however, and one or both sides are recalcitrant, the *kokwet* reconvenes – time and time again, if necessary – to provide alternative solutions until both sides are satisfied. The logical implications of this procedure are that we have a process of arbitration that searches for compromises, rather than a process of adjudication that provides a unilateral decision. But the traditional judicial mechanism, in the absence of coercive sanctions, could not always necessarily come up with a negotiated settlement, and we should be aware of the fact that many disputes remain unresolved.

In the past there had been coercive sanctions, and even capital punishment that was carried out by the immediate agnatic relatives of the wrongdoer. Conceptually, the Kipsigis made no clear distinction between what we understand as the difference between criminal and civil law. Today, the imposition of state law and the application of coercive sanctions are fully understood. Again, in contrast to today, the past reliance on supernatural sanctions has diminished and the weight of public opinion no longer has the same efficacy that it once possessed. The courts provide an alternative avenue for the resolution of disputes that is perceived by many as being more efficient and effective.

Returning, however, to one of the historical variables mentioned above, the British had recognized customary law as valid, when the parties involved were Africans. The magistrate's court, apart from dealing with cases brought directly before it, also essentially becomes the first court of appeal for *kokwet* decisions. In fact, the magistrate's court would not normally hear a civil case unless there had been a prior hearing at the *kokwet* level, and representatives of the *kokwet* had to appear and inform the court of that decision. An examination of court records over a twelve-month period[4] revealed that out of 104 civil cases heard before the court that involved a prior *kokwet* decision, the magistrate accepted 59 per cent of the those decisions, while rejecting only 16 per cent. In the remaining 25 per cent of the cases he accepted the *kokwet*'s decision in principle, but modified its terms in one way or another.

What in effect was happening was that the court was backing up the decisions of the *kokwet*. In the long run, this enabled the *kokwet* to make unilateral decisions rather than having to go into the complexities of finding negotiated and arbitrated solutions. Magistrates' courts in Kenya were equipped with a set of two volumes entitled, *Restatement of African Customary Law – Kenya*, edited by Eugene Cotran (1968, 1969). In accordance with government policy, magistrates were appointed to their jurisdictions in tribal areas that were not their own. It was the most efficient way that a magistrate from one tribal group could familiarize himself with the customary law of another tribal group. Cotran set up law panels for each tribal group, comprising former presidents and members of African courts and other specialists such as chiefs or elders. On the basis of questionnaires and discussions he compiled the codification that is the basis of the *Restatement*. The Kenyan Attorney-General, writing in the Foreword to Volume I, makes it clear that the *Restatement* has no statutory effect. He views it more as a guide that would enable the application of customary law. In fact, the magistrates often used the *Restatement* as if it were a statutory instrument, which again contributed towards the issuance of adjudicated, unilateral decisions rather than the traditional compromises.

But the *Restatement* did not refer to land law, which constitutes an issue in its own right and is relevant to the theme of this chapter. As noted above, the Kipsigis, prior to the colonial period, were pastoralists and for pastoralists the concept of land is radically different from that of cultivators. What is more meaningful is the idea of territory. Maybe 'terrain' would be a more appropriate concept, for territory has more of a political implication. Since the subject of this volume is Land, Territoriality and Identity, the idea of 'territory' is understood in the context of this chapter as spatial rather than political. In the past there had been no notion of landownership. Cattle were owned property, characterized by complex ownership rights, and were driven over wide expanses of territory on which there was usually no lack of natural resources – grazing and water. Territory was certainly contested on an inter-tribal basis, although cattle-theft was a more economically profitable occupation. The extent to which, if at all, territory was contested between Kipsigis is not known. The inter-tribal wars in the pre-colonial period might indicate that the Kipsigis perceived a political definition of a territory that was theirs as opposed to it belonging to others. The political limits of a territory under those circumstances were the lines beyond which the Kipsigis could no longer advance because of resistance.

The British created a new reality. In establishing the Kipsigis 'reserve' they had in fact created a politically defined territory, which was now clearly associated with the tribal identity. The Kipsigis began to understand the concept of land when the British took it away from them and reallocated it to British settlers. The spatial concept merged with the political. The *Pax Britannica* did not allow for tribes to move out of their tribal areas. Ostensibly, the white settlements were to constitute buffer zones between the warring tribes. But what ultimately came to be known as the 'White Highlands' were choice portions of arable land given to the settlers. At this early stage of colonization the Kipsigis hardly regarded themselves as the 'owners' of the territory they had been allotted as the 'reserve'. But as time passed they regarded themselves as the ex-owners of the territories that had been alienated from them for the benefit of the white settlers.

The Kipsigis pernicious pastoral proclivity, mentioned on p. 161 was the prime factor that brought about land enclosure. The maintenance of large herds of cattle was not compatible with cultivation, which, over time, was going to be the mainstay of the Kipsigis economy. Even if cattle were to become secondary as an economic resource, they were still highly valued for their social importance – for contracting marriages, for establishing social ties with other Kipsigis, as well as for their aesthetic appeal to a traditionally pastoral people. Crops had to be guarded against the ravages of cattle, making land enclosure an inevitable process.

When serious cultivation began around 1925, maize plots were unfenced. There was at that time a substantial amount of litigation over damage to crops by roaming cattle, and it became obvious that the enclosure of these plots was inevitable. According to Pilgrim, it was members of the junior age sets who expanded their landholdings for cultivation *circa* 1935 (1961: 50). At that time these men were young, mission-influenced and were being encouraged by the administration to engage in serious cultivation. The reaction of the senior age sets was, for the most part, to move away. The other alternative has been stated by Pilgrim: 'The means of stopping a man from extending his area of cultivation was to establish by a dispute in court that he had no right to cultivate beyond certain limits from where another's rights began. This setting of boundaries between neighbours and the planting of hedges, or building of fences which is entailed, was the beginning of enclosure' (1961: 50).

Manners has pointed out that the initial process was of an *ad hoc* nature (1967: 295). Only a few individuals initially engaged in 'land grabbing' and established their claims by ploughing large tracts of land, irrespective of the fact that these tracts were way beyond their subsistence needs. One of Manners' informants justified the process of fencing on the grounds that land used for subsistence cultivation in the past had been fenced off (1967: 293–4). Within a few years virtually all land became enclosed, causing a serious problem of overstocked cattle on insufficient grazing ground. Land disputes became frequent, and even though one might expect that in the absence of indigenous land law, resolutions would be sought in the native courts, this was not the case. Pilgrim notes that in the year 1935 only five cases of land disputes were taken to the Native Divisional Court in Buret, and from then until 1945 no other land cases for that court were recorded. Pilgrim goes on to state, 'it appears to have been the policy of the District Administration in letting developments of individual property rights over land take place through the action of indigenous authorities, so long as it seemed to be proceeding with reasonable efficiency and equitably in that way' (1961: 50). Insofar as equity was concerned, both Manners and Pilgrim note definite inequities in the apportionment. Some people gained large tracts throughout the reserve, others gained nothing and even lost. The members of the senior age grades, during that period, who were the more substantial cattle-owners, were inclined to move away from the enclosed areas in order to seek land for unlimited grazing.

One of the main implications of land enclosure is that of land ownership. He who encloses land is essentially laying claim to that piece of land. Insofar as the Kipsigis were concerned, there were no prior rules governing the ownership of land, apart from a single custom, to which reference will be made below. As long as land was freely available for enclosure, the transition to land ownership was slow and uncomplicated. Kipsigis did not rush into cultivation. Many pastoralists throughout the world, including the Kipsigis, regard farming as a demeaning and unappealing occupation. 'Ownership' began to constitute a problem as land grew scarce and the Kipsigis found themselves competing with each other in the process of land enclosure. As it became clearer that the economic future was going to be that of cultivation, 'land grabbing' began on a serious scale and disputes over land ownership became the order of the day. Neither the *kokwet* nor the colonial administration had the tools to resolve these disputes.

The Kipsigis had always engaged in a secondary form of cultivation on an extremely minor scale. This was the cultivation of certain kinds of grain in the immediate vicinity of a man's house. The limited purpose of this cultivation was for the manufacture of home-brewed beer, which plays a very important role in Kipsigis social life. It was a shared understanding among the Kipsigis that cattle owners would be held liable if they allowed their cattle to stray onto these small plots and damage the crop. But this in no way implied that the land on which the crop was being grown was 'owned' in any sense of the word. Any implication of tort referred to the damage caused to the crop. This liability held as long as the damaged party was cultivating his plot. As soon as he stopped the cultivation, the land reverted back to the public domain and cattle could roam over it at will.

The customary perception of the legal status of land approximates the idea of a usufructuary right. As long as he is using it, working it, he has the exclusive right to do so. As soon as he ceases to use or work it, the right ends and the land reverts once again to the common weal. This principle was extended and extrapolated in order to resolve the plethora of disputes over land ownership during the initial period of 'land grabbing'. If a litigant could demonstrate a greater intent to use the land than his opponent, he would win his case. Not only would he win his case, he would win it unilaterally to the complete exclusion of the other side. This is a far cry from the traditional outcomes of Kipsigis dispute settlement – arbitration and compromise. The precedents grew naturally out of the principle, an escalation of qualifications required to define 'greater intent to use land'. If two men laid claim to the same plot of land, the one who could demonstrate that in fact he was actively enclosing the plot was deemed to be showing greater intent of future use and thus won his case. But as it became common knowledge that the act of 'enclosure' constituted the decisive criterion, there was a corresponding increase of cases in which both parties to the dispute were enclosing the same plot. If, however, one of the litigants could demonstrate greater intent of usage by simultaneously enclosing and clearing the field in preparation for its use, he would obtain the edge over his rival. The constraints became progressively more sophisticated as they escalated. The building of a hut on the plot demonstrated the element of the owner's intent as regards future permanency of interest. But the construction of Potemkin-like empty huts had, in the long run, to give way to those huts within which a wife and children could be installed.

The legal implications of enclosure were felt soon after the physical process of the enclosure had more or less been completed. Even though the shared under-standings, as described above, served to resolve the disputes pertaining to the process of enclosure itself, there were no criteria for dealing with the problems of land inheritance. In addition to this, many hundreds of Kipsigis were demobilized from the army at the conclusion of the Second World War. These men returned home to find that they either had no land at all or that an inadequate portion had been put aside for them. The *kokwotinwek* were in no position to handle cases of this nature, and the native courts faced a spate of these cases from 1945 onwards.

Initially, the elders had one sole principle governing land tenure from the pre-enclosure period. A man had rights over a piece of land as long as he was working it. Absenteeism would disqualify that man's rights, even if he had enclosed the land. Men could still maintain plots in different places so long as they had a household in residence on each plot and members of the household actually worked the land. But inheritance constituted a difficult problem. The only existing customary rules relating to inheritance referred to the inheritance of cattle. In essence, these rules stated that after putting aside a number of head of cattle for ceremonial purposes, plus additional cattle for the support of widow(s), as well as *kaniyok* (brideprice) cattle for unmarried sons, the rest of the cattle is divided equally among all sons. Without considering the problems of land fragmentation, or the virtues of primogeniture in the prevention of land fragmentation, the elders adopted the principle of the equal distribution of land among all sons. This analogy of equality in inheritance surely derived from the custom of equality in the inheritance of cattle.

As long as the original plots were sufficiently large, the first series of inheritance disputes, as well as the litigation brought by the returning soldiers, were by and large dealt with to everyone's satisfaction. But with the passage of time the problem of land fragmentation loomed large as a consideration in the judicial process. The courts had not yet worked out an adequate position *vis-à-vis* land inheritance that could resolve the problem of fragmentation. Dissatisfaction with decisions, rendered on the basis of the simplistic solution of equality in land inheritance, achieved expression in a sudden rise of appeals to District Officers and the African Appeals Court during the period 1952–7. Whereas the normal volume of appeals in all cases was 1–2 per cent, the volume became 25–30 per cent in land inheritance cases during that same period (Saltman 1977: 80–1).

In response to this situation, the administration convened a Kipsigis Law Panel, comprising Kipsigis elders in the main part, to formulate a statement of land law. This statement would constitute the basis for recommended municipal laws to the County Council of the Kipsigis. The report was submitted in four parts, the third part of which refers to land inheritance. The preamble to this section shows the clearest break with tradition:

> [T]he Kipsigis, who by tradition and custom were nomadic pastoralists, have never had customs regarding inheritance of land. They had, and still have, customary rules regarding the inheritance of livestock, but the Law Panel does not consider that the principles governing these rules can be applied to land inheritance. The Law Panel is therefore faced with the task of formulating rules in regard to the inheritance of land which are in conformity with current thought and might be acceptable to the tribe as a whole. In formulating these rules the members of the Law Panel were deeply conscious of the dangers of land fragmentation and recognized that at all costs, this deadly process must be avoided. With this, the Law Panel declared the following principles . . .

A series of detailed procedures and rules relating to the inheritance of land follows, the most important element of which is the definition of a 'minimum economic holding'. This is defined as fifteen acres in the high grassy zone and as twenty-five acres in the lower, more arid zone. Such a holding is deemed indivisible.

The provisions for achieving an equitable system of inheritance in the event of a piece of land being indivisible are as complex as any contemporary Western codification of law. Under no circumstances can they be perceived as customary law and, if anything, constitute a very definite break with pre-existing custom. The complexity of these provisions is such that they defy sensible application at the *kokwet* level. Some of the provisions, such as one demanding that every landowner make a written will, have no bearing on the reality of the Kipsigis situation. That these rules were not adopted at any level is quite clear. In the *kokwet* of Kiplelji, it is fitting testimony to the non-adoption of these rules that, at the time of the field study in that *kokwet,* only 18 per cent of the plots were above fifteen acres, while 39 per cent of all plots were less than five acres.

Neither did the courts apply the recommendations of the Law Panel. On the other hand, Cotran's *Restatement of African Customary Law*, used by the courts as noted above, is brief in its reference to land. But the statements are loosely defined, leaving the magistrate with considerable discretion as to their interpretation.

The Nandi and Kipsigis did not have customary land laws and are in the process of evolving rules of land law at the moment. Subject to this, in cases of disputes that arise today in relation to the inheritance of land, the courts apply the following principles:

1. The sons share the land equally, subject to the proviso that, where the land to be divided is less than an economic unit, the court may direct that the elder sons should seek land elsewhere and be compensated for their share by the youngest son. What constitutes an economic unit should be left for the court to decide.
2. No specific portion of the land is set aside for the widow, but she is entitled to cultivate part of the share of the younger son. Her entitlement terminates on her death.
3. The daughters are not entitled to any share of the land. They live with their mother until they are married.

Referring back to the court statistics, cited above, twenty-seven of the 104 cases recorded were cases over issues of land. Eighty-nine per cent of the land cases involved a prior *kokwet* decision as opposed to 59 per cent of prior *kokwet* decisions in the total sample. The overall rejection rate of *kokwet* decisions was 16 per cent, whereas in the land cases that figure fell to 12 per cent. He also accepted 67 per cent of the prior *kokwet* decisions without imposing any modifications, which is significantly higher than the 59 per cent overall unqualified acceptance for all categories of cases. While twenty-seven cases do not constitute a significant sample, it still confirms the trend established through participant-observation field study of the *kokwet* in its judicial capacity. This revealed that the settlement of land cases was being effectively carried out by the *kokwet,* and that the result was land fragmentation. A necessary conclusion appears to be that the development of land law among the Kipsigis has arisen through the modification of pre-existing custom rather than as a result of introducing alien concepts into their legal culture.

It is interesting to note how an indigenous shared understanding is transformed into consistent precedent, by means of which problems created by a new reality can be resolved. The terms of reference were those of Kipsigis perceptions. It was an original solution to a problem from alien sources. There was an objective difficulty for Kipsigis to transform their way of thinking from territoriality to land.

Translating this into familiar terms enabled them to conceptualize the problem subjectively and to facilitate a solution. Law is part of a people's identity, an idea developed in some detail by Savigny (1814).

In arguing against Thibaut's proposal for a single and unified code of law for the German States, Savigny claimed that law cannot be made by an interstate committee. In propounding his concept of *Volkgeist*, Savigny states that law is not made by a committee of draughtsmen, but that it grows from a people's experience and character. It is what he describes as 'a common feeling of inner necessity'. Savigny's point of departure is that the true nature of law is to be found in customary law. Stone, quoting Savigny, states the following:

> All law is originally formed in the manner in which in ordinary but not quite correct language, customary law is said to have been formed; that is, it first developed by custom and popular faith and only then by juristic activity. Everywhere, therefore, by internal, silently operating powers and not by the arbitrary will of the law-giver (Stone 1966: 95).

This is apparently true. Kipsigis customary law, as most other legal cultures of customary law, is based on shared understandings. By means of these shared understandings, that are culture-specific (a less pretentious concept than *Volkgeist*), Kipsigis were able to resolve disputes on a consensual basis, even in the absence of coercive sanctions.

When Savigny writes of a people's 'experience and character' or of a 'common feeling of inner necessity', he is obliquely referring to their normative shared understandings. Bohannan (1965) has discussed the relationship between norms and law. He writes of a process of 'double institutionalization' that gives rise to law *per se*. A norm is institutionalized into a custom and a custom is reinstitutionalized into a law:

> All institutions (including legal institutions) develop customs. Some customs, in some societies, are re-institutionalized at another level; they are restated for the more precise purposes of legal institutions. When this happens, therefore, law may be regarded as a custom that has been restated in order to make it amenable to the activities of the legal institutions (Bohannan 1965: 35–6).

The critical points, where these changes take place, are when the shared understandings no longer hold, or where there are no shared understandings from the outset. The Kipsigis had no customary shared understandings as to land ownership for the simple reason that land was never 'owned'. At the point where land ownership became a part of the Kipsigis reality, shared understandings were brought into play to resolve disputes. The colonial authorities, imposing a situation that would implicitly lead to land ownership, had not legislated any land law in order to resolve disputes. The only shared understanding about land was the 'usufructuary' principle (see p. 167). The double institutionalization of the principle can be clearly seen. Initially, it was a shared understanding applying to the damage caused by grazing cattle on a man's usage of land for growing millet for making beer. But if its original intent was to resolve issue of torts, it had to be restated in order to apply to land ownership. As previously quoted, Bohannan has written 'they [the shared understandings] are restated for the more precise purposes of legal institutions'. The principle, as demonstrated, was restated over and over again as the basic shared understanding had to be reformulated to meet the ever-growing complexity of litigants' cases.

For many of the societies discussed in this volume, land and/or territoriality play an important role in the formation of a sense of identity. But identity, in the Kipsigis case, is not a question of either land or territoriality. Identity, or specifically what Savigny called the *Volkgeist*, as expressed in the way Kipsigis resolve their disputes, has its sources elsewhere. The absence of centralized political authority, itself conditioned by the Kipsigis lack of identity with land, characterizes the mode of legal thinking employed by the Kipsigis – that of arbitration and compromise rather than adjudication. Coupled with this was an economy based on cattle and, thus, a natural proclivity to engage in disputes over cattle. As objects of dispute, cattle lend themselves more easily to equitable compromise than does land. For head of cattle can be divided and the future progeny is also divisible. Land fragmentation, beyond a certain point, is economically self-defeating, thus making compromise an inefficient mode of legal reasoning insofar as land disputes are concerned.

The process of double-institutionalization was achieved when the courts gave their formal backing to the *kokwet* decisions in land disputes. Bohannan echoes Savigny, when the latter writes, and I requote

All law is originally formed in the manner in which in ordinary, but not quite correct language, customary law is said to have been formed; that is, it is first developed by custom and popular faith and only then by juristic activity. Everywhere, therefore, by internally, silently operating powers and not by the arbitrary will of the law-giver (quoted in Stone 1966: 95).

Savigny's point was that legal change must take into account the continuity of social experience and its accumulated expression within the legal ideas of the society. This is an integral part of a people's culture; and I equate culture with ethnicity. As already stated, it was not land or territoriality that conditioned the ethnicity of the Kipsigis. It is rather a way of thinking, socially and culturally conditioned, that provides the basis of Kipsigis ethnicity. It was this ethno-cultural specificity that provided the adaptive legal remedies for the radical changes that took place in Kipsigis' adaptations to the changing economic scene.

Notes

1. Land Office Document 2740. Communication from Belfield to Harcourt, 3/4/1914.
2. Article 20, East Africa Order in Council 1902.
3. *Kokwotinwek* is the plural form.
4. Silibwet/Bomet magistrates court, July 1968 to July 1969.

References

Bohannan, P. (1965), 'The Differing Realms of Law', *American Anthropologist*, Special Issue, 67(6): 33–42.

Cotran, E. (1968), *Restatement of African Customary Law – Kenya*, Vol. 1: *The Law of Marriage and Divorce*, London: Sweet & Maxwell.

—— (1969), *Restatement of African Customary Law – Kenya*, Vol. 2: *The Law of Succession*, London: Sweet and Maxwell.

Langat, S.C. (1969), *Some Aspects of Kipsigis History Before 1914*, NGANO Nairobi Historical Studies, Nairobi: East African Publishing House.

Manners, R.A. (1967), 'The Kipsigis of Kenya: Culture', Change in a "Model" East African Tribe , in J. Steward (ed.), *Contemporary Change in Traditional Societies*,

Vol. 1, Chicago: University of Illinois Press.

Orchardson, I. Q. (1961), *The Kipsigis*, Abridged, edited and partly rewritten by A. J. Matson, Nairobi: East African Literature Bureau.

Peristiany, J. G. (1939), *The Social Institutions of the Kipsigis*, London: Routledge and Kegan Paul.

Pilgrim, J. (1961), *The Social and Economic Consequences of Land Enclosure in the Kipsigis Reserve*, (mimeographed), Kampala: East African Institute of Social Research.

Saltman, M. (1977), *The Kipsigis: A Case Study in Changing Customary Law*, Cambridge: Schenkman Publishing Co.

Savigny, F. K. von (1814), 'Über die Notwendigkeit eines allgemeinen bürgerlichen Rechts für Deutschland', in A. F. J. Thibaut, Civilistisch Abhandlungen, Heidelberg.

Stone, J. (1966), *Social Dimensions of Law and Justice*, Sydney:Maitland Publications.

9

Land, Territory and Identity in the Deterritorialized, Transnational Caribbean

Jean Besson

The 'Caribbean experience' has been invoked as a paradigm for the post-modern world. For example, as Bill Maurer (1997) notes, James Clifford challenged Claude Lévi-Strauss's vision in *Tristes Tropiques* (1961) of 'an invincible monoculture embracing the entire world' since the Second World War by arguing that:

> Alongside this narrative of progressive monoculture a more ambiguous 'Caribbean' experience may be glimpsed. In my account Aimé Césaire, a practitioner of 'neologistic' cultural politics, represents such a possibility – organic culture reconceived as inventive process or creolized 'interculture.' The roots of tradition are cut and retied, collective symbols appropriated from external influences. For Césaire culture and identity are inventive and mobile. *They need not take root in ancestral plots* [my emphasis]; they live by pollination, by (historical) transplanting (Clifford 1988: 15, references omitted, quoted in Maurer 1997: 10).

Simultaneously, the Caribbean itself has been portrayed as characterized by the absence of regional and national identities, resulting from the eradication of indigenous populations and the fracturing of the region through long and pro-nounced colonization (Mintz 1971a, 1989; see also Thomas-Hope 1984). This crisis of identity has been linked to the themes of deterritorialization, flight and exile – such as migration, marronage,[1] the Rastafarian movement and the concept of 'adventure' (e.g. Olwig 1987; Campbell 1980; Barrett 1977; Wardle 1999) – and to the 'shallowness' of kinship and the 'weakness' of community (Wagley 1960: 8–9; Mintz 1971a: 38–9; Beckford 1972: 76–7), and to 'a high degree of indiv-idualization' (Mintz 1989: xviii; see also Young 1993).

In partial contrast to these perspectives and to Clifford and Césaire, this chapter shows how the 'Caribbean experience' of deterritorialization, flight and exile, invention and creolization has itself taken 'root in ancestral plots' in Caribbean lands and Caribbean territories as a basis for forging transnational identities. This paradox is reflected in return- and circulatory-migration, and in creole land tenures which enable all descendants of the original landholder – whether male or female, migrant or resident – to retain inalienable rights to 'family land' and common land. These enduring landholding systems, based on such unrestricted cognatic descent,[2] have linked generations through time and space in the face of 500 years of globalization and dispersal through forced and voluntary migration.

The first part of this chapter outlines the 'crisis of identity', which has been identified for the Caribbean region and especially for the island of Jamaica, and highlights the related themes of exile, marronage, migration and adventure. The second section explores the seemingly contradictory processes of Caribbean creolization and invention. The third part of the chapter integrates these two preceding themes by focusing on my fieldwork in the west-central area of Jamaica,[3] exploring how the paradox of alienation and creation is crystallized in the ancestral land of kin groups and communities. The fourth and final section widens the analysis by charting parallels throughout the Caribbean region and by engaging with Maurer's (1997) 'recharting' of the 'Caribbean experience'.

The 'Crisis' of Caribbean Identity

As Sidney Mintz has noted, the essence of the Caribbean *oikoumenê*[4] is the forging, through historical processes, of this societal region as Europe's oldest colonial sphere, and the responses of the colonized, including rebellion, marronage and cultural resistance (Mintz 1970, 1971a, 1971b, 1974, 1989, 1996a). The lengthy and pronounced colonial impact, involving the conquest of territories by different and often rival European powers – Spanish, Dutch, Danish, British, French and Swedish[5] – has however also been seen as fracturing the region. Over thirty years ago, Mintz (1968: 310) argued that '[A]ny effective pan-Caribbean consciousness is still lacking, in large part because of the traditional cultural links between particular islands and their former or present mother countries.' At the turn of the millennium, there are still Dutch and British colonies (for example, the Dutch Antilles, the British Virgin Islands and Montserrat) and French overseas *départements* (French Guiana, Guadeloupe and Martinique)[6] in the Caribbean region.

Elizabeth Thomas-Hope has likewise highlighted the colonial fragmentation of the Caribbean region and the related crisis of identity:

The colonial fragmentation of the region meant that the term *West Indies* evolved to denote a group of colonial enclaves, each the possession of a European power . . . The region's identity therefore, became associated with distant metropoles; the inhabitants, their colonial subjects; the institutions, the derivations of other cultures; . . . The term West Indies and its implied connotations robbed the region of any acknowledged character of its own, so that even the local creation of new cultural forms, new identities of interest and affiliations went unrecognised. The people in the region itself, well tutored in the views of their colonial overlords, saw themselves through the eyes of Europeans, as European subjects. Later, in reaction to this, but still looking outside the region for a local identity, they found some satisfaction in stressing their ancestral roots in Africa and Asia. (Thomas-Hope 1984: 1)

The Rastafarian movement, with its central concepts of 'Zion' and 'Babylon' denoting the African homeland and exile through slavery in Jamaica, has been seen as the most extreme manifestation of the latter theme (e.g. Lowenthal 1972: 250); while a parallel has been drawn between the Rastafarian movement – whose exile-ethos has spread throughout the non-Hispanic Caribbean (Campbell 1985; de Albuquerque 1980) – and the Jamaican tradition of 'flight' or marronage (Barrett 1977: 30–8), which was widespread in African-America (Price 1996).

Thomas-Hope's path-breaking work on the establishment of a Caribbean migration tradition after Emancipation highlighted the significance of emigration for the ex-slaves in attaining a sense of freedom. In an early article, focusing on the movements from the British West Indies to the Hispanic Caribbean territories in the century after Emancipation, she concluded that '*[O]nly* through emigration could the former West Indian slaves attain the sense of freedom for which they yearned' (Thomas-Hope 1978: 66; emphasis added). In that article emigration was seen as the unique alternative to plantation agriculture, as it was argued that '[T]he estates held the worst of past memories, and *even on small-holdings there was no deep-felt attachment to land*' (ibid.; emphasis added). Thomas-Hope (1980, 1986, 1992, 1995) has since shown that this British West Indian migratory tradition typifies Jamaica and the eastern Caribbean islands, especially the Leewards, up to the present time, while her overview of Leeward Island movements has highlighted the parallel between migration and marronage (Thomas-Hope 1995). Focusing on the Leeward Island of Montserrat, Stuart Philpott (1973) has likewise argued that West Indian societies are 'migration-oriented'.

In addition to the fracturing of Caribbean regional identity, Mintz (1971a: 20, 1989: xiii) has identified 'the prevailing absence of any ideology of national identity that could serve as a goal for mass acculturation' as a defining feature of the region. He portrays the problem of national identity as being most pronounced in the non-Hispanic Caribbean (Dutch, French and British) variant[7] – especially in the British territories (Mintz 1971a: 34–5, 1989: 251–328). Mintz's argument is paralleled by Lowenthal's (1972: 250-92) analysis of the crisis of 'racial and national identity' in West Indian (that is, non-Hispanic Caribbean) societies. Lowenthal opens his discussion by referring to the elite, the middle class and the Rastafarians in Jamaica:

> A striking feature of West Indian identity is the low esteem in which it is locally held. West Indians at home often wish they were not West Indian . . . The wish is often realized in imagination; they easily persuade themselves they are something else. This delusion is most prevalent in the elite and middle class, but the desire extends throughout the social order; both Kingstonian suburbanites and West Kingston Ras Tafari believe themselves to be citizens of some remote land . . . Instead of rejecting the system, West Indians deny their own identity. (Lowenthal 1972: 250)

Likewise, Olwig's initial portrayal of the Leeward Island of Nevis (part of the independent state of St Kitts-Nevis) was of '[A]n externally-oriented society' (1987: 154), where nationhood does not rest on an 'innate attachment to the native land' (ibid.: 153) and where even for those not 'able to emigrate, the extra-local field of social and economic relations will probably continue to be a more relevant framework for life than a nation state' (ibid.: 169). Most recently the uprooting theme has been elaborated, in the Jamaican context, in terms of a narrative of flight and 'adventure' (Wardle 1999).

Caribbean Creolization and Invention

Despite Mintz's (1971a, 1989) preoccupation with the absence of Caribbean regional and national identities, his work on the region also richly portrays a process of creolization and cultural invention. Mintz argues that: 'Caribbean creolization began five centuries past, with migration and resettlement, forced transportation, the stripping of kinship and community, the growth of individuality on a new basis, and the appearance of the first true creoles – things of the Old World, born in the New' (Mintz 1996a: 301).

Elsewhere he defines such creolization as a process of 'indigenization' (Mintz 1996b: 43) or localization, entailing the invention or re-creation of culture in new social contexts, rooted in the adaptation and/or resistance of the slaves and their descendants (Mintz 1974, 1989, 1996a; Mintz and Price 1992). Indeed, Mintz (1980: 15) has argued that the Caribbean region reflects 'the most remarkable drama of culture-building in the modern world' (see also Mintz 1996a).

For Mintz, this 'drama of culture-building' has especially occurred in the new social contexts of Caribbean 'reconstituted' peasant adaptations created in response and in resistance to the plantation system (Mintz 1989: 132–3).[8] These peasant formations include the 'squatters', the 'early yeomen', the 'proto-peasantry', the 'runaway peasantries' or maroons, and post-slavery peasant adaptations persisting to the present day (Mintz 1989: 146–79; see also Besson 1995b). The 'squatters' were of 'mixed cultural and physical origins' (Mintz 1989: 147): escaped slaves (early maroons), free persons of colour and white deserters, who created new creole cultures by drawing on Arawak, African and European traditions. They emerged from the early post-Conquest period in the sixteenth-century Greater Antilles colonized by Spain. Such peasantries, who were escaping from colonial control and the early Hispanic plantations, squatted illegally in the interiors of these large islands (Cuba, Hispaniola, Puerto Rico and Jamaica), where they were largely self-contained in terms of production and consumption (with some 'smuggling through illegal ports' (ibid.)), but were sooner or later wiped out by the escalating plantation system. This eradication occurred more swiftly in those territories subsequently seized by the non-Hispanic colonizers, who first intensified the Greater Antillean slave plantations in the late seventeenth and eighteenth centuries; namely, in French Saint-Domingue and British Jamaica.[9]

The 'early yeomen' were the Euro-Creole peasantry that evolved in the Lesser Antilles (such as British Barbados and French Martinique) in the mid-seventeenth century, as Europeans who had served their indenture on early non-Hispanic plantations and received post-indenture land grants turned their backs on the plantations to take up small-scale diversified cultivation for subsistence, also producing 'tobacco, indigo, and other products for European markets' (Mintz 1989: 149). They too, however, were soon wiped out by the escalating eighteenth-century non-Hispanic slave-plantation system (ibid.: 148–51, 1978: 85).

The 'proto-peasantry' (Mintz 1989: 151–2), who were particularly significant for Caribbean culture-building, were African and Afro-Creole slaves who created a peasant-like adaptation within the plantation system itself,[10] in the eighteenth and early nineteenth centuries, especially in the non-Hispanic colonies. Here, with the early burgeoning of the plantation system, the planters faced the problem of feeding their slaves, especially with increasing warfare in the region and the rising cost of imported food. Therefore, wherever topography allowed, planters allocated hilly plantation backlands and mountains, unsuited to growing sugar-cane for export, to the slaves for growing their own provisions. The slaves, however, developed the provision-ground system well beyond the planter rationale, producing surpluses for sale in internal markets beyond plantation boundaries. For example, in Jamaica at the zenith of plantation slavery in 1774, slaves controlled 20 per cent of the island's currency through their marketing activities (ibid.: 199). In addition, the proto-peasant economy was elaborated by the slaves to provide the basis of kinship, community, and customary land tenure and transmission (Mintz 1979, 1989: 180–213; Besson 1992, 1995c, 1995d, 2000). The proto-peasantry would also lead to post-slavery peasantization and to the consolidation of Caribbean culture-building. Such proto-peasantries were especially highly developed in British Jamaica and in neighbouring French Saint-Domingue but also, for example, typified

British Guiana (now Guyana), the French West Indies (especially Martinique), the British Windward Islands (Dominica, St Vincent, St Lucia and Grenada), Monserrat, Nevis and Barbuda in the Leewards, and the Danish West Indian island of St John (Mintz 1979, 1989: 151–2, 180–213; Besson 1992, 1995c).

The 'runaway peasantries', who escaped from slavery and established auto nomous maroon communities beyond plantation boundaries (Mintz 1989: 152–3), typified the entire span of New World slavery and were widespread throughout African-America, as Price (1996) has also shown. Maroon societies lived under constant threat of war from European plantation–military regimes, and were therefore established in virtually inaccessible areas such as mountains, swamps, forests and ravines. Maroons produced for subsistence through hunting, gathering and cultivation; raided plantations for goods and livestock; and sometimes traded surreptitiously at public market-places (Mintz 1989: 152–3; Price 1996; Campbell 1990; Besson 1998b). Some maroon communities were wiped out in war, while others won freedom and legal rights to land through treaties with European colonial governments forced to sue for peace. Such treaties were forged in Brazil, Colombia, Cuba, Ecuador, Hispaniola, Jamaica, Mexico, and Suriname. The most significant and longest surviving maroon societies persist today in the non-Hispanic Caribbean territories of Suriname and Jamaica (Genovese 1981: 51; Price 1976, 1996; Besson 1997).

After emancipation (1838 onwards), and revolution in Saint-Domingue (1791– 1804), post-slavery peasantries emerged in the nineteenth century, evolving especially from the proto-peasant adaptation in the non-Hispanic Caribbean territories. Of particular significance was the exodus of emancipated slaves from the British West Indian plantations after 1838; a flight that was later reflected elsewhere in the Caribbean region, such as in French Martinique and Danish St John after emancipation in 1848 (Besson 1992, 1995c). Jamaica's free village system (Paget 1964; Mintz 1989: 157–79) was the vanguard of this post-slavery peasant movement and such free villages (often founded in alliance with Non-conformist, especially Baptist, missionaries), and other post-slavery peasant communities, persist today throughout the Caribbean region including Jamaica. Through his fieldwork in Haiti and Jamaica, Mintz (1960, 1983, 1989: 180–250, 1996c) has explored the peasant house-yard complex as the nucleus of creole culture, and peasant institution-building in production, marketing and cuisine; while his case study of the Baptist-founded free village of Sturge Town in the Jamaican parish of St Ann pioneered the historical anthropology of Caribbean post-slavery villages (Mintz 1989: 157–79; see also Mintz 1987; Carnegie 1987a; Besson 1987b).

My own research in eight 'reconstituted' peasant communities (see Mintz 1989: 132) in the west-central area of Jamaica, in the parishes of St Elizabeth and Trelawny, bordering St Ann, has developed the creolization and culture-building perspectives pioneered by Mintz (see also Mintz and Price 1992; Price 1996). The communities that I studied include 'free villages', evolving from the 'proto-peasant' adaptation and founded at the vanguard of the Caribbean post-slavery flight from the estates; a 'runaway peasant' community that is the oldest corporate maroon society in African-America; and a currently emerging Rastafarian-Revivalist 'squatter-peasantry'.[11] All these peasant adaptations are still hemmed in by persisting plantations, now reinforced by the bauxite and tourist industries. These communities are also enmeshed in transnational networks and in return- and circulatory-migration. In addition, all the communities reflect the complex articulation of uprooting and rooting in relation to ancestral land, territory and identity.

Jamaican Maroons, Free Villagers and Squatter-Peasants

The paradoxical themes of Caribbean alienation and creation are reflected to a pronounced degree in the west-central area of Jamaica, where I have conducted recurrent long-term fieldwork over the period 1968-98. This area was central to the plantation-slave economy of the island, which by 1700 had become the world's leading sugar producer (Walvin 1983: 35) and which in the eighteenth century (with neighbouring French Saint-Domingue)[12] was one of the two most profitable dependencies the world has ever known – based on the forced migration of African slaves and the continued exile of their descendants in Europe's New World. This exile ethos is reflected in the oral traditions and cosmologies of the communities that I studied. In addition, these communities originate in various forms of flight (marronage, the post-emancipation flight from the estates, and a further flight from a contemporary free village) and are also typified by pronounced traditions of migration. Yet this area of Jamaica also manifests intensive rooting, cultural invention and identity formation (cf. Besson 1995b, 1997, 2000, 2001). These seemingly contradictory themes are crystallized in the creole tenures of ancestral family land and common land which are at the heart of the communities; in the rituals and oral histories focused on these lands; and in return- and circulatory-migration. This section of the chapter outlines these complementary themes. I look first at deterritorialization, flight and exile; then at creolization and cultural re-creation, and the rooting of transnational identities in the 'ancestral plots' of this post-colonial Caribbean territory.

Deterritorialization, Flight and Exile

The Atlantic slave trade provided the main basis of New World plantation labour from the early sixteenth century to the late nineteenth century.[13] This forced deterritorialization and migration entailed the exile of over fifteen million Africans (Inikori 1982: 20), especially from western Africa (from Senegal to Cape Negro (Patterson 1973: 113)), to Plantation-America; and about 'one-third of all enslaved Africans who reached the New World alive' were taken to the Caribbean region (Mintz 1996a: 294), where slavery was most extreme (Mintz 1989: 22; Lowenthal 1972: 41–4). The colony of Jamaica, encountered by Columbus in 1494, conquered by the Spanish in 1509 and captured by the British in 1655, became the most pronounced example of Caribbean plantation-slave society (Williams 1970: 152, 154; Robotham 1977: 46; Mintz 1989: 35). At least 662,000 enslaved Africans were imported to Jamaica (Mintz 1989: 60): especially Coromantees from the Gold Coast (now Ghana), particularly from the Akan-speaking Ashanti people; Ibos from the Niger and Cross delta areas (now Nigeria); and large numbers from the Congo (Patterson 1973: 113–44; Brathwaite 1968: 337–8).

Of these enslaved African men and women, many were taken to the west-central area of Jamaica, including the adjoining parishes of St Elizabeth and Trelawny, where the island's plantation system was most profitable – in the fertile intermontane valleys and on the coastal plains. Here, too, slave resistance became highly developed through rebellion and marronage. These manifestations of exile included the establishment of the Leeward Maroon communities of Cudjoe's Town and Accompong's Town in the interior wilderness of the precipitous *karst* Cockpit Country Mountains straddling the parishes of St Elizabeth, Trelawny and St James, and the 1831 slave rebellion which led to the abolition of slavery in 1834 and 'full freedom' in 1838.[14] The Leeward Maroon polity had earlier gained its freedom by a treaty with the British, in March 1739, after Jamaica's First Maroon War (1725–39) and the defeat of the colonists through guerrilla warfare.

In Jamaica's Second Maroon War of 1795–96, the maroons of Cudjoe's Town (renamed Trelawny Town after the treaty) in the parish of St James were betrayed by the British and exiled to Nova Scotia. However, Accompong's Town (now known as Accompong Town or Accompong), in the parish of St Elizabeth, persists today as the oldest surviving corporate maroon society in African-America and is one of the communities that I studied. Their history of exile and marronage, or flight from slavery, is commemorated in oral tradition and cosmology reaching back to early African ethnic groups and to the 'First-Time Maroons' (Colonel Cudjoe and his Captains, Quaco, Cuffee, Johnny and Accompong) who fought the war and won the peace; and to the Myal slave religion, a spirit possession cult (based on African principles) which was perceived to protect the slaves from the sorcery of exile and enslavement (Schuler 1979; Besson 1995a; Besson and Chevannes 1996). Myalism was likewise seen by the maroons as protecting their flight into the forest, and the Myal Dance or Play is still performed in Accompong each year, on 6 January (said to be Colonel Cudjoe's birthday), to protect the contemporary community by renewing links with the First-Time warrior-heroes (Besson 1995d, 1997, 2000). Oral tradition recounts that the early maroon ancestors were Congos and Coromantees (especially Ashantis) enslaved in Jamaica, who escaped from the plantations on the plains,[15] and that these two 'tribes' (deterritorialized from their African homelands) forged an alliance in the mountain forest against the colonial regime. These African ethnicities are symbolized by cairns and boulders in the bush marking reputed ancient African ethnic burial grounds. Since the building of the rocky road to Accompong Town in the 1940s, a new tradition of flight has typified Accompong; namely, overseas migration to North America and Britain. Today, the Leeward Maroon polity is a deterritorialized transnational community with a dispersed adult voting population[16] of around 3,300 persons – some of whom reside (twice exiled) in London and Bradford, England.

Leeward Maroon traditions of flight and exile also link Accompong to its neighbouring community of Aberdeen in St Elizabeth. Aberdeen is a post-slavery village, which evolved from the proto-peasant plantation-slave community on Aberdeen estate bordering the Leeward Maroon polity. Archival research, fieldwork and oral history interviews locate the founding of post-slavery Aberdeen around 1845 in a migratory movement or flight of ex-slaves from Aberdeen estate to squat on plantation backlands (such as Island Mountain),[17] south of Aberdeen estate and nearer to the plains (Besson 1997, 2000, 2001). Oral traditions in both Aberdeen and Accompong also tell of military and conjugal alliances between the Aberdonian slaves and the early Leeward Maroons, and many modern Aberdonians claim Leeward Maroon descent and have voting rights in the dispersed Leeward Maroon polity. The theme of flight and exile also recurs in contemporary Aberdeen, with the oral tradition of the African-Prince Maroon – a reputed ancestor, in eight ascending generations from the youngest descendants, of a central Aberdonian family line, who is said to have been an African Prince exiled on a slave ship to Jamaica and who then fled from a plantation on the plains into Accompong's Town. Oral history further states that one of his descendants 'came out' from Accompong after Emancipation in 1838 (around 1845) to squat on land in Aberdeen, nearer to the plains. Today members of this descent line are part of the transnational Aberdeen community, dispersed through migration (in the face of persisting land monopoly by corporate plantations and bauxite mines in St Elizabeth) to New York in the United States and to London and Bradford, England. Aberdeen's migratory tradition overlaps with that of Accompong, but stretches further back to the post-emancipation period and the flight of freed slaves from the plantations into free villages and overseas (to Colon in Panama, from which some ex-slaves returned).[18]

The free villages of Trelawny (at least twenty-three were established) were the very vanguard of the flight from the Jamaican and British West Indian estates, in and after the year of Emancipation, 1838 (Paget 1964; Mintz 1989; Besson 1992, 1995c). The five Trelawny free villages that I studied – New Birmingham/The Alps, Wilberforce/Refuge, Grumble Pen/Granville,[19] Kettering and Martha Brae

– were founded, in association with the Baptist Church,[20] in this wider context (Besson 1984b). Trelawny free villagers today are very conscious of this history of the flight from the estates, which is likewise reflected in the naming of some of the communities (as discussed below), and their oral traditions also tell of the exile of their enslaved African and Afro-Creole ancestresses and ancestors. For example, in Wilberforce/Refuge (founded in 1838, named by the English Baptist missionary William Knibb after the abolitionist William Wilberforce, but renamed Refuge by ex-slaves in the context of their flight from surrounding sugar-estates such as Oxford), many of the villagers claim descent (four ascending generations from the oldest living persons) from one of three sisters, or fictive shipmate sisters,[21] brought on a slave ship from Africa to Jamaica and exiled on different plantations. The Refuge ancestress is said to have been taken to Oxford sugar estate, which now borders the free village. Her grandchildren, including slaves nicknamed 'Queenie',[22] 'Poor Man' and 'Hard Time' who were known to elderly villagers, told their grandchildren of the exile of slavery, as recounted to me in the following extract recorded in 1983:

> Of course my grandmother Queenie, she knew a little of slavery . . . The old people told me that in the days of slavery, the slaves lived in little huts, and in the mornings they are called up into a big yard, and they call it a big pen, like how you gather up animals, and you are taken out to work by a task master . . . And they had food in a big long trough for the people . . . And many people were beaten with whips when they did not work, and of course they had a very hard time . . . (quoted in Besson 1984b: 14–15)

Likewise in The Alps, Trelawny's first free village (established in 1838 on a former coffee slave-estate at The Alps in the northern foothills of the Cockpit Country, but named New Birmingham by William Knibb after the English home-town of the abolitionist Joseph Sturge), many of the villagers claim descent from a holy man in Africa, exiled through slavery in Jamaica;[23] other villagers tell of another ancestor who, as a slave boy, was put to work in a plantation hogmeat gang.[24] In the free village of Kettering (founded in 1841 on a former pimento estate, surrounded by sugar plantations, and named after Knibb's home town in England), there are similar oral traditions of slaves exiled in Jamaica. One such tradition concerns a pregnant slave ancestress who was flogged in a pit, with a cat-o'-nine-tails, for refusing to work on nearby Harmony Hall estate; another tradition tells of an ancestress who was a slave girl in a hogmeat gang. In the free villages of Granville (named by Knibb after the abolitionist Granville Sharp, but known by ex-slaves as 'Grumble Pen' due to land disputes in the struggle for land) and neighbouring Martha Brae, established and consolidated in the sugar-plantation heartlands in the mid-1840s, similar oral traditions relate the experiences of exiled slave ancestors and ancestresses, including children, on plantations such as Merrywood, Green Park, Irving Tower and Holland (Besson 1984b, and forthcoming).[25]

In all of these Baptist free villages, which persist today hemmed in by corporate plantations and the burgeoning tourist industry of the world-famous Jamaican north coast, the themes of flight and exile are underlined by the Revival-Zion cult, the Rastafarian movement and a pronounced tradition of overseas migration. The Revival-Zion cult is rooted in the Jamaican Myal slave religion, which was especially strong in the Trelawny plantation heartlands and which, as outlined earlier, was based on African principles and was perceived to protect the exiled slaves from the sorcery of slavery. The Revival cult today (which evolved from the control of Baptist Christianity by Myalism) portrays a spirit pantheon and supernatural causation; the Rastafarian movement (which coexists in these villages with the Baptist church and the Revival cult) highlights exile in 'Babylon' and a spiritual return to Africa or 'Zion'. Therefore (along with the Myal Dance in the Accompong maroon community which focuses on *another time*; namely, the First-Time Maroons and the days of marronage), the creole cosmologies of these villages elaborate the themes of flight and exile by focusing on *another world* (the Revival spirit pantheon) and *another place* (a spiritual return to Africa) (Besson 1995a, 1995b).

Actual migration from these communities, however, has been primarily to Jamaica's capital city of Kingston, and to other Caribbean areas, Central and North America and Britain. Five main patterns of overseas migratory flight, reflecting wider island trends, have typified these communities (especially the free villages) since emancipation in 1838.[26] First, oral tradition tells of migrations to Central America among the emancipated slaves in the nineteenth century. This migration was shaped by labour demand for construction work in Panama on the trans-Isthmian railway and canal and on the Costa Rican banana plantation railroad. The second main movement was to Central America and Cuba in the early twentieth century, to work on the Panama Canal, Costa Rican banana plantations and Cuban sugar estates. The third migration was to the United States, to work in the Manpower Schemes of the Second World War and then on the post-war Farmwork Scheme. The fourth pattern, following the McCarran–Walter Act of 1952 which curtailed immigration into the United States, was the large-scale migration to Britain, especially to England, in the decade 1952-62. The fifth and current trend, following restrictive legislation in Britain in 1962 (the Commonwealth Immigrants Act), and in 1981 (the British Nationality Act), and the loosening of entry restrictions to North America in the 1960s, is to the USA and Canada for farm labour and domestic work schemes. As mentioned previously, in the case of the Accompong maroon community the road built in the 1940s has facilitated overseas migration to the United States and to Bradford and London, England (as was already the case in the neighbouring non-maroon free village of Aberdeen in St Elizabeth).

In recent years there has been another, more local, flight from the Trelawny free village of Martha Brae: an exodus of landless tenants, who have established a satellite squatter settlement during the thirty-year period of my long-term, recurrent fieldwork (1968-98) on a part of Holland plantation (bordering the village) owned by the Trelawny Parish Council (successor to the Trelawny planter Vestry).[27] Here the themes of exile and flight have come full circle, as descendants of exiled slaves return to 'capture' land on a plantation where their enslaved ancestors had been a proto-peasantry, and where Revival-Zionists and Rastafarians (with their cosmology of exile in 'Babylon' and spiritual flight to Africa or 'Zion') have given the squatter settlement the name of Zion.

Creolization, Ancestral Plots and Transnational Identities

In contrast to the themes of deterritorialization, flight and exile – looking to Africa, the Americas and Europe – in the eight communities that I studied, are the processes of Caribbean creolization or 'indigenization'/localization (Mintz 1996b: 43) and cultural re-creation or invention in adaptation and resistance to colonially derived land monopoly and imposed Euro-American styles of life (see Mintz 1989: 132–3). The peasant formations themselves, and their lifestyles, represent variations on this theme: as mentioned previously, Accompong Town is the oldest surviving corporate maroon society in African-America; Aberdeen and the Trelawny villages originated in proto-peasant adaptations on slave plantations and were re-established as free villages at the forefront of the post-slavery flight from the estates; while Zion is a recently reconstituted squatter-peasantry. The communities, which remain hemmed in by persisting plantations and by the more recent bauxite and tourist industries, are still characterized by creole peasant economies (see Besson 1984a, 1988, 1997, 1998b; Mintz 1989: 225–50). Ritual and belief in all of the communities likewise reflect Caribbean culture building, manifested in the creation of the Myal and Revival cults and in the Rastafarian movement (Besson 1995a, 1997; Besson and Chevannes 1996). Systems of kinship, marriage and descent also reflect the process of creolization, as do oral tradition and language (Besson 1987b, 1995d). All of these dimensions of cultural creativity – the peasant economy, religion, kinship, creole language and oral history – are crystallized in the 'ancestral plots' of family land and common land at the core of these communities (Besson 1984a, 1984b, 1997, 2000). These creole tenures, based on kinship and community, also articulate with return- and circulatory-migration and enable the rooting of trans-national identities (see Besson 1995c).

In Accompong, the themes of dispersal, flight and exile (enslavement, marronage and migration) have (in contrast to Clifford and Césaire) taken 'root in ancestral plots' within the wider framework of the ancestral maroon commons. Through the treaty of March 1739, the Leeward Maroon polity won freedom and legal rights to 1,500 acres[28] of marginal common land, which they had already appropriated through guerrilla warfare and squatting (Kopytoff 1979; Campbell 1990). This land is said by contemporary maroons to have been transmitted to them from the First-Time Maroons: 'Cudjoe seh [said] the land is for the born and unborn'. The themes of exile, flight and dispersal are rooted in these commons, especially in the still-evolving burial patterns which articulate with oral tradition and Myal ritual and chart the commons as sacred space (Besson 1997, 2000, 2001). As noted earlier, the Accompong maroons claim descent from Congos and Coromantees exiled in Jamaica who fled into the mountain wilderness, where they forged an alliance against the plantation–military regime, and these African ethnic identities are symbolized by cairns and boulders in the bush marking reputed African 'tribal' burial grounds. These burial grounds encompass the sacred 'Kindah' grove: an area of grassland and jutting limestone 'cockpits' surrounding the 'Kindah Tree' (a fruitful common mango tree) – a microcosm of the *karst* topography of the Leeward Maroon commons. It is under the Kindah Tree itself that the two 'tribes' are said to have forged their alliance, through intermarriage, against the colonial regime. The Kindah grove therefore symbolizes the transition from African ethnicities to Jamaican maroon ethnicity. This creole maroon identity is further rooted in the ancestral common land through the reputed burial grounds of the 'First-Time' warrior-heroes: maroons born in the Jamaican wilderness, who fought the war and won the peace. Colonel Cudjoe – who had a Coromantee father, but who was himself born in marronage and who ordered his followers to speak Jamaican Creole English rather than the languages of Africa (Kopytoff 1976) – is said to be buried about a mile from Kindah at the sacred 'Old Town' grove.[29] At Old Town, stones mark Cudjoe's reputed resting place (and that of the ancestress-heroine 'Nanny', said to have been his sister[30]) under a jutting cockpit mountain covered profusely with cocoon vines which provided both camouflage and food during the First Maroon War. Cudjoe's captains (Quaco, Cuffee, Accompong and Johnny) are said to be buried in another grove, between Old Town and Kindah, where stones mark their reputed graves in grassland under shade trees.

More recent generations of maroons are buried in the cemetery of the Presbyterian (now United) church, which was established in Accompong by the invitation of the maroons in the late nineteenth century (Kopytoff 1987: 473; Besson 1997), and this graveyard serves as a symbol of the creole maroon community. Jamaican creole maroon identity is further symbolized by the Kindah Tree (rooted at the heart of the ancestral common land), which bears a sign proclaiming 'We are Family'. This statement crystallizes the endogamous cousin conjugality (said to derive from the 'tribal' alliance), the interweaving bilateral kinship networks created in marronage, and the dispersed overlapping unrestricted cognatic family lines descended from the First-Time Maroons.[31] These unrestricted descent lines hold and transmit usufructuary rights to house yards and provision grounds, carved out of the deep forest, within the wider framework of the commons. These family lines are now further rooting in the ancestral land through burial in kin-group house yards; an interment pattern that has been emerging during the period of my fieldwork in Accompong from 1979–98.[32]

These 'ancestral plots' of house yards and provision grounds, and the ancestral common land itself, remain strong referents for maroons who have migrated from the community to other parts of the island or overseas. All Leeward Maroons, whether resident or migrant, retain inalienable rights in the Accompong commons; and any member of the dispersed cognatic descent lines descended from the First-Time Maroons may return to live on and cultivate such land. These co-heirs include maroon migrants overseas, especially in the United States and England; and the architectural landscape of maroon house yards is currently being transformed, with concrete houses gradually replacing cottages of wood or wattle and daub, through return- and circulatory-migration and by migrant remittances. Concrete tombs and vaults are likewise supplanting the earlier interment patterns of cairns and stones, and are powerful symbols of kin-group identity for migrant kin abroad. In addition, the annual Myal ritual on 6 January (said to be Colonel Cudjoe's birthday) at Kindah and Old Town, at the heart of the commons, draws migrant maroons from elsewhere in the island and overseas back to their ancestral land and links First-Time and contemporary, transnational maroons through time and space.[33]

While ancestral common land (encapsulating ancestral plots), elaborated by oral tradition and Myal ritual, is the key referent for transnational maroon identities, 'family land' (based on unrestricted cognatic descent and originating in the proto-peasant adaptation of plantation-slave communities) reinforced by Revival ritual and oral history serves a similar role in the neighbouring post-slavery community of Aberdeen and in Trelawny's free villages (Besson 1984a, 1984b, 1988, 1995c, 1995d, 2000). In Aberdeen, while other small-scale tenures (such as purchased and rented land) exist in relation to parcelled lands, family lands form the core of the community and are reinforced by burial in house yards through Revival mortuary ritual (which articulates with Pentecostalism in this formally Moravian community).[34] Such ancestral plots, which provide an economic foothold in the face of the surrounding corporate plantations (such as Appleton Estates, which manufactures sugar and rum for the world economy), bauxite mines and the developing south coast tourist industry, are also significant symbols of 'home' for many members of the unrestricted cognatic descent lines who are dispersed through migration elsewhere in the island or in North America and Britain. Such is the case with the family land of the descendants of the 'African-Prince Maroon'.[35] As mentioned earlier, one of the Prince's male descendants is said to have 'come out' from Accompong around 1845 (seven years after emancipation), to live nearer to the plains of St Elizabeth, and to have acquired sixteen acres of mountain land in Aberdeen. This land, which is said to have been obtained through squatting and then by purchase, has been orally transmitted to all of his descendants[36] – some of whom have migrated to New York in the United States and to Bradford, England. Any member of this family line may return to live on the land or may be buried there; in 1998, the family burial plot contained at least twenty-three graves and tombs of this transnational family line. This 'ancestral plot' therefore links African, Caribbean, Black British and African-American identities across the globe and through centuries of forced and voluntary exile, flight and dispersal.

Similar themes recur throughout the Trelawny Baptist free villages (where Revival cults coexist with Baptist churches), which were established earlier (from 1838) at the forefront of the flight from the estates. 'Old Families' with family lands, descended and transmitted through unrestricted cognatic descent from emancipated slaves, form the core of these communities which are hemmed in by corporate plantations and the highly developed north coast tourist industry. In the free village of Martha Brae, while a community cemetery replaced yard burial in the early twentieth century (due to the village's proximity to the parish capital of Falmouth), there are several overlapping unrestricted, partially dispersed cognatic descent lines with small plots of family land. One such family-land estate is the symbol of the transnational Minto Old Family, whose members are in Canada, the United States and Britain as well as elsewhere in the island and the village (where some members of the descent group have obtained their own small plots of land through purchase or rental, or by 'capturing' land in the satellite squatter settlement of Zion) and on the family land itself. This family land (which comprises three minuscule ancestral plots, totalling only a few square chains in size) was consolidated by the ancestor William Minto, an ex-slave from Irving Tower sugar plantation bordering the village, who settled in Martha Brae with his parents (emancipated slaves, great grandparents of the oldest living generation) and purchased land there. William Minto also established a tradition of return migration in the early post-emancipation period in the nineteenth century, by emigrating to Port Limon in Costa Rica and then returning to the village.

Other Old Families in Martha Brae reflect similar themes. For example, several members of the Thompson Old Family (which overlaps with an Old Family in the neighbouring free village of Granville) migrated throughout the twentieth century to Cuba, Costa Rica and the United States. The family land (just over an acre in size) in Martha Brae, purchased by an ex-slave ancestor from Irving Tower plantation, remains the symbol of this transnational descent group. This group included the trustee of the family land, Mr T (a grandson of the ex-slave), who returned to live there in 1962 after many years of circulatory migration to Cuba and the United States. Since Mr T's death in 1985, his wife (who has only a life interest in the land) and children (who are among the co-heirs) have continued to live there.

Similar themes of ancestral plots, linking transnational descent groups, recur in the Trelawny free villages of Granville, Kettering, Refuge and The Alps, where burial in family-land house yards still continues but where the architectural landscape is being transformed (as in Accompong, Aberdeen and Martha Brae) through the building of concrete houses and vaults financed by migrant pensions and remittances. Such has been the case, for example, with the Wallace family land in Granville, which has been transmitted through seven post-slavery generations and which has ancestral graves and a wooden chattel cottage from the early post-emancipation period. By 1983, the living members of this descent group were entirely dispersed elsewhere in Jamaica and in Britain. However, by 1995, there were two concrete houses on the land built through circulatory migration and migrant pensions and remittances. One of these houses serves as a family-land 'hotel' for members of the transnational descent group, who return to visit. In addition, in Granville as elsewhere in Trelawny and Jamaica, Revival-Zion mortuary ritual draws together such transnational family lines, whose members return from North America and Britain for burials of deceased kin in ancestral plots and for related Revival wakes in free villages and urban communities (Besson and Chevannes 1996).

Moreover, as the case of Mr J in Martha Brae illustrates, 'ancestral plots' are still being created wherever possible from small parcels of purchased land in these free villages in the context of return- and circulatory-migration. After living for many decades as a landless tenant in Martha Brae (to which he migrated from another Trelawny village), Mr J managed to purchase one-third of an acre near the village cemetery. By 1983 (when he was an elderly man in his seventies), he had transformed this bought land into family land for his nine children – who had all migrated overseas – and their descendants, so that any member of this dispersed, unrestricted cognatic descent line could return in time of need. He explained to me his strategy of creating an ancestral plot for his deterritorialized, transnational descendants:

> My land already turned into 'family land'. I give away my land to my seed them [children] – all nine. No-one can molest [exclude] each other. Is just like this: I told them this land is not to sell. *It serve generation, generation, generation* [my emphasis]. Suppose you lef' it for a certain one [individual freehold], that one can dish-out [exclude] other rest. But I leave down there [the land] say is for *nine*. I give them this now that *any part of the world they go and come, they have just where they were born* [emphasis added]. Anywhere they are, they can go and come. And *no-one* out the nine can sell it. So I told them it cannot be sold. They call it 'family land'; it cannot be sold. *So* I told them. Now being these children of today, they have a lot of children. *So grandchildren, and grandchildren and grandchildren, they will inherit* [my emphasis]. (Quoted in Besson 1984b: 9)

In the late 1990s, as a circulatory migrant to Trelawny myself (with 'ancestral plots' in Trelawny and St Elizabeth), I found that Mr J had died and that the family land which he invented had indeed remained as a basis for circulatory residence and transnational identity.

Another variant on this theme of rooting in 'ancestral plots' in the midst of deterritorialization, flight and exile is reflected in Martha Brae's satellite squatter settlement of Zion – which, as mentioned previously, was founded during the period of my long-term, recurrent fieldwork in Trelawny from 1968-98 (Besson 2000, and forthcoming). When I began my fieldwork in Martha Brae in 1968 there were no houses on that part of Holland plantation (bordering the free village) owned by the Trelawny Parish Council. However, by the end of 1968, one chattel cottage had been moved from Martha Brae to 'captured land' there. After an attempted eviction, a court case and a compromise relocation, this founding household created a house yard on the plantation land and another two households squatted there in 1971. All three households were headed by formerly established immigrants to Martha Brae, who had been tenants on the land of other villagers; the third household also brought a Revival-Zion chattel church which they re-rooted in the squatter settlement. By 1979 there were about thirty squatter households, as 'people were *flowing* on the land', and the settlement had been given the name of 'Zion'. By 1996 there were about seventy house yards there, on some thirty acres of captured land, and the Parish Council had surveyed the land with a view to land retrieval, subdivision (in square metres), sale and taxation. By then, the founders of Zion, Mr and Mrs H, were in their seventies and had thirteen children, 'a whole heap' of adult grandchildren, great-grandchildren, and great- great-grandchildren, and were planning to leave their tiny house yard as an ancestral plot for their descendants. In 1998 Mr H died and his family held Revival wakes in the house yard and buried him in the Martha Brae free-village cemetery. At the present time, although no land sales have yet been made at Zion, such sales are anticipated by this 'recon-stituted' squatter-peasantry, who are linked through transnational kinship networks to migrants overseas. In addition to such physical migration to North America and Britain is, as mentioned previously, the spiritual return to Africa made by the many Rastafarians who (along with Revival-Zionists) have squatted in the settlement. However, despite their exile ethos and outward view to Africa, these Rastafarians have invented their own 'Zion' by rooting in the Caribbean territory of Jamaica at the very heart of 'Babylon'.

Recharting and Rethinking the Caribbean Experience

The preceding section has illustrated the co-existence of Caribbean alienation and creation, uprooting and rooting, crystallized in the 'ancestral plots' of family land and common land in the eight communities that I studied in the west-central area of Jamaica – at the core of the Caribbean region. This paradox of deterritorialization, flight and exile coexistent with creolization and invention, and rooting in ancestral land, can be widely identified throughout the Caribbean, especially in the non-Hispanic territories where the crisis of identity has been portrayed as most extreme (see pp. 176–8). As my earlier work has shown (e.g. Besson 1979, 1984a, 1987a, 1995c, 2000), unrestricted cognatic landholding descent systems enabling migrants to return to family land[37] can be identified, not only throughout Jamaica but also in Haiti and Providencia, the Virgin Islands of Tortola and St John, the Leeward islands (Antigua, Nevis and now-erupting Montserrat), the Windward Islands (Dominica, Martinique, St Lucia, St Vincent and Grenada), Carriacou and Bequia in the Grenadines, Barbados, Trinidad and Tobago, and in some Guyanese villages and urban Suriname. In addition, similar cognatic descent systems interweave with common land in Barbuda, the Bahamas, on the coastlands of Suriname and Guyana, among the Windward Island Caribs of Dominica and St Vincent, and the Black Caribs of Belize; as among the Jamaican Leeward Maroons discussed earlier in this chapter, and as is also the case among the Windward Maroons in the eastern mountains of Jamaica (Bilby 1996; Besson 1997).

In addition, the identification of these cognatic landholding systems has been drawn on by Elizabeth Thomas-Hope in her recent and classic work on return- and circulatory-migration. In contrast to her earlier view that emigration was the only route to forging free Caribbean identities, and that 'even on small-holdings there was no deep-felt attachment to land' (Thomas-Hope 1978: 66), her later inter-pretation of Caribbean migration highlights the unrestricted landholding systems which enable migrants to return:

> Land-tenure practices among the rural populations of most Caribbean countries further accommodate the sequential or long-term absence of household and family members, giving a sense of security of tenure to those who stay, as well as to those who migrate. This system of inheritance is based on an ideology of cognatic descent whereby children of either sex inherit rights to land from both parents (Besson 1984[a]; 1987[a]). Closely interconnected with the entire institutional structure which evolved, land tenure practices of this type provided the newly formed peasantries – the future small-farming populations of the Caribbean – with a measure of security in the event of migration. This is a security hardly measurable in economic terms, but highly significant in symbolic and psych-ological terms. (Thomas-Hope 1992: 5; see also 1995: 169)

The analysis of these Caribbean landholding systems, based on unrestricted descent and enabling migrants as well as residents to root in 'ancestral plots', has likewise illuminated Karen Olwig's recent interpretations of the migration-oriented Leeward Island of Nevis and the American Virgin Island of St John. As mentioned previously, in an important early article highlighting the pronounced tradition of emigration in Nevis (where the development of a post-slavery peasantry was particularly constrained by persisting plantations) since Emancipation, Olwig (1987:

153) questioned an assumed 'innate attachment to the native land' as a basis for nationhood, highlighting instead the orientation of Nevisian children to migrant relatives in Brooklyn and Brixton. However, in that same volume (Besson and Momsen 1987), Janet Momsen and myself (ibid.: 3) drew attention to another, complementary view of Nevis; namely, a continued attachment both by residents and migrants to even government land settlements – where, as Momsen (1987: 63) showed, many 'farmers could trace their family's presence on a particular estate back through the period of sharecropping to slave days', and where '[E]ven without land ownership settlers have often attempted to ensure that their heirs, resident or absentee, are allowed to take over occupance of the settlement plot' (ibid.: 65; see also Besson 1992, 1995c). This complex interrelation of the global and the local has been skilfully developed by Olwig in her later work on 'global culture, island identity' in Nevis, which recognizes migrants' attachment to their native territory and to family lands there to which they can return (Olwig 1993: 97–8, 110–11 n.5, 130–1, 1995: 112, 115–16).

In a recent account of Nevis, Olwig (1997a) further highlights the 'attachment to place' among Nevisians overseas and extends this methodology to illuminate cross-cultural analysis of the articulation of the global and the local:

> On the basis of a study of a West Indian community I shall argue that the strong propensity to migrate found among West Indians is counterbalanced by an *equally strongly developed notion of attachment to place*. In order to understand West Indian life it is therefore necessary to study the role of both *fixed places* and changeable and ever-expanding global networks of relations. I suggest that a useful concept in such studies may be found in the notion of 'cultural sites,' cultural institutions which have developed in the interrelationship between global and local ties. These cultural sites attain their significance because they are *identified with particular places*, at the same time as they accommodate the global conditions of life which have long characterized the West Indies. It is suggested that such cultural sites may be useful focal points in anthropological studies of the more general global and local condition of human existence. (Olwig 1997a: 17, my emphases)

In developing her argument, Olwig focuses on the 'family house' and 'family land', underwriting her Nevisian data with reference to the pan-Caribbean analysis of family land (Besson 1987a, 1995c) and concluding that family land on Nevis 'constitutes an important linchpin in the global family networks' (Olwig 1997a: 25).

The pan-Caribbean perspective on cognatic landholding systems binding migrants to their homelands (Besson 1979, 1984a, 1987a, 1992, 1995c) has likewise illuminated Olwig's (1985, 1994, 1997b) classic work on the American Virgin Island of St John. Olwig's rich monograph, *Cultural Adaptation and Resistance on St John: Three Centuries of Afro-Caribbean Life* (1985), highlighted the significance of ego-focused bilateral kinship networks of exchange, rooted in proto-peasant and post-emancipation communities and continuing as a basis of cultural identity in the contemporary tourist society where much of the island is now an American National Park. Olwig critiqued traditional interpretations of the Afro-American family in the Caribbean region for focusing on household structure and matrifocal family forms. 'With few exceptions', she argued, 'there has been little discussion of kinship structure as such, much less of the larger sociocultural systems' (1985: xi). However, despite her data on St Johnian family land (some of which has been retained despite the National Park), her emphasis on ego-focused bilateral networks as the essence of Caribbean kinship overlooked the ancestor-focused unrestricted cognatic descent systems at the heart of Caribbean family land.[38] Moreover, as my review of Olwig (1985) showed, the invention of family land was a significant mode of adaptation and resistance among the St Johnian peasantry to the plantation system; family land was also more than a system of land use (as Olwig argued at that time), being a central symbol of Afro-Caribbean autonomy and identity that also enabled return migration (Besson 1989; see also Besson 1995c: 89–91). In her later work on St John, Olwig (1994, 1997b) has explored more fully these dimensions of family land as cultural heritage and symbolic resource among the proto-peasantry and post-slavery migrants:

> Family land never was primarily an economic resource, to be exploited by people for their own private gain. It provided rather a place of belonging and rooting, first for the freed slaves living within the confines of the plantation society, later for the global network of relatives who were scattered in various migration destinations. (Olwig 1997b: 156–7)

Olwig's widened perspective on St Johnian and Nevisian family land has also enriched the predecessor to this volume, *Migrants of Identity: Perceptions of Home in a World of Movement* (Rapport and Dawson 1998: 17; Olwig 1998: 225–36).

In addition to (and often articulating with) descent, ritual binds Caribbean migrants to ancestral plots and territories. As discussed earlier in this chapter, non-maroon Jamaican migrants return for Revival mortuary ritual for kin interred in family land and in free-village and urban cemeteries, while Jamaican Leeward maroon migrants return for Myal rituals on ancestral common land. Jamaicans also return to their homeland for the annual August Independence celebrations which, from 1962 to 1997, replaced Emancipation commemorations. Migrants likewise return to other Caribbean territories to participate in national rituals. In Nevis, where 'every year . . . thousands of Nevisian migrants . . . make pilgrimages to their former home in order to visit family and re-establish their cultural roots', the annual August Culturama festival 'attracts a great number of Nevisians living and working abroad' (Olwig 1990: 17–18). Carnival in Trinidad, which may be seen as 'a quest for national identity' (van Koningsbruggen 1997) and which has spread to other Caribbean territories such as Antigua (Manning 1977), has long played a similar role. In Barbados, the national 'Crop Over' ritual draws 'Barbadians living abroad back home' (Gmelch and Gmelch 1997: 168); while in Montserrat, before the recent volcanic eruptions of Chance's Peak, migrants remained 'very much a part of the Montserratian social system' (Philpott 1973: 154) and community rites of passage marked both their departure and return to this British Caribbean territory (ibid.: 154–64) – where ancestral plots of 'generation land' and 'family land' had long symbolized belonging and enabled migrants to return (ibid.: 124–8).

The British Virgin Islands (BVI), like Montserrat, is also a British Caribbean territory. However Bill Maurer (1997), in his fine monograph *Recharting the Caribbean: Land, Law, and Citizenship in the British Virgin Islands*, stresses the differences between the BVI and the rest of the Caribbean region in relation to land, territory and identity. In addition, while Maurer sympathizes with Clifford's (1988: 15) view (discussed in the Introduction to this chapter) that the Caribbean and its diaspora may be seen as a microcosm of the contemporary world, he posits an urgent need to rechart the 'Caribbean experience' in four main areas of anthropological debate (Maurer 1997: 10–16; Besson 1999).[39] First, while agreeing that the reformulation of identities among West Indian migrants in North America and Britain may be seen as reflecting post-modern processes, Maurer questions the romanticization of this experience in terms of 'mixing and hybridization' (1997: 13), for such notions of 'nature' may also generate new cultural rhetorics of exclusion – as in the BVI, where new categories of nationals and foreigners have been created out of former British subjects since the 1981 British Nationality Act. Second, Maurer aims to rechart Caribbean Studies, with its emphasis on either social structure, household and family or African retentions and culture change, by turning attention to 'the role of the state and law in shaping family or in changing cultures', and thereby to highlight 'the problematics of colonialism, colonial discourse, and national identity in state contexts' (ibid.). Maurer explores the paradox of the BVI as a self-governing territory with its own laws and legislature, symbolizing its nation-statehood, and its colonial relationship with Britain[40] – whose common law is the foundation of BVI law-and-order society, which provides the basis for tourist development and global financial offshore services. Third, by focusing on BVI exclusion of immigrants (in a context where race–class hierarchies are supposedly diminishing), Maurer identifies the potential of liberal law, based on equality, for generating hierarchical inequalities of race, class and gender. Fourth, he aims to show, by exploring the legal reformulation of the 'natures' of land, kinship, race, place and nation in the BVI, how liberal state law may constitute new kinds of persons and identities.[41]

In Chapter 6 of his 1997 book (which focuses especially on the island of Tortola), 'Making Family, Making Genealogy: One Hundred Years of Family Land', Maurer addresses the family-land literature (e.g. Besson 1979, 1984a) to elaborate his thesis.

Drawing on my argument that Caribbean family land is a creole institution rooted in unrestricted cognatic descent (which maximizes scarce land rights and formerly forbidden kinship lines among descendants of chattel slaves, and enables migrants to return), rather than in restrictive colonial codes (such as primogeniture) or African restricted unilineal retentions, he further highlights the role of family land in creating Caribbean identities by his documentation of the BVI case. However, Maurer sees his analysis as shifting ground in the so-called 'family-land debate' (e.g. Carnegie 1987b; Crichlow 1994), which includes the questions of whether family land is an 'institution' and whether the landholding kin groups are restricted. Substituting 'phenomenon' for 'institution', he argues that BVI (and Barbadian) descent groups are in fact restricted; stresses the centrality of law in creating Caribbean identities; and highlights the link between British 'common law' and Caribbean 'custom'. He also asserts that my analysis of unrestricted descent depends 'on a weak notion of "family"', while Carnegie (1987b) stressed ambiguous 'genealogy'; contends that neither view explains 'how Caribbean peoples talk and think about Caribbean family land' (p. 203); and concludes that '[T]he family/genealogy distinction maps almost too neatly onto the so-called plural society debate' (p. 204).

However, both Carnegie (1987b) and myself (Besson 1974, 2: 1–113, 1984a: 76 n.7, 1987a: 38 n.3, 1987b, 1988, 1995e) advanced 'intersystem' analyses of 'custom' and 'law', in contrast to Smith's (1965) plural society approach. I had also argued (1974: Chapter 7) that, even at a conceptual level, custom and law in Jamaica are not as separate as Smith and Clarke (1953, 1966) contended; for Jamaica's legal system not only differs from, but also draws on English common law in certain ways.[42] In addition, I have shown that since the days of slavery family land has overturned the British West Indian primogeniture on which the colonial plantation system was based and is now shaping the writing of laws in Commonwealth Caribbean territories (Besson 1984a: 76 n.9, 1987b, 1988; 2000; see also Carnegie 1987b: 97 n.3).[43] Indeed, Maurer himself might have taken more account of the articulation of 'custom' and 'law' by exploring the institution-building rooted in the slavery past and its contribution to Caribbean perceptions of Caribbean family land; and had he followed through the culture-building thesis beyond 1988 (e.g. Besson 1992, 1995c, 1995d), it would have been difficult to overlook my protrayal of the strength of Caribbean kinship (genealogy and family). Moreover, Maurer's attempt to demonstrate 'restriction' in landholding descent groups focuses on affinity (1997: 198, 201) rather than on descent, while his own delineation elsewhere of BVI land tenure richly portrays a British West Indian landholding system recharted through creolizing unrestricted cognatic descent (Maurer 1996: 353–4). Therefore, as throughout the rest of the non-Hispanic Caribbean, the retention of land rights by absent kin in BVI ancestral plots provides a basis for transnational identities at the interface of the local and the global, and of hierarchy and equality,[44] even in this British colonial territory.

In recharting the 'Caribbean experience', Maurer (1997: 13, 31–3, 119, 264) highlights Olwig's (1993) analysis of the role of the state and law, the local and global, and hierachy and equality in the Leeward Island of Nevis. However, as I have shown earlier in this section, Olwig's analysis itself was enriched by the pan-Caribbean view of family land and its unrestricted cognatic descent systems enabling migrants to return (Besson and Momsen 1987; Besson 1987a, 1995c; Olwig 1993, 1995, 1997a). Moreover, in her recent work on the American Virgin Island of St John (which has likewise been enhanced by the pan-Caribbean family-land perspective), Olwig (1997b: 138) shows that 'after the instituting of American rule family land became recognized by the legal system'. Therefore both the British and the American Virgin Island cases underline, rather than undermine, the significance of Caribbean 'ancestral plots' in transforming colonial law and creating new natures of land, territory and identity, thereby reinforcing the more far-reaching rethinking of Clifford's (1988) view of the 'Caribbean experience' suggested in this chapter.

The argument of this chapter, which has focused on the Caribbean paradox of uprooting and rooting through the post-slavery and post-modern invention of transnational identities linked to ancestral lands and territories, is further underlined by Mary Chamberlain's (1997) perceptive monograph, *Narratives of Exile and Return*. Focusing on Barbados and its diaspora, but generalizing to the wider Caribbean, Chamberlain highlights the importance of ties among Barbadian migrants to their ancestral homeland for forging diaspora identities, and the likely strengthening of these ancestral links in the future through return migration:

> although the different Caribbean communities [in Britain] have joined together in pursuit of common political, economic, social and cultural goals, nevertheless the island communities still retain an awareness of cultural distinctiveness and, with the young Barbadians cited here, a determination to construct autonomous Barbadian identities in Britain which, if the current trends towards return continues, is likely to be enhanced rather than diminished by time. (Chamberlain 1997: 132)

Notes

1. Escape from slavery.
2. In contrast to restricted unilineal systems (which trace descent through only one gender) and to restricted cognatic systems (which trace descent through both genders but restrict membership through residence), unrestricted cognatic

descent includes both residents and absentees as well as males and females. In the case of the Caribbean region, during plantation slavery such unrestricted systems invented by the slaves transformed African unilineal descent and maximized customary land rights and family lines among chattel slaves who were legally landless and kinless and who were considered property themselves. Since Emancipation, unrestricted cognatic landholding systems have maximized scarce land rights and kinship lines as bases of security and identity among the descendants of chattel slaves and have enabled migrants to return. For a more detailed discussion of unrestricted cognatic descent systems see Besson (1979, 1987a, 1992, 1995c, 1995d).

3. The fieldwork on which this chapter is based was undertaken in eight Jamaican rural communities in the parishes of Trelawny and St Elizabeth during the thirty-year period 1968-98. Fieldwork in the eastern Caribbean from 1992–4 has contributed to the Caribbean regional perspectives drawn on in this chapter. I am grateful to the Economic and Social Research Council, the Carnegie Trust, the Nuffield Foundation and the British Academy for financial assistance.

4. For a discussion of the concept of *oikoumenê* in relation to the Caribbean region see Mintz (1996a).

5. With the Spanish-American War, the United States also became a colonizing power in the Caribbean in 1898. Puerto Rico and the American Virgin Islands (formerly the Danish West Indies, sold to the USA in 1917) illustrate these Euro-American colonial ties.

6. In addition, St Barts is a dependency of Guadeloupe and therefore part of the French state; while the small island of St Martin/Sint Maarten is divided between France and the Netherlands.

7. Mintz argues that in the non-Hispanic Caribbean territories, a rapid and steady escalation of the plantation system led to the swift eradication of early peasant formations (e.g. the 'squatters' and the 'early yeomen', see pp. 178–81 of this chapter); in addition, the planters identified more strongly with the metropoles and were often absentee. He posits that, in contrast, some sense of national (creole, local) identity developed in the Hispanic territories of Cuba, Puerto Rico and Santo Domingo/Dominican Republic: due to neglectful Spanish rule; a strong distinction between local Spanish colonists and Spaniards in Europe; a slower development of the plantation system; and the related consolidation of squatter-peasantries. Hoetink (1985) adds that more rigid colour-class hierarchies therefore typified the non-Hispanic territories, while the Hispanic variant developed a socio-racial continuum reinforced by more inter-racial marriages and a homogeneous Hispanic-American religious culture rooted in Catholicism. Mintz makes a special case for French, Catholic Saint-Domingue/post-revolutionary Haiti as straddling the two variants. Patterson's (1973) analysis of (non-Hispanic/British/Protestant) Jamaica during

slavery highlights the theme of planter absenteeism as being at the basis of Jamaica's 'non-society'.

8. Mintz (1989: 132) defines peasantry in general as 'a class (or classes) of rural landowners producing a large part of the products they consume, but also selling to (and buying from) wider markets, and dependent in various ways upon wider political and economic spheres of control', qualifying elsewhere the criterion of landowning by referring to a 'peasantry' as 'those small-scale cultivators who own or *have access to* land' (ibid.: 141; my emphasis). From this viewpoint, Caribbean small-scale agriculturalists are '*reconstituted* peasantries, having begun other than as peasants – in slavery, as deserters or runaways, as plantation laborers, or whatever – and becoming peasants in some kind of resistant response to an externally imposed regimen' (ibid.: 132). More specifically, Mintz (ibid.: 132–3) argues that 'Caribbean peasantries represent *a mode of response* to the plantation system and its connotations, and *a mode of resistance* to imposed styles of life'.

9. This process of extirpation was later reflected in the Spanish colonies, such as Cuba and Puerto Rico, with the intensification of the Hispanic plantations in the late eighteenth and nineteenth centuries (Mintz 1959, 1978: 85, 1989: 82–94, 148).

10. The proto-peasantry are the classic illustration of Mintz's (1989: 76) idea of 'resistance' based on 'adaptation'. The proto-peasant adaptation can also be portrayed as a mode of 'opposition' (rather than 'resistance') to the slave plantations, since this 'contestation' developed *within* (rather than *outside*) the plantation system itself (cf. Burton 1997: 6) – in contrast to the maroons.

11. Mintz's (1989) work conveys that the squatter-peasant adaptation has been wiped out in the Caribbean region. However, my fieldwork shows that this mode of peasantization is re-emerging (see also Besson 1995a, 1995b, 2000).

12. Saint-Domingue was the western third of the island of Hispaniola and was ceded by the Spanish to the French in 1697. After the Saint-Domingue slave revolution (1791-1804), the former French colony became the independent republic of Haiti.

13. The importation of slaves to the Americas began by 1505, within a few years of Columbus's landfall on the Caribbean island of Guanahani (in the Bahamas chain) in 1492, and continued until the total abolition of slavery in the western hemisphere in 1888 despite the abolition of the British slave trade in 1807.

14. From 1834–8 there was a period of 'Apprenticeship' for the former slaves.

15. Coromantees and their descendants dominated the Leeward Maroons in the eighteenth century, and 'Congo' runaways settled 'deep in the western woods' of Jamaica after the treaty (Kopytoff 1976: 38, 40).

16. Elections for the Colonel of the Leeward Maroons are held every five years.

17. Island Mountain was part of the plantation mountain lands of Island Estate. A part of the contemporary Aberdeen community ('Lower Aberdeen') was founded on a subdivision of Island Estate, while the older core of the community ('Upper Aberdeen') includes Island Mountain.

18. Moravian Church records for St Elizabeth include the information that ex-slaves from this area of Jamaica migrated to and from Colon in Panama (*Periodical Accounts*, Volume 33, 1885).

19. Some Jamaican free villages were typified by dual naming around the time of their establishment, reflecting the interplay between British visions and creole views (Besson 1984b; cf. Mintz 1989: 157–79). In addition to some of the Trelawny Baptist free villages, as discussed in this chapter, the Moravian community of Aberdeen in St Elizabeth (previously discussed) was known by the English name Ockbrook to the Moravian missionaries (see Hastings and MacLeavy 1979), while the ex-slaves named the free village after their Afro-Scots plantation-slave community (see Besson 2000).

20. For a more detailed discussion of the paradoxical relationship between the slaves/ex-slaves and the Baptist missionaries, especially the Reverend William Knibb, slaves' missionary stationed in Trelawny, see Besson (1995a).

21. See Mintz and Price (1992: 43–4) on the significance of the fictive-kinship shipmate bond for culture-building throughout African-America, and Besson (1995d) for a discussion of this in relation to the villages that I studied.

22. The nickname 'Queenie' may have referred to the ritual role of a Kumina 'Queen', deriving from Myalism in the evolution to Revivalism (with its Revival-Zion and Pukumina variants) (see Besson 1995a; Besson and Chevannes 1996).

23. This exiled ancestor is said to have gained access in enslavement to the Bible and other books, to have taught himself to read, and to have been severely punished (beaten) for his learning. In addition to the oral tradition of this dispersed, unrestricted cognatic descent group and their family land collected by me in The Alps (Besson 1984b), I am grateful to a member of this Old Family who I met in London, England, for providing further details of this ancestor and for permission to cite this information. That this informant had been born in the United States, had not yet visited The Alps, but had treasured this oral tradition from her elders in the diaspora, underlines the central point in this chapter regarding the significance of ancestral plots for the rooting of transnational identities.

24. Slaves on Jamaican plantations were divided into work gangs based on physical strength and age. As Patterson (1973: 59) notes, '[T]he hogmeat gang consisted of young children between the ages of four or five and nine and ten. They were employed in minor tasks such as collecting food for the hogs, weeding and the like.'

25. Granville was founded in 1845 by Knibb in the year of his death and (in contrast to The Alps and Refuge) the English name that he gave the village was retained. Martha Brae had been the first colonial town in the eastern part of the parish of Old St James and, when the parish was subdivided into St James and Trelawny in 1771, became Trelawny's first parochial capital. It was eclipsed by the new port and town of Falmouth around 1800 and was appropriated by ex-slaves (in association with the Baptist church) in the flight from the estates (Besson 1984b, 1987b, 2000, 2001, and forthcoming).

26. For a fuller discussion of these migratory trends, for example in relation to gender, see Besson (1998a).

27. During the slavery and early post-emancipation periods, local government was conducted by Parish Vestries which were in the hands of the plantocracy. Vestries were subsequently replaced by Parochial Boards and then by Parish Councils. In the case of the ex-slaves who squatted in the colonial town of Martha Brae, the Vestry retrieved such land for sale, registration and taxation (Besson 2000) – as is currently being undertaken by the Parish Council in Martha Brae's satellite squatter settlement of Zion, as discussed later in this chapter (see p. 191).

28. This was later increased to 2,559 acres (Campbell 1990: 127, 181–3).

29. For a more detailed discussion of the meaning of the 'Old Town' grove see Besson (1997, 2000).

30. As discussed more fully elsewhere (Besson 1995d, 1997, 2000, 2001), the appropriation by the Leeward Maroons of the Windward Maroon ancestress 'Nanny' as Cudjoe's sister symbolizes the origin of their unrestricted cognatic descent system (which includes males and females, migrants and residents, and which transformed the restricted unilineal systems of West and Central Africa – as well as overturning restricted colonial primogeniture) through the brother-sister sibling bond.

31. See note 30 above.

32. Burial in house yards typified the proto-peasantry and, as will be seen below in the discussion of the free villages, has characterized many non-maroon peasant communities since emancipation.

33. The Myal Dance or Play, in which ancestral spirit-possession is enacted and perceived, occurs directly beneath the Kindah Tree and also includes a ritual feast at the Kindah grove and a pilgrimage to Old Town (Besson 1997, 2000, 2001).

34. The Moravians were the first slave missionaries in Jamaica, but were not as successful as the Baptists (Patterson 1973: 209–15). On the contemporary impact of American Pentecostalism in Jamaica, see Austin-Broos (1997).

35. Although Aberdeen is a non-maroon free village evolving from the proto-peasantry, it has a special relationship with the Acccompong maroon community

as Aberdeen slave plantation bordered the maroon commons. Oral traditions of the two communities (regarding military and conjugal alliances) overlap and some Aberdonians claim Leeward Maroon descent (Besson 1997, 2000, 2001).

36. The oral tradition regarding this land is reinforced by historical, archival and genealogical evidence.

37. In some Caribbean territories family land is known as 'generation land', 'generation property', or 'children's property'.

38. See Besson (1979, 1987a) for a discussion of the contrast between ego-focused and ancestor-oriented kin groups, drawn from the anthropological literature beyond the Caribbean region.

39. My discussion of Maurer (1997) in this chapter both draws on, and develops my review of his book (Besson 1999).

40. The British Virgin Islands became a self-governing colony in 1956 after the dissolution of the wider Leeward Island colony governed from Antigua.

41. Maurer concludes that not only does globalization foster BVI national identity, but also BVI national law-writing has entrenched colonial rule and reinforced the world economy by creating a major tax haven for global finance markets. He argues that BVI discourses do not challenge the system of dominance; for both British Virgin Islanders and immigrants (from elsewhere in the Caribbean) stress liberal individualism. 'Choice' is perceived to work through creolizing 'articulatory practices', which 'produce momentary stabilizations of and sources for identity' – such as '"ethnic" stereotypes; "races" and communities bound to "places"; "families" and "genealogies"; "land" and "country"; "classes" and "parties"; "states" and "societies"; "individuals" who owe nothing to society; and "nations"' (Maurer 1997: 264). For Maurer, '[T]he "Caribbeanization of the world" narrative is itself one such transition narrative, one that stabilizes "the Caribbean" and "the world" just at a moment when offshore finance (among other things) makes that separation more a fiction than ever' (ibid.). In this way, Maurer argues, the Caribbean may provide paradigms for recharting post-modern identities.

42. I am grateful to my late father, Kenneth M. McFarlane, the longest-serving Attorney-at-Law on Jamaica's north coast (who worked for fifty-three years in the parishes of Trelawny, St James and Hanover), for his help in my analyses of the interplay between 'custom' and 'law' in Jamaica. The responsibility for those anthropological analyses are, of course, mine alone.

43. For example, the 1976 Status of Children Act in Jamaica and the 1981 Family Law Act in Barbados, which include illegitimate children as intestate heirs, thereby moving closer to the egalitarian ethos of family land.

44. For a fuller consideration of the interplay between hierarchy and equality in the Caribbean see Besson (1993).

References

Austin-Broos, D. J. (1997), *Jamaica Genesis: Religion and the Politics of Moral Orders*, Chicago: University of Chicago Press.

Barrett, L. E. (1977), *The Rastafarians: The Dreadlocks of Jamaica*, London: Heinemann.

Beckford, G. L. (1972), P*ersistent Poverty: Underdevelopment in Plantation Economies of the Third World*, New York: Oxford University Press.

Besson, J. (1974), 'Land Tenure and Kinship in a Jamaican Village', Unpublished Ph.D. Dissertation (2 vols.), University of Edinburgh.

—— (1979), 'Symbolic Aspects of Land in the Caribbean: The Tenure and Transmission of Land Rights among Caribbean Peasantries', in M. Cross and A. Marks (eds), *Peasants, Plantations and Rural Communities in the Caribbean*, Guildford: University of Surrey and Leiden: Royal Institute of Linguistics and Anthropology, pp. 86–116.

—— (1984a), 'Family Land and Caribbean Society: Toward an Ethnography of Afro-Caribbean Peasantries', in E. M. Thomas-Hope (ed.), *Perspectives on Caribbean Regional Identity*, Centre for Latin American Studies, University of Liverpool Monograph Series No. 11, pp. 57–83.

—— (1984b), 'Land Tenure in the Free Villages of Trelawny, Jamaica', *Slavery & Abolition*, 5(1): 3–23.

—— (1987a), 'A Paradox in Caribbean Attitudes to Land', in J. Besson and J. Momsen (eds), *Land and Development in the Caribbean*, London: Macmillan, pp. 13–45.

—— (1987b), 'Family Land as a Model for Martha Brae's Two Histories', in C. V. Carnegie (ed.), *Afro-Caribbean Villages in Historical Perspective*, ACIJ Research Review No. 2, African-Caribbean Institute of Jamaica, Kingston, Jamaica, pp. 100–32.

—— (1988), 'Agrarian Relations and Perceptions of Land in a Jamaican Peasant Village', in J. S. Brierley and H. Rubenstein (eds), *Small Farming and Peasant Resources in the Caribbean,* Manitoba Geographical Studies 10, University of Manitoba, Winnipeg, pp. 39–61.

—— (1989), 'Review of Karen Fog Olwig, *Cultural Adaptation and Resistance on St John*, in *Plantation Society in the Americas*, 2: 345–48.

—— (1992), 'Freedom and Community: The British West Indies', in F. McGlynn and S. Drescher (eds), *The Meaning of Freedom: Economics, Politics, and Culture after Slavery*, Pittsburgh and London: University of Pittsburgh Press, pp. 183–219.

—— (1993), 'Reputation and Respectability Reconsidered: A New Perspective on Afro-Caribbean Peasant Women', in J. H. Momsen (ed.), *Women and Change in the Caribbean*, London: James Currey, pp. 15–37.

—— (1995a), 'Religion as Resistance in Jamaican Peasant Life', in B. Chevannes (ed.), *Rastafari and Other African-Caribbean Worldviews*, Institute of Social Studies, The Hague/London: Macmillan, pp. 43–76.

—— (1995b), 'Free Villagers, Rastafarians and Modern Maroons: From Resistance to Identity', in W. Hoogbergen (ed.), *Born Out of Resistance,* Utrecht: ISOR Press, pp. 301–14.

—— (1995c), 'Land, Kinship and Community in the Post-Emancipation Caribbean: A Regional View of the Leewards', in K. F. Olwig (ed.), *Small Islands, Large Questions:*

Society, Culture and Resistance in the Post-Emancipation Caribbean, London: Frank Cass, pp. 73–99.

—— (1995d), 'The Creolization of African-American Slave Kinship in Jamaican Free Village and Maroon Communities', in S. Palmié (ed.), *Slave Cultures and the Cultures of Slavery,* Knoxville: University of Tennessee Press, pp. 187–209.

—— (1995e), 'Consensus in the Family Land Controversy', *New West Indian Guide,* 69 (3/4): 299–304.

—   (1997), 'Caribbean Common Tenures and Capitalism: The Accompong Maroons of Jamaica', in B. Maurer (ed.), *Common Land in the Caribbean and Mesoamerica,* Special Issue, *Plantation Society in the Americas,* IV (2/3): 201–32.

—— (1998a), 'Changing Perceptions of Gender in the Caribbean Region: The Case of the Jamaican Peasantry', in C. Barrow (ed.), *Caribbean Portraits: Essays on Gender Ideologies and Identities,* Kingston, Jamaica: Ian Randle, pp. 135–55.

—— (1998b), 'Gender and Development in the Jamaican Small-Scale Marketing System', Paper Presented at The Third RGS/IBG British-Caribbean Seminar, Resources, Planning and Environmental Management in a Changing Caribbean, University of the West Indies, Kingston, Jamaica, July.

—— (1999), Review of Bill Maurer, *Recharting the Caribbean: Land, Law and Citizenship in the British Virgin Islands,* in *The Journal of the Royal Anthropological Institute,* 5(3): 506–7.

—— (2000), 'The Appropriation of Lands of Law by Lands of Myth in the Caribbean Region', in A. Abramson and D. Theodossopoulos (eds), *Land, Law and Environment: Mythical Land, Legal Boundaries,* London: Pluto Press, pp. 116–35.

—— (2001), 'Empowering and Engendering Hidden Histories in Caribbean Peasant Communities', in T. Bremer and U. Fleischmann (eds), *History and Histories in the Caribbean,* Madrid: Iberoamericana; Frankfurt am Main: Vervuert, pp. 69–113.

—— (forthcoming), *Martha Brae's Two Histories: European Expansion and Caribbean Culture-Building in Jamaica,* Chapel Hill: University of North Carolina Press.

—— and Chevannes, B. (1996), 'The Continuity–Creativity Debate: The Case of Revival', *New West Indian Guide/Nieuwe West-Indische Gids,* 70(3/4): 209–28.

—— and Momsen, J. (1987), 'Introduction', in J. Besson and J. Momsen (eds), *Land and Development in the Caribbean,* London: Macmillan, pp. 1–9.

Bilby, K. M. (1996), 'Ethnogenesis in the Guianas and Jamaica: Two Maroon Cases', in J. D. Hill (ed.), *History, Power, and Identity,* Iowa City: University of Iowa Press, pp. 119–41.

Brathwaite, E. (1968), 'Jamaican Slave Society, A Review', *Race,* IX(3): 331–42.

Burton, R. D. E. (1997), *Afro-Creole: Power, Opposition, and Play in the Caribbean,* Ithaca, N.Y.: Cornell University Press.

Campbell, H. (1980), 'Rastafari: Culture of Resistance', *Race & Class,* 22(1): 1–22.

—— (1985), *Rasta and Resistance: From Marcus Garvey to Walter Rodney,* London: Hansib.

Campbell, M. C. (1990), *The Maroons of Jamaica 1655–1796: A History of Resistance, Collaboration and Betrayal,* Trenton: Africa World Press.

Carnegie, C. V. (1987a), 'Introduction', in C. V. Carnegie (ed.), *Afro-Caribbean Villages in Historical Perspective,* Kingston: African-Caribbean Institute of Jamaica, pp. iv–x.

—— (1987b), 'Is Family Land an Institution?', in C. V. Carnegie (ed.), *Afro-Caribbean Villages in Historical Perspective*, Kingston: African-Caribbean Institute of Jamaica, pp. 83–99.

Chamberlain, M. (1997), *Narratives of Exile and Return*, London: Macmillan.

Clarke, E. (1953), 'Land Tenure and the Family in Four Selected Communities in Jamaica', *Social and Economic Studies*, 1(4): 81–118.

—— (1966), *My Mother Who Fathered Me: A Study of the Family in Three Selected Communities in Jamaica*, (2nd edn), London: Allen and Unwin.

Clifford, J. (1988), *The Predicament of Culture*, Cambridge, Mass.: Harvard University Press.

Crichlow, M. A. (1994), 'An Alternate Approach to Family Land Tenure in the Anglophone Caribbean: The Case of St Lucia', *Nieuwe West-Indische Gids*, 68(1/2): 77–99.

de Albuquerque, K. (1980), 'Rastafarianism and Cultural Identity in the Caribbean', *Revista/Review Interamericana*, 10(2): 230–47.

Genovese, E. D. (1981), *From Rebellion to Revolution: Afro-American Slave Revolts in the Making of the New World*, New York: Vintage Books.

Gmelch, G. and Gmelch, S. B. (1997), *The Parish Behind God's Back: The Changing Culture of Rural Barbados*, Ann Arbor: The University of Michigan Press.

Hastings, S. U. and MacLeavy, B. L. (1979), *Seedtime and Harvest: A Brief History of the Moravian Church in Jamaica, 1754–1979*, Bridgetown: Cedar Press.

Hoetink, H. (1985), '"Race" and Color in the Caribbean', in S. W. Mintz and S. Price (eds), *Caribbean Contours*, Baltimore, Md.: Johns Hopkins University Press, pp. 55–84.

Inikori, J. E. (1982), *Forced Migration: The Impact of the Export Slave Trade on African Societies*, London: Hutchinson University Library for Africa.

Kopytoff, B. K. (1976), 'The Development of Jamaican Maroon Ethnicity', *Caribbean Quarterly*, 22(2/3): 33–50.

—— (1979), 'Colonial Treaty as Sacred Charter of the Jamaican Maroons', *Ethnohistory*, 26(1): 45–64.

—— (1987), 'Religious Change among the Jamaican Maroons: The Ascendance of the Christian God within a Traditional Cosmology', *Journal of Social History*, 20(3): 463–84.

Lévi-Strauss, C. (1961), *Tristes Tropiques*, (trans. J. Russell), New York: Criterion Books.

Lowenthal, D. (1972), *West Indian Societies*, London: Oxford University Press.

Manning, F. E. (1977), 'Cup Match and *Carnival*: Secular Rites of Revitalization in Decolonizing, Tourist-Oriented Societies', in S. F. Moore and B. G. Myerhoff (eds), *Secular Ritual*, Assen: Van Gorcum, pp. 265–81.

Maurer, B. (1996), 'The Land, the Law and Legitimate Children: Thinking through Gender, Kinship and Nation in the British Virgin Islands', in M. J. Maynes *et al.* (eds), *Gender, Kinship, Power: A Comparative and Interdisciplinary History*, New York: Routledge, pp. 351–63.

—— (1997), *Recharting the Caribbean: Land, Law, and Citizenship in the British Virgin Islands*, Ann Arbor: The University of Michigan Press.

Mintz, S. W. (1959), 'Labor and Sugar in Puerto Rico and Jamaica, 1800–1850', *Comparative Studies in Society and History*, 1: 273–81.

—— (1960), 'Peasant Markets', *Scientific American* 203: 112–22.

—— (1968), 'Caribbean Society', in *International Encyclopedia of the Social Sciences*, Vol. 2, New York: Crowell Collier and Macmillan, pp. 306–19.

—— (1970), 'Creating Culture in the Americas', *Columbia University Forum*, 13: 4–11.

—— (1971a), 'The Caribbean as a Socio-cultural Area', in M. M. Horowitz (ed.), *Peoples and Cultures of the Caribbean*, Garden City: Natural History Press, pp. 17–46.

—— (1971b), 'Toward an Afro-American History', *Cahiers D'Histoire Mondiale*, 13: 317–31.

—— (1974), 'The Caribbean Region', in S. W. Mintz (ed.), *Slavery, Colonialism and Racism*, New York: Norton, pp. 45–71.

—— (1978), 'Was the Plantation Slave a Proletarian?', *Review*, 2(1): 81–98.

—— (1979), 'Slavery and the Rise of Peasantries', in M. Craton (ed.) *Roots and Branches: Current Directions in Slave Studies*, Toronto: Pergamon Press, pp. 213–42.

—— (1980), 'Cultural Resistance and the Labor Force in the Caribbean Region', Paper Presented to the Cornell University Conference, Latin America Today: Heritage of Conquest, 3–5 April.

—— (1983), 'Reflections on Caribbean Peasantries', *Nieuwe West-Indische Gids*, 57(1/2): 1–17.

—— (1987), 'The Historical Sociology of Jamaican Villages', in C. V. Carnegie (ed.), *Afro-Caribbean Villages in Historical Perspective*. Kingston: African-Caribbean Institute of Jamaica, pp. 1–19.

—— (1989), *Caribbean Transformations*, New York: Columbia University Press.

—— (1996a), 'Enduring Substances, Trying Theories: The Caribbean Region as *oikoumenê*', *The Journal of the Royal Anthropological Institute*, 2(2): 289–311.

—— (1996b), 'Ethnic Difference, Plantation Sameness', in G. Ostindie (ed.), *Ethnicity in the Caribbean*, London: Macmillan, pp. 39–52.

—— (1996c), 'Tasting Food, Tasting Freedom, in S. W. Mintz (ed.), *Tasting Food, Tasting Freedom: Excursions into Eating, Culture, and the Past*, Boston, Mass.: Beacon Press, pp. 33–49.

—— and Price, R. (1992), *The Birth of African-American Culture*, Boston, Mass.: Beacon Press.

Momsen, J. (1987), 'Land Settlement as an Imposed Solution', in J. Besson and J. Momsen (eds), *Land and Development in the Caribbean*, London: Macmillan, pp. 46–69.

Olwig, K. F. (1985), *Cultural Adaptation and Resistance on St John: Three Centuries of Afro-Caribbean Life*, Gainesville: University of Florida Press.

—— (1987), 'Children's Attitudes to the Island Community: The Aftermath of Out-Migration on Nevis', in J. Besson and J. Momsen (eds), *Land and Development in the Caribbean*, London: Macmillan, pp. 153–70.

—— (1990), 'Cultural Identity and Material Culture: Afro-Caribbean Pottery', *Folk*, 32: 5–22.

—— (1993), *Global Culture, Island Identity: Continuity and Change in the Afro-Caribbean Community of Nevis*, Philadelphia, Pa.: Harwood.

—— (1994), *'The Land is the Heritage': Land and Community on St John*, St John Oral History Assocation Monograph No. 1, University of Copenhagen, Denmark.

—— (1995), 'Cultural Complexity after Freedom: Nevis and Beyond', in K. F. Olwig (ed.), *Small Islands, Large Questions: Society, Culture and Resistance in the Post-Emancipation Caribbean,* London: Frank Cass, pp. 100–20.

—— (1997a), 'Cultural Sites: Sustaining a Home in a Deterritorialized World', in K. F. Olwig and K. Hastrup (eds), *Siting Culture: The Shifting Anthropological Object,* London: Routledge, pp. 17–38.

—— (1997b), 'Caribbean Family Land: A Modern Commons', in B. Maurer (ed.), *Common Land in the Caribbean and Mesoamerica,* Special Issue, *Plantation Society in the Americas,* IV(2/3): 135–58.

—— (1998), 'Epilogue: Contested Homes: Home-making and the Making of Anthropology', in N. Rapport and A. Dawson (eds), *Migrants of Identity: Perceptions of Home in a World of Movement,* Oxford: Berg, pp. 225–36.

Paget, H. (1964), 'The Free Village System of Jamaica', *Caribbean Quarterly,* 10(1): 38–51.

Patterson, O. (1973), *The Sociology of Slavery: An Analysis of the Origins, Development and Structure of Negro Slave Society in Jamaica,* London: Granada Publishing.

Philpott, S. B. (1973), *West Indian Migration: The Montserrat Case,* London: Athlone Press.

Price, R. (1976), *The Guiana Maroons,* Baltimore, Md.: The Johns Hopkins University Press.

—— (1996), *Maroon Societies: Rebel Slave Communities in the Americas* (3rd edn), Baltimore, Md.: Johns Hopkins University Press.

Rapport, N. and Dawson, A. (eds) (1998), *Migrants of Identity: Perceptions of Home in a World of Movement,* Oxford: Berg.

Robotham, D. (1977), 'Agrarian Relations in Jamaica', in C. Stone and A. Brown (eds), *Essays on Power and Change in Jamaica,* Kingston: Jamaica Publishing House, pp. 45–57.

Schuler, M. (1979), 'Afro-American Slave Culture', in M. Craton (ed.), *Roots and Branches: Current Directions in Slave Studies,* Toronto: Pergamon Press, pp. 121–55.

Smith, M. G. (1965), *The Plural Society in the British West Indies,* Berkeley: University of California Press.

Thomas-Hope, E. M. (1978), 'The Establishment of a Migration Tradition: British West Indian Movements to the Hispanic Caribbean in the Century after Emancipation', in C. G. Clarke (ed.), *Caribbean Social Relations,* Liverpool: Centre for Latin American Studies, University of Liverpool Monograph Series No. 8, pp. 66–81.

—— (1980), 'Hopes and Reality in the West Indian Migration to Britain', *Oral History,* 8(1): 35–42.

—— (1984), 'Caribbean Identity: A Matter of Perception', in E. M. Thomas-Hope (ed.), *Perspectives on Caribbean Regional Identity,* Liverpool: Centre for Latin American Studies, University of Liverpool Monograph Series No. 11, pp. 1–4.

—— (1986), 'Caribbean Diaspora: The Inheritance of Slavery', in C. Brock (ed.), *The Caribbean in Europe,* London: Frank Cass, pp. 15–35.

—— (1992), *Explanation in Caribbean Migration,* London: Macmillan.

—— (1995), 'Island Systems and the Paradox of Freedom: Migration in the Post-Emancipation Leeward Islands', in K. F. Olwig (ed.), *Small Islands, Large Questions,* London: Frank Cass, pp. 161–75.

van Koningsbruggen, P. (1997), *Trinidad Carnival: A Quest for National Identity*, London: Macmillan.

Wagley, C. (1960), 'Plantation-America: A Culture Sphere', in V. Rubin (ed.), *Caribbean Studies: A Symposium* (2nd edn), Seattle: University of Washington Press, pp. 3–13.

Walvin, J. (1983), *Slavery and the Slave Trade*, London: Macmillan.

Wardle, H. (1999), 'Jamaican Adventures: Simmel, Subjectivity and Extraterritoriality in the Caribbean', *The Journal of the Royal Anthropological Institute*, 5(4): 523–39.

Williams, E. (1970), *From Columbus to Castro: The History of the Caribbean 1492–1969*, London: André Deutsch.

Young, V. H. (1993), *Becoming West Indian: Culture, Self, and Nation in St Vincent*, Washington, DC: Smithsonian Institution Press.

List of Contributors

Simone Abram: Lecturer, Department of Town and Regional Planning, University of Sheffield.

Fiona Armitage: Social Anthropologist, Oxford.

Jean Besson: Senior Lecturer, Department of Anthropology, Goldsmiths College, University of London.

Shulamit Carmi: Sociologist, Jerusalem.

Davina Cooper: Professor of Law, Keele University.

Dorothy Kennedy: Director, British Columbia Indian Language Project.

Joanna Pfaff-Czarnecka: Professor, Faculty of Sociology, University of Bielefeld.

Henry Rosenfeld: Emeritus Professor of Anthropology, University of Haifa.

Michael Saltman: Associate Professor of Anthropology, University of Haifa.

Index